CarTech®

A History of
Ford's Legendary 4x4

FORD
Bronco

TODD ZUERCHER

CarTech®

CarTech®, Inc.
838 Lake Street South
Forest Lake, MN 55025
Phone: 651-277-1200 or 800-551-4754
Fax: 651-277-1203
www.cartechbooks.com

Edit by Wes Eisenschenk
Layout by Connie DeFlorin

ISBN 978-1-61325-414-1
Item No. CT634

Library of Congress Cataloging-in-Publication Data
Names: Zuercher, Todd, 1969- author.
Title: Ford Bronco : a definitive history of Ford's legendary SUV / Todd Zuercher.
Description: Forest Lake, MN : CarTech, [2019] | Includes index.
Identifiers: LCCN 2018050503 | ISBN 9781613254141
Subjects: LCSH: Bronco truck--History. | Ford trucks--History
Classification: LCC TL230.5.B76 Z84 2019 | DDC 629.223--dc23
LC record available at https://lccn.loc.gov/2018050503

Written, edited, and designed in the U.S.A.
Printed in China
10 9 8 7 6 5 4 3

DISTRIBUTION BY:

Europe
PGUK
63 Hatton Garden
London EC1N 8LE, England
Phone: 020 7061 1980 • Fax: 020 7242 3725
www.pguk.co.uk

Australia
Renniks Publications Ltd.
3/37-39 Green Street
Banksmeadow, NSW 2109, Australia
Phone: 2 9695 7055 • Fax: 2 9695 7355
www.renniks.com

Canada
Login Canada
300 Saulteaux Crescent
Winnipeg, MB, R3J 3T2 Canada
Phone: 800 665 1148 • Fax: 800 665 0103
www.lb.ca

TABLE OF CONTENTS

DEDICATION

To my wife, Andrea, for helping me to find my "yes." Your support has
meant everything to me and made this book possible.
To my parents, Herman and Marian Zuercher, whose purchase of a 1969
Ford Bronco changed my life in ways I never imagined.

ACKNOWLEDGMENTS

When my wife, Andrea, and I were married a few years ago, I apparently told her that writing a book about the history of the Ford Bronco was one of the things on my bucket list. However, when Wes Eisenschenk offered me the opportunity to write this book, I honestly wanted to say no. I already had a "real" job as an engineer, was raising a family, had no shortage of hobbies, and was writing a few articles a year for Bronco Driver magazine and other outlets. Andrea helped give me some perspective on the opportunity and reminded me of that bucket list comment from a few years earlier. I realized I had a book "in me," and my no turned to a yes. Thank you, Dre, for your encouragement, and Wes, for the opportunity to do this project. Who could have imagined that a simple Facebook Messenger message about research on another work would lead to this.

As I began to write, I was reminded that automotive writers have always, in a way, been heroes of mine. The ability to convey information and engender certain emotions in a compelling manner is a skill I have long admired. In my formative years, I counted automotive scribes such as Jimmy Nylund, Moses Ludel, and Tom Madigan as my chief influences. As an adult, Peter Egan, Tom Cotter, Peter Brock, Jim Allen, and Colin Comer have been those I admired and looked up to the most.

No one creates a book totally on their own, and this volume was no exception. Chief contributors who helped with the creation of this work were: Andrew Norton, Terry Marvel, Tim Hulick, Drew Peroni, Chris House, Jack Niederkorn, Ed Gudenkauf, Dennis Bragg, Dave Kunz, Rick Williamson, Cliff Brumfield, and David Grinch. Willie Stroppe's memories of the 1977 Balloon Chase and other Bronco racing facts were particularly meaningful and helpful.

A special thanks goes to George Peterson and Dick Nesbitt for their help and recollections regarding Project Shorthorn and the resulting 1978 Bronco. I also owe a huge debt of gratitude to Don Wheatley, who led the engineering team that designed the 1978 Bronco and who was the coinventor of the Twin-Traction Beam front axle introduced in the 1980 Bronco. A delightful Saturday afternoon in July was spent reminiscing about his endeavors. Time spent with Parnelli Jones at his office in Torrance, California, is always a treat, and the interview for this book was no different. Thank you, Parnelli, for your time, and a big thanks to Jimmy Dilamarter, who always helps with logistics and puts up with my pestering emails.

Photos are a huge part of a historical record and pulling together images for this book was a large effort. Thanks to all who contributed photos to help make it possible. In particular, I am grateful for the help from: Al Rogers (Freeze Frame Image LLC), Jim Ober (Trackside Photo), Boyd Jaynes (Boyd Photo), Warren Crone (Ford Images), and Thomas Voehringer (Petersen Archives), who dug deep into the archives for some of the photos in the book.

Finally, all the production data in this book beyond the general totals for each year comes from Kevin Marti and his Marti Reports. Marti Auto Works is licensed by Ford Motor Company with the complete database of all Ford, Lincoln, and Mercury vehicles built from 1967 to the present. It has supplied statistics for this book. These statistics are copyrighted and used by permission of Marti Auto Works and Ford Motor Company. Marti Auto Works sells individual reports on vehicles and these are available at martiauto.com.

For all the people I've been able to connect with and reconnect with during the writing of this book, I'm so glad I said yes to this opportunity and the journey.

FOREWORD by James Duff, Founder, James Duff Enterprises

When my friend Todd Zuercher asked me to write a foreword for this book, I was honored, and happy to hear that one of the Bronco's leading historians would be chronicling the story of our favorite vehicle.

I bought my first Ford Bronco in 1967 while working as a body and paint man at Walker Buerge Ford in Los Angeles. I spent some time running the local sand dunes and taking home Broncos from the dealership at night and outfitting them with heavy-duty aftermarket parts.

With encouragement from Bill Stroppe, I decided to try my hand at desert racing. My career started off with a bang as my codriver took the first leg of the 1969 Baja 500. At more than 100 mph, a hay truck stalled in the middle of the road comes at you real quick. Although he missed hitting it, we caught the edge of the pavement into the ditch and did 3.5 rolls end over end, corner to corner! I put it all back together and ran it all season long, circle-track racing against Steve McQueen, James Garner, and Ray Harvick. We were back for the Mexican 1000 that fall. Desert racing was in its infancy and I was fortunate to race with the greats, including Bill Stroppe, Mickey Thompson, Parnelli Jones, James Garner, Walker Evans, and Rod Hall.

At the time, parts to toughen up my Bronco were scarce, so I made many of them myself. I built products to hold up to the rigors of off-road racing while making them accessible to everyone, which soon grew into our business: Duffy's Bronco Service.

Racing gave way to family four wheeling when the kids came along. My wife Judy and I helped form the first Bronco-only club: Broncos West 4WD Club in Los Angeles. The club frequented Pismo Beach, Glamis, Big Bear, and other Southern California hot spots.

The business continued to grow and I developed parts for other four-wheel-drive vehicles. A devastating warehouse fire in 1978 forced us to sell off the majority of our product line to

In the early days, James "Duffy" Duff raced off-road with the greats. Many of his products were developed from lessons learned on courses in Baja and the southwestern United States. Here he plows through the silt at the 1970 Mint 400.

In the 1970s, the Duff family posed with their two signature vehicles: Mrs. Duff's *and* Pony Express *on the sand at Pismo Beach.*

The Duff family is shown here in 2014. Since their relocation to Knoxville, the business and the Bronco fleet have grown as the popularity of the Bronco has soared. James and Judy Duff are enjoying retirement these days while Suzy and her husband, Michael, manage day-to-day operations of the business.

Mickey Thompson Shock Co. Thankfully, it didn't want the Bronco parts side of the business, so my wife Judy kept on selling those parts out of the garage and I kept designing new parts while working for M/T. In 1980, I won a SEMA Best New Off-Road product award for my camber adjusters for the new Ford Twin-Traction Beam front ends, a product that is still produced today.

Soon, Judy and I moved to the small town of Sequim, Washington, and reorganized as James Duff Enterprises. We started out small, and with the kids' help, rebuilt the business, first as a strictly mail-order operation and then to a proper store/showroom to help serve the burgeoning early Bronco restoration craze. We patented degreed polyurethane C-bushings to help solve caster problems on lifted trucks and also designed and developed parts for the Bronco II and the big Broncos when they entered the market.

Our kids, as you might expect, both ended up with in automotive-related careers. Richard became an international car designer. Suzy took over the reins of our business when we finally decided to retire. By then, the business had outgrown Sequim, so the decision was made to move to Knoxville, Tennessee, where we have enjoyed many successful years in a business that keeps on growing in a beautiful region of the country.

Todd Zuercher wrote me a letter as a young teenager more than 35 years ago, telling me of his plans for his dad's Bronco. Over the years, we've 'wheeled with him at many events in Arizona and California. To his utter embarrassment, a few years ago I pulled out that letter and shared it with him and a group of his friends around the campfire in Arizona. I've enjoyed reading his historical articles in the Early Bronco Registry's *Horsing Around* newsletters and in more recent years, his many contributions to *Bronco Driver* magazine. As one of the primary historical chroniclers of our favorite vehicle, we're happy that he's put together a history for us all to enjoy.

The Bronco has provided not only our livelihood but a lifetime of experiences, memories, and many wonderful friendships during the past 50 years. We're excited about the future, particularly with the introduction of a new Bronco and where Suzy will take it. Here's to many more years behind the wheel of our favorite rigs!

FOREWORD by Parnelli Jones

As many of you know, I've basically been a Ford guy for most of my career—whether it was racing a Ford product or a race car powered by Ford—and over the years, I had some pretty good success. When I decided to reduce my oval track and road racing schedules, an opportunity came my way via my old friend Bill Stroppe, who at a party one night, challenged me to try off-road racing. My reaction was that I didn't think that it would be my bag. Whereupon Bill, ever the master at goading someone on, replied that I probably wasn't man enough. Well, that was like waving a red flag at a bull, and Bill got exactly what he wanted. The rest, as they say, is history.

The Ford Bronco, to me, was the perfect vehicle; it had all kinds of uses, and buyers just loved it because it could do just about anything on the street or highway. Needless to say, it also turned out to be a fabulous platform for off-road adventures of all kinds, including racing. I can hardly believe that this vehicle was introduced by Ford to the public 53 years ago, and yet today it is still highly sought after for restoration purposes and nostalgia events. Not only that, the Bronco is just plain fun to drive.

Todd Zuercher and I have known each other for several years, and he is still, to me, the most enthusiastic Bronco owner and historian I've ever met. You will feel his pride of Bronco history exuding from these pages. It is truly a pleasure and honor for me to be asked to write the foreword to

Capturing the spirit of the evening, Parnelli Jones shared a story during the Early Bronco Registry's "Evening with the Legends" held during the Bronco 40th Anniversary Celebration in 2006. (Photo Courtesy Steve Sampson)

this chronicle and pictorial record of the long Bronco history. Long live the Ford Bronco!

Parnelli Jones
January 14, 2019

INTRODUCTION

"What do I do? What do I do?" cried my mother. It was the annual woodcutting season in ranch country north of Prescott, Arizona, and our 1969 Ford Bronco, affectionately dubbed *Broncitis*, had just slid into a ditch.

The winter months in northern Arizona can bring heavy precipitation, which turn the local dirt roads into a sloppy, slippery mess once the sun thaws the frozen surface each day. Following my father in a truck loaded with firewood, our Bronco slithered left to right across his tracks, like a small boat trying to follow in the wake of an oceanliner. Pointing the vehicle in the desired direction of travel meant judicious application of the throttle, followed by a flurry of elbows as Mom turned the large steering wheel to counteract the pendulum-like motions of the rear of the vehicle.

And that's how we ended up in the ditch. And how I ended up in the driver's seat—again.

Switching seats made both of us immediately happier. Several years away from legally obtaining my driver's license, I was happiest behind the wheel in Arizona's remote backcountry, learning the skills to operate the Bronco on challenging roads. Mom was happiest when she could enjoy the view from the passenger's seat while her husband or one of her sons drove.

That Bronco went on to become my driver's training vehicle, carrier for my first date, partner for countless backcountry exploration adventures, research and development platform, and model for countless photos and articles. More recently, it carried my beautiful bride and I away from our wedding.

My love affair with the Ford Bronco is just one of thousands that have unfolded over the more than 50 years since its introduction. Talk to a longtime owner, or a group of enthusiasts, and they'll all have stories of how the bobtail from Ford played a special part in shaping their lives and their most favorite memories. From family vacations to hunting and camping trips to simple run-of-the-mill commutes, these are the stories that give voice to the true legend of the Ford Bronco in American culture.

The Bronco started making history from almost the moment it was introduced. Magazine writers thrashed them around the backcountry, and high-performance enthusiasts soon had fenders cut, larger tires installed, and high-performance engines stuffed between the frame rails. On the practical side, service station operators and small business owners found them to be great plow trucks and delivery vehicles.

Owners went on to make memories with their trucks; whether they were one of the fairly crude early models or a plush Eddie Bauer Edition with leather seats and pile carpeting. Through all its iterations, the Bronco has been known as a tough, capable four-wheel-drive vehicle that combined its utilitarian nature with enough sportiness to engender strong emotions from owners, passengers, and those who admired them in action.

This book recounts some of the most iconic moments in the life of the Ford Bronco: its historic development, the technical details of each generation, its rich racing legacy, celebrity owners, appearances in numerous movie and TV roles, its part in the O. J. Simpson chase, and most important, the many stories of everyday owners that comprise a fascinating history of this remarkable vehicle in the American automotive landscape. Even more than that, it is a love story for the Ford Bronco, a truck that captured my heart and that I hope will enlighten yours.

The author's 1969 Bronco at the top of Imogene Pass in southern Colorado in 1991 is a little sport and a little utility. The tow strap on back of the Bronco was used to tow a 2WD Nissan pickup to the top; the author's younger brother (right) had just ridden his mountain bike to the summit from Telluride.

IN THE BEGINNING

"We think of the Bronco as neither a conventional car nor a truck, but as a vehicle which combines the best of both worlds. It can serve as a family sedan, a sports roadster, a snow plow, or as a farm or civil defense vehicle. It has been designed to go nearly anywhere and do nearly anything."

The Bronco was not Ford Motor Company's first foray into the world of sport utility vehicles (SUVs) that bridged the gap between cars and trucks. In fact, the seeds were planted almost 25 years earlier when Ford became one of the producers of the ubiquitous World War II Army Jeep. When Bantam Motor Company and Willys Motors could not keep up with Jeep production in the fall of 1941, the vast resources of Ford Motor Company were brought to bear in helping produce vehicles for the war effort. Ford produced almost 278,000 quarter-ton 4x4s, known as GPWs, in nearly four years of production, earning the love and respect of veterans (GIs) throughout the various theaters of the war.

When those GIs returned from the war, they married, started families, and bought surplus Jeeps. The little trucks, in turn, birthed a new form of recreation in the United States in the years following the war, allowing families to explore the country's rugged backcountry. Legions of young men and women took their first turn behind the wheel in Jeeps, and the small utility vehicles served faithfully as snow plows, farm runabouts, ranch hands, maintenance vehicles, and errand runners. The Jeep line received a few upgrades in the 1950s, but the advent of the interstate highway system and higher speeds meant that the surplus war trucks and their younger brethren started to fall behind.

In 1960, the vehicle segment that is now known as the SUV market consisted of about 11,000 vehicle sales annually, with the majority belonging to the Jeep brand. In 1961, the International Scout was introduced and the market immediately expanded to 32,000 vehicles per year. In the year before the Bronco was introduced, the market had stabilized at about 40,000 units with Jeep and International capturing 85 percent of those sales and foreign-made units, such as the Toyota Landcruiser and Nissan Patrol, comprising the rest. Ford estimated there were about 200,000 SUVs on the road at the time of the Bronco's introduction.

This increased growth in the utility vehicle market was not lost on Ford. In the early 1960s, the company embarked

This pristine 1966 U13 Roadster is believed to have been built during the first week's production in August 1965. A dealership vehicle for the first 17 years of its life, it was not titled until 1983. After some time on a wheat farm in North Dakota, Donald and Drew Peroni purchased it in 2000 and performed a frame-off restoration. The Bronco has traveled about 12,000 miles in its life. (Photo Courtesy Freeze Frame Image LLC, Al Rogers)

on a detailed marketing survey to determine what enthusiasts might be looking for in a new utility vehicle. Ford interviewed hundreds of potential customers about what they liked and disliked most about their current utility vehicles, without revealing they were doing the research under the auspices of the Ford Motor Company.

At the press introduction of the Bronco, Ford Division's general manager Donald N. Frey noted that in conversations with customers, many were intensely loyal to their vehicles and didn't want to change a thing but upon further questioning revealed some things that they *did* want. The young warriors who had driven the Jeeps in World War II were now in their 40s and 50s and wanted a tough vehicle that could do everything a Jeep could but with more comfort and more interior room. They wanted a vehicle that could cruise at highway speeds with more ease than the old Jeeps and they wanted cabs that were better insulated and better sealed against the rain. They wanted nicer paint jobs, more rust protection, and smoother-riding suspension systems. And although they wanted improvements over the existing offerings in the utility four-wheel-drive market, they didn't want "too many fancy frills." There was room for new ideas in this market segment, and luckily, the Bronco was poised to step in.

Development

Details on the timeline of the Bronco's original development cycle are limited as the design principals involved are deceased. The earliest mention of the Bronco in Ford official documentation is October 1963.

Minutes from the February 12, 1964, Product Planning Committee (comprised of top Ford Motor Company planning executives) meeting reveal that a five-year vehicle life cycle was assumed for financial planning purposes but that Ford thought the Bronco would run for much longer than five years. Ford believed that the International Harvester Scout and Jeep would not change much in the following years, giving Ford a competitive advantage with the Bronco that would last for several years. Ford president Lee Iacocca remarked that if the Bronco was successful, General Motors would enter the market within a few years, and he felt that Chrysler would not be a threat to Ford's sales for a long time. Remarkably, all of these predictions came true in the following half-dozen years. At the conclusion of the February 12 meeting, the Product Planning Committee viewed the first styling model of the Bronco in the Rotunda styling studio and gave its approval. Ten days later, the committee gave its approval for a $10 million proposal to develop the Bronco.

Meanwhile, engineers were already hard at work on the design aspects of the new filly. According to notes of the

Believed to be the earliest known photo of a Bronco, this shot from Ford's styling studio shows what Ford's stylists were thinking in 1964. No drivetrain exists in this mockup and it's likely made of clay. In this view, you can see the 1966-only liftgate latch assembly and the full door has been mocked up. Hubcaps are from a Ford car. (Photo Courtesy Ford Motor Company)

Looking remarkably similar to production trucks, sharp-eyed readers can note some differences. The grille treatment looks familiar but changed for production. The driver's side of the Bronco has the 1967-and-later-style hubcaps and a mockup of the fiberglass door insert used in the 1966–1968 roadsters. (Photo Courtesy Ford Motor Company)

Advanced Development Group in April 1964, the full-size chassis layouts of major components were completed for a mechanical prototype build, and feasibility of the new Mono-Beam/coil-spring front suspension was verified during the first quarter of 1964.

In a Society of Automotive Engineers (SAE) paper published in early 1966, Ford engineer Paul Axelrad noted that no less than 10 complete package layouts were made before the final selection was determined. With an overall length of 152 inches, the wheelbase was expanded and contracted on several occasions before 92 inches was selected as the final number. The engineering team found 92 inches gave a good balance between approach, departure, and ramp break-over angles.

The break-over angle was determined to be the most important of the three based on Ford's owner surveys and internal testing. Thus, Ford designed the Bronco to beat or equal the break-over angles of its primary competitors (the CJ-5 and Scout). In addition, Ford engineers carefully considered the various interactions of wheelbase, track width, and wheel turn angle to meet the Bronco's design goals of maneuverability, ride comfort, and stability.

Retired Ford engineer Larry Wynne worked in Light Truck Engineering during those years and recalls that five or six engineers, under the leadership of Group Leader Paul Axelrad, were responsible for the mechanical development of the Bronco. Wynne notes that Light Truck Engineering consisted of only about 35 to 40 engineers during that time and his memory of those long-ago years was that the Bronco was not the primary focus during those years; that honor belonged to the Twin I-Beam front suspension that debuted on the Ford light-duty pickup trucks in 1965.

Wynne's strongest memory from the Bronco development story isn't of engineers sitting at desks crunching numbers or creating drawings, but instead it involves a test trip out West with prototypes of the new trucks. A caravan of three Broncos along with a Scout and a Jeep were the test vehicles. In Arizona, the vehicles were traversing rough terrain when the Scout rolled on a hillside and several men were injured. One man broke his collarbone and another broke his pelvis and right arm. According to another engineer's account, Axelrad himself rolled one of the vehicles and was knocked unconscious.

Due to the first generation's unique styling, many people believe that the Bronco was a wholly unique vehicle that didn't share many parts with other existing Ford vehicles. However, Ford initially intended to use as many existing parts as possible to minimize the fixed investment. The rear quarter panels from the 1964 F-100 Styleside box were reused with some minor modifications for the sides of the Bronco body. Floorpan assemblies and the tailgate (both resized) from the same truck were also used.

Ford outsourced engineering design services for the body-in-white, seats, trim, and body electrical system to the Budd Company in Philadelphia, Pennsylvania. Budd built engineering prototype bodies using reworked 1964 Styleside F-100 sheet metal. The front-end sheet metal for the initial prototypes was made from low-cost tooling produced from plaster casts of the clay model.

For the production trucks, the engines were modified versions of powerplants already offered in Ford's lineup. Exterior items such as headlights, trim rings, turn-signal lenses, and taillight lenses were reused from Ford's car and truck models. The bucket seats in the 1966 Bronco were two Mustang buck-

**Frisky, trail-breaking Bronco
(with Budd-built parts)**

Ride Ford's Bronco anywhere. Its four driving wheels
dig in to take you there and bring you back.
It's got the muscle for chores. Sport-loving design for play.
And, like 27 other leading cars, it has quality components*
made by *Budd* COMPANY
AUTOMOTIVE DIVISION · DETROIT, MICH.

*Budd products include fenders, hoods, roofs, doors, body panels, chassis frames, wheels, hubs, drums, disc and drum brakes.

The Budd Company did much of the development work on the Bronco prototypes for Ford and also built Bronco bodies for Ford for the first several months of production in 1966. This rare ad highlights Budd's relationship with the Bronco and other 1960s vehicles.

ets. Knobs on the dash and the instrument cluster were also borrowed from the Ford light truck cab. Even small items such as the transfer case shifter knob came from the existing Ford parts list (F250 4x4).

Introducing the Bronco

Ford introduced the 1966 Bronco to the buying public at a press conference in Dearborn, Michigan, on August 11, 1965. On that warm, humid Wednesday, Ford Division president Donald Frey announced the Bronco to the press, stating, "We think of the Bronco as neither a conventional car nor a truck, but as a vehicle which combines the best of both worlds. It can serve as a family sedan, a sports roadster, a snow plow, or as a farm or civil defense vehicle. It has been designed to go nearly anywhere and do nearly anything." Adding the Bronco name to the line that already included the Mustang, Frey wryly remarked, "We wanted a new 'in' car to add to our 'horse

Blaze a Bronco trail to where the fun is!

Roadster is great for the great outdoors! Convertible vinyl top and doors available.

Wagon takes the whole family...anywhere!

Sports utility does all kinds of chores...in all kinds of places.

Bronco, the new 4-wheel · drive from Ford!

Unexpected traction, unexpected action, exciting things happen to driving when all four wheels provide the drive! Whether you collect big-game trophies or just the kids at school, you'll get a new lift from going when Bronco supplies the go!

You'll have a lot more fun in '66—if Bronco has a part in it! Bronco is the new kind of sports car with 4-wheel drive.

Your Bronco will take you up hills too steep for roads. Over beach sand. Through unplowed snow (plow it, too, if you wish). Bronco will take you into the woods for hunting. And right to the banks of lakes and streams for swimming and fishing.

Smooth six-cylinder power gives you the muscle you need for rough terrain... and the speed for expressway cruising.

Husky radius rods permit the use of soft-riding coil springs up front. So Bronco is a comfortable car for every-day family needs—shopping, running errands, driving to school or work.

Let Ford's frisky Bronco bring a new kind of living into your life!

Multiply Bronco's usefulness with these extras!

SNOW PLOW	WINCH	LIMITED-SLIP AXLE
SKID PLATES	TOW HOOKS	POWER TAKE-OFF
REAR SEAT	BUCKET SEATS	FREE-WHEELING HUBS
RADIO	OVERLOAD SPRINGS	TRAILER HITCH

Ford Bronco/66

Bronco: new kind of sports car!

NEW 4-WHEEL DRIVE Bronco takes you where the action is. Deep into woods for hunting, through snow to good skiing, over sandy beaches to where the fishing is best. Plenty of oomph from a smooth six-cylinder powerplant and 4-wheel traction take Bronco wherever you dare to drive it. Transmission is fully synchronized for smooth downshifting. Bronco is a great performer on the road too. No annoying whine in 2-wheel drive, even at highway speeds. You get a soft, sedan-like ride from Bronco's rugged Mono-Beam coil-spring front suspension. Try the Wagon, Roadster or Sports Utility at your Ford Dealer's now. One's just right for you.

New fun one from **Ford**

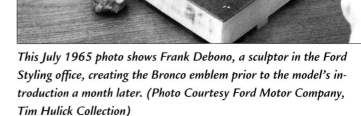

This July 1965 photo shows Frank Debono, a sculptor in the Ford Styling office, creating the Bronco emblem prior to the model's introduction a month later. (Photo Courtesy Ford Motor Company, Tim Hulick Collection)

"It fits, I'll take it!"

The Bronco was heavily advertised in its initial year. Smiling, happy passengers in a variety of models were shown enjoying their new Fords, particularly the roadsters. While her well-dressed parents look on in glee, a small child seems to be traumatized by a small blue creature in front of the new blue Bronco wagon (top).

This September 1965 Ford publication cartoon bears witness that Ford designed the Bronco to be attractive to hunters. No deer were harmed in the Bronco's development, but there were likely many brought home in Broncos over the years following its introduction. (Photo Courtesy Ford Motor Company)

It's the fall of 1965 and Bonnie Dykes, executive secretary at Don Sanderson Ford in Glendale, Arizona, finds herself behind the wheel of a brand-new 1966 Bronco roadster while a group of salesmen check out the various features of the new bobtail. (Photo Courtesy Sanderson Ford)

This large banner is the only one of its kind known to exist. The late Dave Metz, who owned the banner, had given it to his friend, Tim Hulick, who proudly displays it at events and shows throughout the country. (Photo Courtesy Tim Hulick)

stall,'" referring to the Mustang as Bronco's "big brother."

Fry continued, "We think the small utility vehicle will be one of the new 'in' cars. It will be popular with the college crowd, with the active lively people who can go places and do things, and with families as a second or third car . . . with the Bronco, we expect to attract into the market a sizable number of persons who have never been utility vehicle owners—people who have succumbed to the lure of the great outdoors, skiers, hunters, fishermen, and 'fun' families who have been bitten by the camping bug or who just enjoy doing different things together . . . We also expect it to appeal to people in hundreds of service industries."

Fry also noted that the Bronco could be easily serviced at nearly 6,400 Ford dealerships throughout the country, offering quick repairs and easy access to parts. This was a not-so-subtle dig at the competition in the market segment; International dealers numbered 4,764 and Jeeps were available at only 2,152 locations.

Models

At its introduction for the 1966 model year, the Bronco, carrying the U model designation, was offered in three models: U13 Roadster, U14 Sports Utility, and U15 Wagon.

U13 Roadster

The least expensive model, retailing for a base price of $2,336.82, was the Roadster (U13 model). Offering the most basic of amenities and with such items as a top and doors on the options list, the roadster was the most direct competitor to the Jeep CJ-5.

This early 1966 Bronco was discovered in the small northern New Mexico town of Eagle Nest. It is recognized as one of the few survivor 1966 roadsters on the road today with the original dealer accessory Whitco top still in place. (Photo Courtesy Tim Hulick)

Highlighted against the Milwaukee skyline, this beautiful 1966 roadster represents the best of the breed. Ford produced 4,090 of the spartan roadsters for 1966, and few remain today. This Peacock Blue roadster has the sporty rocker stripes and no locking hubs on the front axle. (Photo Courtesy Tim Hulick)

U14 Sports Utility

The U14 model was denoted as the Sports Utility and featured a short top, which made the Bronco resemble a small pickup truck. It had seating for two (bucket seats) or three (bench seat) with a steel bulkhead panel separating the seats from the cargo area. The Sports Utility, which retailed for $2,479.93, was most often the workhorse of the bunch. It was popular with service station owners and municipalities where the vehicle's combination of an enclosed cab with a small cargo-carrying area was advantageous and carrying more than two people was not required. In time, the Sports Utility simply became known as the "half cab" among owners and enthusiasts.

The smiles on these boys' faces say it all. How much more fun could you have than climbing around in the back of a new 1966 U14 half cab? Complete with the 1966-only hubcaps and rocker stripes, this truck would be highly prized by collectors today.

This early 1966 U14 half cab calls Carrier, Oklahoma, home. It was built in September 1965 and sports an eyebrow grille, chrome bumpers ($28.75), 1966-only wheel covers ($22.48), and the 1966-only red rocker stripe ($12.55). (Photo Courtesy Bobby Tennell)

U15 Wagon

Retailing for $2,551.19, the most popular model by far was the U15 model, a wagon, with a full-length hardtop and seating for up to five people. In time, it was the only model offered. The wagon, if optioned with two bucket seats, offered an open pass-through area to the optional rear seat. Wagons were also offered with a bench seat with a bulkhead (identical to the half cab bulkhead) if the rear bench seat was not ordered.

Bearing the number 524 on the rear liftgate glass, this prototype was likely very close to production ready. The fenders carry roadster mirrors, which command premium prices with restorers and enthusiasts. (Photo Courtesy Ford Motor Company)

Reviews

The Bronco's introduction was widely covered in the motoring press in the fall of 1965. Most impressions were formed from driving several prototypes at the Ford proving grounds in June 1965, with articles appearing shortly after the official August introduction.

Magazines were generally positive in their initial impressions, saving the negative points for later tests, and the car-centric automotive media followed that pattern.

The Bronco's coil-spring front suspension was well received by nearly all writers, who noted its superior ride quality and the anti-dive characteristics of the design, a feature touted extensively by Ford at its introduction. *Science and Mechanics* magazine noted that "as a highway vehicle, the Bronco more than holds its own . . . Cornering is excellent . . . progressive-rate rear leaf springs offer a good ride without sacrificing carry capacity."

Four Wheeler magazine stated, "Ford engineers have come up with extra-ordinary paved road ride. Because the noise level is already far below average for four-wheel-drive (4WD)

One of the earliest shots from the driver's seat of a Bronco was taken in June 1965 when Motor Trend *editors traveled to the Ford Proving Ground in Dearborn for their first drive of Ford's new filly. A Rotunda tachometer and Falcon horn button are visible in front of the nattily attired driver. (Photo Courtesy Motor Trend Group, LLC)*

rigs, long trips are far less fatiguing. On the trail, this springing combination pays off in an extremely comfortable ride over all but the roughest of trails."

Jan Norbye, writing in *Popular Science,* went so far as to say, "The Bronco behaved like a real sports car." The Bronco's extremely good maneuverability (turning circle of less than 34 feet) was also universally praised. The coil springs allowed the front wheels to be cut up 37 degrees; far tighter than on comparable leaf-sprung vehicles.

Highway travel was a mixed bag with reviewers. Zero-to-60 tests ranged from 15.8 seconds (*Mechanix Illustrated*) to a more believable 25.4 seconds (*Science and Mechanics*). Most testers noted that they topped out the Bronco speed at between 80 and 85 mph. *Popular Science* again was positive, noting that "the ride was better than in many taxicabs, the directional stability excellent, the noise level inside the vehicle quite tolerable."

Science and Mechanics opined, "As a highway vehicle, the Bronco more than holds its own. It's quieter than most other four wheel drives."

Tom McCahill, writing in *Mechanix Illustrated* magazine, felt that the 170-ci 6-cylinder "proved more than ample for keeping the Bronco up with fast-moving traffic. For many miles, it cruised over Michigan's freeway at 70 mph without distress."

Car Life had a different take, "A tour of Southern California freeways immediately demonstrated the low-geared Bronco should be given its head in back country. A comfortable highway cruise for this particular Bronco was 55 mph—

slow by the majority of freeway standards. A speed of 60 mph created tight winding of the smallish engine and audible workings of transmission and transfer cases."

The reason for the disparity in testers' impressions is likely due to differences in test vehicles' axle ratios, with testers finding the 4.11:1 ratio acceptable and the optional 4.57:1 axle ratio too low for sustained highway travel.

Four Wheeler, looking at the new truck from an off-roader's perspective, felt that the hub assemblies on the front axles stuck out too far and would be targets for passing rocks. They also felt that the locking hubs might be undone by passing rocks or branches, leaving the driver in a potentially dangerous position if the hubs were accidentally unlocked.

McCahill, the dean of automotive writers in the mid-1960s, faulted the Bronco for the lack of what he referred to as a "stump-catcher." That, according to McCahill, was essentially a thick steel skidplate that hung from the front bumper to below the lowest point on the front axle, thereby protecting the front of the "adventure car" from low tree stumps hidden in the grass (common in the South) and from sharp rocks (out West). He also recommended steel armor protection for the crankcase and the transmission and felt that the bumpers were too flimsy.

After all the pros and cons of the new Bronco were considered, *Car Life* probably summed up the new truck best by stating, "The International Harvester Scout, the Toyota Land Cruiser, the Kaiser Jeep, and the Land Rover all have idiosyncrasies which those people accustomed to conventional vehicles find disturbing. Of the total group, the Bronco seems to possess fewest of these detractions which would prevent buyer transition from passenger car to four-wheel-drive sports-utility vehicle."

That's exactly what Ford Motor Company was aiming for when it introduced the Bronco.

Engines

Following their penchant for using as many existing parts as possible, Ford selected examples from their existing engine families to drop into the Bronco's engine compartment.

170 I-6

At the Bronco's introduction, the sole powerplant offered was the 170-ci 6-cylinder engine, euphemistically called the "spirited Big Six power" in early sales brochures. The 170 offered a maximum gross horsepower rating of 105 at 4,400 rpm and a maximum gross torque rating of 158 ft-lbs at 2,400 rpm. Bronco's standard engine bested all of its competition. The closest was Scout's 152-ci 4-cylinder, which came within 3.3 ft-lbs of Bronco's net torque rating.

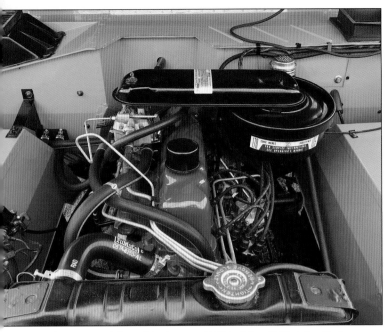

The Bronco debuted in August 1965 with a 170-ci 6-cylinder engine and a gross output of 105 hp. Often referred to as the "Falcon Six," it was actually sourced from the Econoline van line and used solid lifters instead of the Falcon's hydraulic units. The 1966 radiator had an offset cap; all other years' radiators were centered. (Photo Courtesy Tim Hulick)

The 170-ci Six was known as the "Falcon Six," having been introduced as an upgrade to the original 144 ci in the Falcon lineup in 1961. With a bore of 3.5 inches and stroke of 2.94 inches, the oversquare engine featured four main bearings and an intake manifold that was integrally cast with the cylinder head, limiting its performance potential. The compression ratio was a healthy 9:1. Typical of inline 6-cylinder engines, the 170's torque curve was fairly flat, with 90 percent of maximum torque developed at an engine speed of 1,000 rpm. The Bronco version of the engine was actually developed from the Econoline van version of the engine, which featured solid mechanical lifters in lieu of the hydraulic lifters used in the Falcon engines.

Because Ford engineers knew that the Bronco would see more angles and inclines that cars would never travel, they modified the 1-barrel carburetor and mechanical fuel pump to provide a positive fuel supply under all conditions. On top of the carburetor, an oil-bath air cleaner was added for maximum air filtration. The Bronco's oil pan held 7 quarts of oil; the Econoline version made do with 4.5 quarts.

The road tests of the first Broncos didn't specifically complain about the lack of power with the 170, but instead obliquely made comments such as "No power options exist now, but compartment is big enough for a V-8" (*Popular Science*) and "A V-8 could easily slip in there" (*Car Life* photo caption).

Ford clearly intended to install a V-8 between the frame rails of its pony. As early as the first quarter of 1964, Ford documents indicated that Advanced Development Engineering was working on studies to provide for a 289-ci V-8 engine in the truck.

289 V-8

The 289 V-8 was introduced in the Bronco on March 2, 1966, and as a result, the Bronco leaped to the top rung of the horsepower and torque ratings ladder in the sport utility stable.

The 289 was the latest iteration of Ford's small-block V-8 family that was introduced in July 1961 as a small, compact, lightweight V-8 to replace the Y-block series of engines. Using thin-wall casting techniques to save weight, and displacing 221 ci, the engines were first introduced in the mid-size 1962 Ford Fairlane and Mercury Meteor cars. In mid-1962, the displacement grew to 260 ci, with the displacement again increased to 289 ci by 1964.

At the time of the Bronco's introduction, three iterations of the 289 were in production. It had become a popular engine because of its widespread use in the Mustang and was a natural fit for the Bronco with its size and power output.

For the Bronco, Ford selected the 2-barrel version, which had the lowest compression ratio (9.3:1) and the lowest torque peak (282 ft-lbs at 2,400 rpm) of the three versions. The installation of the V-8, which Ford described as "the power of a tractor and the performance of a Mustang" was met with universal

Motor Trend testers were quite exuberant in their appraisal of the new Bronco V-8 in the September 1966 issue. You can only imagine what the landing was like when the little bobtail half cab returned to terra firma. (Photo Courtesy Motor Trend Group, LLC)

The 289 V-8 was introduced in the Bronco lineup in March 1966, immediately vaulting the Bronco to the top of the horsepower list in the segment. The 1966–1968 V-8 Broncos, in their original configuration, had sealed radiators with an expansion reservoir tank with a cap mounted between the radiator and the engine. Many of these tanks have been discarded. (Photo Courtesy Tim Hulick)

acclaim. In its September 1966 issue, *Motor Trend* summed it up well: "Ford's Bronco with its standard 6-cylinder engine is quite capable of unseating an unstrapped rider in somewhat less than the standard rodeo time of 8 seconds. But now with an optional 200-hp, 289-cubic-inch V-8, it packs the violence of a Braham bull . . . 200 hp feeding into a 4:57-ratio limited slip differential is somewhat akin to whipping water in a Waring blender." The 289 offered the option of either a paper air filter or an oil-bath air filter.

Transmission

The 1966 Broncos used 3-speed manual transmissions with a shifter mounted on the column, a configuration used on the F-Series pickups at the time. Because the remainder of the segment vehicles used floor-mounted shifters, Ford touted the column shifter as a plus that gave more seating room for front-seat passengers. Consumer reaction was mixed, and Hurst introduced a floor-shift conversion within a year of the Bronco's introduction that proved to be very popular with Bronco owners for many years.

The 6-cylinder 3-speed, known as the HEF, had ratios of 3.41, 1.86, and 1.00:1. When the 289 V-8 was introduced, an almost identical transmission with slightly higher torque capacity, known as the HEF/RAN/RAT, was used. First and second gears had slightly higher (lower numerically) ratios of 2.99 and 1.75:1. Because the engines were different lengths, the cast-iron

adapters were of differing lengths so the transfer case and transfer case crossmember could stay in the location in the vehicle regardless of the engine and transmission.

Recently, a retired Ford engineer revealed in an interview that he was responsible for the redesign of the adapters after the initial configuration failed during testing right before the vehicle's introduction. The engineer noted with a wry smile that he received "lots of help" in the redesign.

The 6-cylinder 3-speed transmissions were backed by a 9-inch-diameter clutch with a 9.375-inch unit as a heavy-duty option. The 289 3-speed had an 11-inch clutch between it and the engine.

Transfer Case

In choosing the Dana 20 transfer case for the Bronco, Ford selected one of the best transfer cases ever used in 4WD vehicles. This transfer case, which featured a cast-iron housing and used steel gears (not chains), enjoyed a sterling reputation for longevity and strength; Jeep specified it for its J4000 1-ton trucks.

Ford learned from its preproduction surveys that customers wanted quieter drivetrains on their 4WDs. The Spicer 18 transfer case, which had been used in Jeeps since their introduction and in Scouts until 1965, was a so-called "offset design" (the input and output shafts were not colinear), requiring an intermediate shaft and gears as part of the power transmission from the input shaft to the output shaft. The extra gears generated noise, particularly at highway speeds, which consumers found tiresome.

The Dana 20 was a "straight through" or "silent drive" design, highly touted at the Bronco's introduction. Because the input and output shafts were colinear, there were no gears moving in the transfer case when operated in two-wheel drive (2WD), resulting in much less gear train noise. And although the Scout 800 had started using the Dana 20 in 1965, the International Harvester unit had a low range ratio of 2.03:1, compared to the 2.46:1 low ratio of the Bronco Dana 20, which was much more desirable for those enthusiasts looking for the lowest possible crawl ratio.

The mid-1960s was also a time when manufacturers were moving from the twin-stick transfer case shifters to single sticks to make shifting into 4WD less confusing and intimidating for first-time 4WD owners. Jeep had made the jump to a single-stick transfer case in its CJ-5 with the introduction of the 225-ci V-6 engine in 1965, and Ford followed suit with the Bronco (its F-Series 4x4 pickups always had them).

The single transfer-case shifter found on the 1966 Broncos is a textbook example of engineering revisions during production as customer feedback revealed weaknesses.

The initial shifter design was a single lever topped with a traditional shifter knob denoting the shift pattern, similar in design to the shifters used in other vehicles but longer in length, presumably to ease shifting effort. Several testers in early magazine reviews noted that the resulting shifter position was very close to the column-mounted transmission shifter when it was in third gear. *Four Wheeler*, in particular, noted that the shifter knob tips were less than an inch apart, and they feared that a driver may inadvertently shift into 4WD high.

International Harvester, in a period document that compared the Scout to the Bronco, noted that there were reports of the Bronco shifter breaking off at the transfer case due to the increased leverage of the long lever. The obvious agenda of a competitor's document notwithstanding, broken shift levers were reported by other 1966 owners.

Apparently, Ford listened to these complaints and later production models used a shorter version of the same shifter. Late in the model year, coinciding with the introduction of the V-8, Ford made a switch again to a shifter topped by a chrome T-handle. The handle housed a push-button assembly that actuated a gated plate at the base of the assembly to lock the shifter into the specific gearing options in the transfer case.

These first T-handle shifters had boots similar to, but larger than, the first-generation 1966 shifters. The driver still had to rely on the shift-pattern decals on the dash to determine exactly what gear the transfer case was in, and it likely took some time and finesse for owners to figure this out. The base of the shifter was modified as well with a stronger configuration that worked well for the next six model years.

Ford used double Cardan U-joints at the transfer end of the front and rear driveshafts in the Bronco. This allowed the transfer case to be mounted higher inside the frame for additional ground clearance.

Axles and Suspension

Although Ford used solid axles front and rear on the Bronco, as did other 4WD manufacturers in the 1960s, the outboard ends of the front axle were revolutionary at the time. According to Axelrad's SAE paper, Ford originally planned to use a Dana 27 closed-knuckle axle (used by CJ-5 and Scout) but decided to go with the Dana 30 front axle instead when it learned of its upcoming release.

Dana 30

Dana promised 500 pounds more capacity than the Dana 27 with the Dana 30 through the use of thicker walled, larger tubes. The 2,500-pound capacity rating fit neatly between the competition (2,000 pounds) and full-size pickups (Dana 44 with a 3,000-pound rating). More important, it featured the

The 1966–1967 locking hubs were optional ($66.08), and they are unique to those years. In 1968, Ford switched to a bright housing with a red dial.

industry's first open-knuckle design, which allowed much tighter turning angles than its closed-knuckle cousin (37 versus 29 degrees). Axelrad noted that the full advantage of the Bronco's coil-spring front suspension could not be realized without the use of the open knuckles due to the steering angle limitations of the closed-knuckle design.

Because the open-knuckle design required new sealing and lubrication strategies, Ford did extensive laboratory and road testing of the new axle seals to ensure that they were satisfactory. Road testing in sand, dirt, and gravel took place in northwestern Arizona surrounding the Arizona Ford Proving Grounds in Yucca. As a result of this testing, some seals and bearings were modified before production began.

The Dana 30 proved to be a good first volley across the bow of competitors in terms of upgraded axles. It gave up just a bit of ground clearance (1 to 1.5 inches) to go along with the slightly increased housing size. Ford did consider using the high-pinion Dana 44 that was introduced in the 1966 Ford F-100, but driveshaft clearance problems precluded its adaptation. Front brakes were of the drum variety and measured 11x2 inches.

The testers' impressions of the brakes were one area that showed how much perceptions and expectations of vehicle performance have changed since 1966. Nearly every test of the first Bronco praised the "large" brakes and their holding power, with some going so far as to exclaim that power brakes were not necessary because the existing setup was so strong and required such low pedal pressure. Those were the expectations in the mid-1960s. In just a few years, with power disc brakes much more prevalent on passenger cars, reviewers complained of fading, pulling, and excessively high pedal effort.

Rear Axle

The Bronco rear axle was Ford's familiar 9-inch (named for the diameter of its ring gear), the first variant of which had been introduced in Ford's 1957 cars. By the time of the Bronco's introduction, the 9-inch rear axle had gained a reputation for strength and ease of gear changes due to its drop-out differential assembly. In the Bronco, it was offered with two capacities: 2,780 pounds and 3,300 pounds, now known as the "small bearing" and "big bearing" rear ends, respectively. Each offered the option of a clutch-type limited-slip (Traction-Lok in Ford-speak) and axle ratios of 4.11 and 4.57:1 behind the 6-cylinder engine. When the V-8 was introduced, Ford added a 3.50:1 ratio to the mix. The 1966 rear axle housing is unique and identifiable from other years of the first generation by an inspection/fill plug on the rear of the housing.

Although the 9-inch rear axle was appreciated for its strength, it did suffer in the ground clearance department compared to the axles offered in the CJ-5 and Scout, hanging 1.5 to 2 inches lower than the competition. The rear brakes on all rear axles had a 10-inch diameter and measured 2.5 inches wide.

The Bronco's header front suspension was one of its strongest selling points when it was introduced and continued to be a prime reason for its success; none of its primary competitors switched to coil springs during the Bronco's lifetime. At its introduction, Ford touted its superior ride characteristics, improved handling, and ability to allow tighter turning circles as its key attributes.

Coil springs generally ride better than their leaf-spring counterparts due to the lack of internal friction inherent in leaf springs. Because the leaf springs on the front of solid-axle vehicles must serve a locating function in addition to providing ride comfort, they end up being stiffer because they are mounted farther inboard from the wheels than coils to achieve an acceptable turning radius.

Ford's radius arm suspension also had excellent anti-dive characteristics, with Ford Bronco engineer Paul Axelrad noting that the Bronco showed 102 percent anti-dive when 70 percent of the braking was accomplished at the front wheels. That is important during panic stops and when performing snowplowing chores with a heavy plow on front.

Body

The Bronco featured body-on-frame construction, combining a ladder frame with a unitized body (the cargo section of the body and the front seat and engine area were all one piece rather than separate structures as on conventional pickup trucks). The Bronco's frame was fully boxed along the length of its two rails and its two primary crossmembers, which made

This test involved test dummies in the front and rear seats, with dummy number-9 eerily looking at the camera as the front of the truck collapses around its legs. The rear-seat dummy has an arm outstretched, likely mimicking the reaction of a passenger in such a collision. (Photo Courtesy Jeff Trapp/Bill Theodoran Collection)

This Bronco intentionally being destroyed is a cringe-worthy moment for enthusiasts today. An instrumented "crash test dummy" is leaning forward in the rear seat. The front buckets are leaning forward and based on the location of the body relative to the axles, it appears the body has shifted forward on the frame. (Photo Courtesy Jeff Trapp/Bill Theodoran Collection)

Caught in mid-roll by the camera, window glass flies across the grass ahead of the rolling truck. A complete drivetrain is visible on this test vehicle, suggesting that a complete vehicle was used for the test. Based on the trees in the background and the terrain, all of these test photos appear to have been taken at the Dearborn Proving Grounds. (Photo Courtesy Jeff Trapp/Bill Theodoran Collection)

SUSPENSION DEVELOPMENT

The development of the monobeam front suspension is a fascinating story. The initial design of the suspension was done in parallel with the development of the famed Twin I-Beam 2WD front suspension, which was introduced on 1965 Ford pickups. In the early 1960s, a feasibility vehicle was built to design and test the monobeam front suspension. Based on a 4WD pickup, it featured a 5-foot cargo bed and rode on a 106-inch wheelbase.

The truck was built in several configurations with both 6- and 8-cylinder engines and 3- and 4-speed transmissions in front of a single-speed transfer case. The evaluation of this vehicle confirmed the desired handling, maneuverability, and performance of the monobeam front axle concept.

The feasibility vehicle's radius arms for the suspension were stamped pieces taken from a Twin I-Beam suspension and modified at the ends to attach to the monobeam axle housing. These radius arms attached to the axle housing with large rubber bushings, which worked fine in testing but were deemed to be unnecessarily complex for production. The final design used forged radius arms that clamped wedges on the axle housing with rubber isolators between the arms and the axles. Ford tested this configuration for 500,000 cycles without failure and deemed it acceptable for production.

A vehicle that uses a leading arm suspension like the monobeam front end with radius arms requires some type of lateral control for the axle as well. Ford chose to use a panhard rod, or track bar in Ford lingo, to locate the front axle. Because the location of the track bar is critical from a vehicle handling standpoint, Ford tested several mounting locations for the bar mounting points and tested them on ride and handling courses to arrive at the ideal configuration. After the mounting points were set, a complete track bar system was fatigue-tested in the laboratory by subjecting it to simulated vehicle loads for more than 1,000,000 cycles without failure.

It's a little-known fact that the first Bronco package study included mirror-image front and rear suspensions. A similar configuration was later used by other manufacturers, but in the early 1960s, Ford decided against coil springs in the rear due to the encroachment into that ever-important ramp break-over area by the radius arms and their mounting brackets.

Instead, Ford used a traditional Hotchkis-type suspension with leaf springs anchoring each rear corner. With the standard 3,900-pound gross vehicle weight (GVW) package, the leaf springs had five leafs and the optional 4,700 GVW package springs had six in their packs. Rear shocks were mounted angling forward from the axle to the frame with stud mounts on top from the Bronco's introduction until March 1966, when Ford switched them to angling rearward with eye mounts on top. The location and mounting configuration remained that way through the end of the first generation's production in 1977.

Due to the Bronco's weight and short wheelbase, the Bronco was never known as a great tow vehicle. Ford did offer a trailer hitch for the Bronco as a dealer accessory and rated the tow capacity at 2,000 pounds.

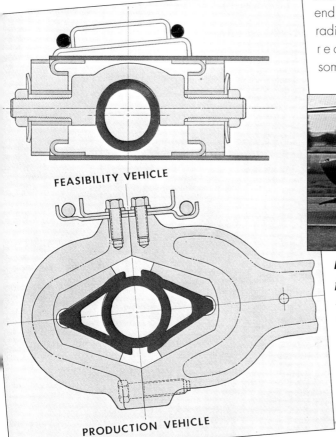

FEASIBILITY VEHICLE

PRODUCTION VEHICLE

Exceeding its rated towing capacity, this 1966 Bronco pulls the most valuable payload ever pulled by a Bronco: the 1966 Le Mans–winning GT40 of Chris Amon and Bruce McLaren. The GT40 sold for $22 million in 2014. (Photo Courtesy John Fowler)

This cross-sectional view shows the attachment of the radius arm to the front axle on the feasibility vehicle (modified 4WD pickup truck) compared to the design used on production Broncos from 1966 to 1979. (Photo Courtesy SAE International)

Bulletin No. 30

January 28, 1966

588 WATER LEAKS – 1966 BRONCO

(1966 Broncos)

Several areas of the 1966 Bronco are susceptible to water leaks, which have been corrected in production as of September 13, 1965. Dealers confronted with customer complaints of Bronco water leaks can make corrections as follows:

1. PROBLEM: Models 97 & 98

Water leaks under the door opening weatherstrip at the "B" pillar at the belt line. The adhesive specified to be used in area shown on Figure 1 was inadvertently omitted.

REPAIR:

Remove the screw attaching the weatherstrip to the "B" pillar. Apply COAZ-19552-A Rubber Cement to the pillar as shown in Fig. 1. Reinstall the weatherstrip.

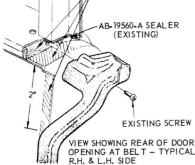

REMOVE WEATHERSTRIP AT TOP END, APPLY C0AZ-19552-A RUBBER CEMENT TO AREAS INDICATED AND REINSTALL WEATHERSTRIP

AB-19560-A SEALER (EXISTING)

2"

EXISTING SCREW

VIEW SHOWING REAR OF DOOR OPENING AT BELT – TYPICAL R.H. & L.H. SIDE

Fig. 1 – Water Leaks – 1966 Bronco – (Article 588)

2. PROBLEM: Models 97 & 98

Water leaks through a hole in the upper rear corner of the roof panel door opening.

REPAIR:

Peel the weatherstrip from the upper rear corner. Apply AB-19560-A sealer to the corner as shown in Fig. 2. Apply COAZ-19552-A Rubber Cement to the flange and reinstall the weatherstrip.

3. PROBLEM: Model 97

Water enters the passenger compartment at the bottom corners of the Panel-Body Front (bulkhead) and the body side.

REPAIR:

Apply AB-19560-A Sealer to the front and back of the Panel-Body Front (bulkhead) as shown in Fig. 3 and 4.

4. PROBLEM: Model 98

The lift gate opening weatherstrip does not provide an adequate seal along the top of the lift gate. This is caused by use of a weatherstrip which is too long between the miter joints, resulting in excess material and an ineffective seal.

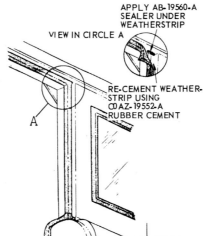

APPLY AB-19560-A SEALER UNDER WEATHERSTRIP

VIEW IN CIRCLE A

RE-CEMENT WEATHERSTRIP USING C0AZ-19552-A RUBBER CEMENT

A

VIEW SHOWING UPPER REAR CORNER OF DOOR OPENING – TYPICAL R.H. & L.H. SIDE

Fig. 2 – Water Leaks – 1966 Bronco – (Article 588)

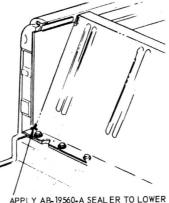

APPLY AB-19560-A SEALER TO LOWER CORNERS OF BODY FRONT PANEL

VIEW SHOWING FRONT OF PANEL-BODY FRONT (BULKHEAD) – TYPICAL R.H. & L.H. SIDE

Fig. 3 – Water Leaks – 1966 Bronco – (Article 588)

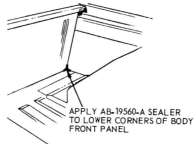

APPLY AB-19560-A SEALER TO LOWER CORNERS OF BODY FRONT PANEL

VIEW SHOWING REAR OF PANEL-BODY FRONT (BULKHEAD) – TYPICAL R.H. & L.H. SIDE

Fig. 4 – Water Leaks – 1966 Bronco – (Article 588)

REPAIR:

Remove the existing C6TB-98404A06-B Weatherstrip. Apply COAZ-19552-A Rubber Cement to the flange. Obtain and install a C6TB-98404A06-C Weatherstrip. (No sketch).

5. PROBLEM: Model 98

Water leaks under the vertical portion of the lift gate weatherstrip due to poor adhesion of the weatherstrip to its mounting flange.

REPAIR:

Peel the vertical portion of the weatherstrip from its mounting flange. Apply COAZ-19552-A Rubber Cement to both faces of the flange in a sufficient amount to insure proper retention and replace the weatherstrip. (No sketch).

6. PROBLEM: Model 98

Roof panel to pickup box weatherstrip leaks at the joint of the body rear corner panel to the body side panel and at the body rear corner panel.

REPAIR:

Loosen the eight (8) bolts on each side of the vehicle securing the roof assembly to the body side, one (1) bolt on each side is located at the tailgate weatherstrip, the other seven (7) are along the joint at the roof to body side. Apply AB-19560-A Sealer to the joint of the body corner panel and the body side panel, also apply sealer to the body corner panel. Refer to Fig. 5. Tighten the bolts.

7. PROBLEM: Model 98

Water enters the vehicle at the outboard junction of the lift gate and tailgate due to the upper weatherstrip on "C" pillar filling with water and overflowing.

REPAIR:

Pull the inboard lip of the weatherstrip down and drill a 3/8" diameter hole in the outboard surface of the weatherstrip assembly and the "C" pillar. See Fig. 6. This will allow the water to drain into the "C" pillar and out of the vehicle.

8. PROBLEM: All Models

The up flange on the cowl top center extension does not extend far enough at each end to drain the water out of the vehicle that enters between the windshield hinge and cowl top panel.

REPAIR:

1. Fabricate from .030 steel stock a right and left hand drain extension and paint them black. See Fig. 7.

2. Loosen the windshield locking knobs.

3. Position the drain extension behind the existing flange as shown in sketch #7 and using the drain extension as a template, drill one 7/64" diameter attaching hole in the cowl top extension.

4. Remove the drain extension and apply a bead of AB-19560-A Sealer as shown on Fig. 7. Secure the extension to the upper cowl with a #6-32 x 3/8" Pan Head Tapping Screw (#51754-S2).

The earliest Broncos had a host of water leakage problems, so Ford issued a series of Technical Service Bulletins with recommended fixes. They usually involved applying copious amounts of silicone sealer and, in one case, drilling 15 holes in the floor under the floor mat so the water could drain. Imagine such a fix being recommended today.

5. Tighten the windshield locking knobs.

9. PROBLEM: All Models

Windshield weatherstrip leaks at outboard area of top windshield frame.

REPAIR:

Loosen the eight (8) bolts attaching the roof to the windshield header sufficiently to apply AB-19560-A Sealer as shown in Fig. 8. Tighten the eight bolts.

10. PROBLEM: All Models

Water enters the vehicle around the brake pedal support bracket attaching bolts and cowl top panel.

REPAIR:

Loosen the nine bolts attaching the pedal support bracket to the cowl top panel and apply AB-19560 Sealer to the holes in the cowl top panel as shown.

11. PROBLEM: All Models

Water enters the vehicle between the heater air inlet duct collar and the opening in the cowl side panel.

REPAIR:

1. Remove the air inlet duct collar assembly from the cowl side panel by removing three attaching screws.

2. Apply a bead of AB-19560-A Sealer around the perimeter of the duct opening in the cowl side panel, and the screw holes. See Fig. 10, view A.

3. Reinstall the air inlet duct collar assembly to the cowl side panel assembly.

11A. PROBLEM: All Models

Water enters vehicle at the mounting surface of the left hand vent air duct due to poor sealing qualities of the air duct gasket to the dash panel and excessive sealer in the drain hole.

REPAIR:

Locate the area of water entry around the air duct gasket and apply AB-19560-A Sealer as required. Detach drain tube from dash panel and remove all excessive sealer found in the drain hole. See Fig. 10, view B.

12. PROBLEM: All Models

Water enters the vehicle between the rear weld flange on the cowl top panel and upper cowl extension near the ends, at the hood hinge pockets, and on the right hand side of lower cowl extension.

REPAIR:

1. Remove if necessary the existing sealer in these areas and apply a daub of AB-19560-A Sealer. See Fig. 11.

2. Fabricate from .030 steel stock a right hand and left hand cowl side drain trough and apply black paint. See Fig. 12. To install the drain troughs, the following procedures are recommended: Right Hand Side Trough

1. Remove the glove compartment from the vehicle.

2. Position the right hand drain trough on the cowl side to locate and drill two 9/64″ diameter attaching holes in the cowl side panel.

3. Locate and hole saw (1) 3/4″ diameter hole in the cowl side panel to drain water out through the pillar area. See Fig. 13.

4. Apply AB-19560-A Sealer between the drain trough and cowl side and along rear edge of trough. See Fig. 13.

5. Attach the drain trough to the cowl side with two (2) #42120-S8 #10-16 x 3/8″ Hex Washer Head Tapping Screws.

6. Reinstall the glove compartment in the vehicle.

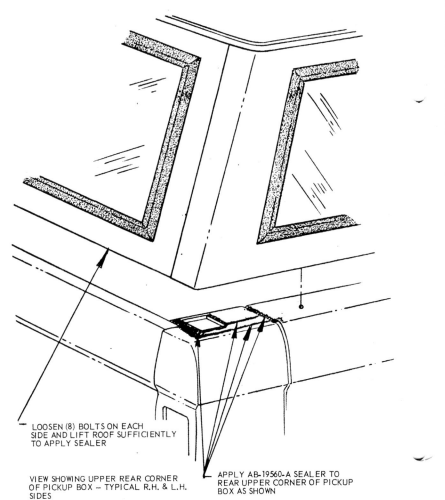

LOOSEN (8) BOLTS ON EACH SIDE AND LIFT ROOF SUFFICIENTLY TO APPLY SEALER

VIEW SHOWING UPPER REAR CORNER OF PICKUP BOX – TYPICAL R.H. & L.H. SIDES

APPLY AB-19560-A SEALER TO REAR UPPER CORNER OF PICKUP BOX AS SHOWN

Fig. 5 – Water Leaks – 1966 Bronco – (Article 588)

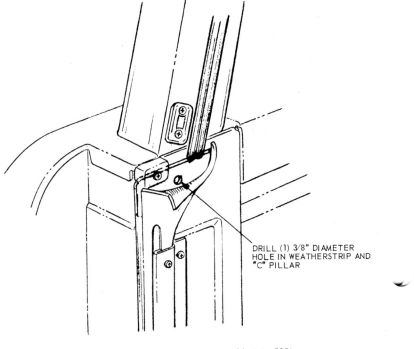

DRILL (1) 3/8″ DIAMETER HOLE IN WEATHERSTRIP AND "C" PILLAR

Fig. 6 – Water Leaks - 1966 Bronco – (Article 588)

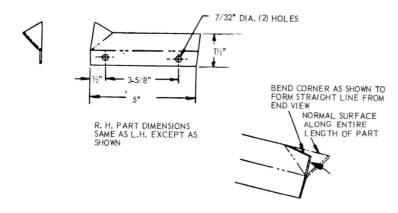

7/32" DIA. (2) HOLES

1½"

½" ⊢ 3-5/8"

5"

R. H. PART DIMENSIONS SAME AS L.H. EXCEPT AS SHOWN

BEND CORNER AS SHOWN TO FORM STRAIGHT LINE FROM END VIEW

NORMAL SURFACE ALONG ENTIRE LENGTH OF PART

VIEW A SHOWING END CONFIGURATION

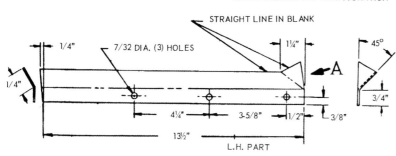

STRAIGHT LINE IN BLANK

1/4" 7/32 DIA. (3) HOLES 1¼" 45°

1/4"

A

3/4"

4¼" 3-5/8" 1/2" 3/8"

13½"

L.H. PART

FABRICATE AND PAINT BLACK (1) R.H. & (1) L.H. TROUGH AS SHOWN. MATERIAL: .030 THICK 2" WIDE STEEL SHEET STOCK

Fig. 12 — Water Leaks — 1966 Bronco — (Article 588)

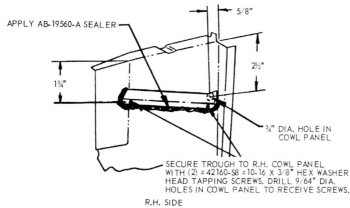

APPLY AB-19560-A SEALER

5/8"

2½"

1¾"

¾" DIA. HOLE IN COWL PANEL

SECURE TROUGH TO R.H. COWL PANEL WITH (2) #42160-S8 #10-16 X 3/8" HEX WASHER HEAD TAPPING SCREWS. DRILL 9/64" DIA. HOLES IN COWL PANEL TO RECEIVE SCREWS.

R.H. SIDE

1¼"

¾" DIA. HOLE IN COWL PANEL

4-5/8"

¾" MINIMUM SLOPE

APPLY AB-19560-A SEALER

SECURE TROUGH TO L.H. COWL PANEL WITH (3) 42160-S8 #10-16 X 3/8" HEX WASHER HEAD TAPPING SCREWS. DRILL 9/64" DIA. HOLES IN COWL PANEL TO RECEIVE SCREWS

VIEWS SHOWING R.H. & L.H. COWL PANELS

L.H. SIDE

Fig. 13 — Water Leaks — 1966 Bronco — (Article 588)

Left Hand Side Trough

1. Position the left hand drain trough on the cowl side to locate and drill three 9/64" diameter attaching holes in the cowl panel.

2. Locate and hole saw 3/4" diameter hole in the cowl side panel to drain water out through the pillar area. See Fig. 13. (Use an offset drill for this operation).

3. Apply AB-19560-A Sealer between the drain trough and cowl side and along rear edge of trough. See Fig. 13.

4. Attach the drain trough to the cowl side with three (3) #42120-S8 #10-16 x 3/8" Hex Washer Head Tapping Screws.

The above correction is covered by Operation No. SP-02228-A-66, 1.1 hrs. (both sides).

13. PROBLEM: Models 97-98 Standard — 96 RPO Doors

Inner door panel cover leaks at lower edges due to excessive sealer plugging the drain holes in inner door panel. REPAIR:

Remove window regulator handle and door latch handle. Remove door inside panel cover plate. Remove excessive sealer from drain holes in door inner panel as shown in Fig. 14. Make certain that all three lower attaching holes are surrounded with sealer prior to re-installation of the cover and handles to the door.

589 EXHAUST MANIFOLD RE-STRICTION

(1966 390, 428 Engines)

When complaints of rough idle, low manifold vacuum (approximately 10" at idle), backfire through carburetor, or poor performance cannot be corrected by normal tune-up procedures on new cars it is advisable to remove the left exhaust manifold and inspect for a restriction.

Flash can block the manifold during the casting process. This can occur between number 6 and 7 ports or number 8 port. If flash is present, the restriction should be removed and the manifold reinstalled.

590 WATER LEAKS IN THE CARGO AREA

(1966 Ranchero)

Field complaints of water in the tool storage compartment have been received on early production 1966 Ranchero pickups. This problem was corrected in production on October 29, 1965, by improved sealing. In the event that water leaks are encountered they can be repaired by loosening the attaching bolts at the forward load floor and adding sealer.

Dealership personnel should note and caution the owner against removing sealer that is squeezed out at the joints and the mounting bolts in the cargo area. Removal of sealer in this area can cause water leaks which can only be corrected by resealing.

WARRANTY STATUS — REIMBURSABLE

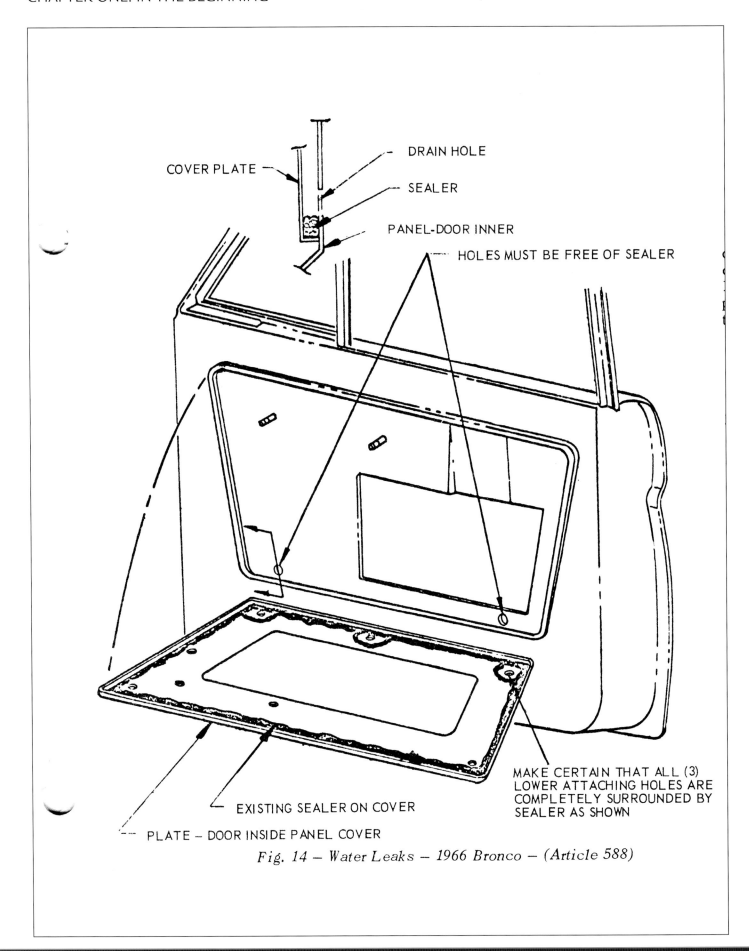

COVER PLATE

DRAIN HOLE

SEALER

PANEL-DOOR INNER

HOLES MUST BE FREE OF SEALER

MAKE CERTAIN THAT ALL (3) LOWER ATTACHING HOLES ARE COMPLETELY SURROUNDED BY SEALER AS SHOWN

EXISTING SEALER ON COVER

PLATE – DOOR INSIDE PANEL COVER

Fig. 14 – Water Leaks – 1966 Bronco – (Article 588)

VIEW SHOWING FRONT EDGE OF DOOR OPENING AT BELT LINE
TYPICAL R.H. AND L.H. SIDE

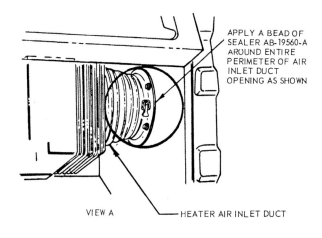

APPLY SEALER AB-19560-A AS SHOWN

FRONT OF VEHICLE

DRILL (1) 7/64" DIA. HOLE & SECURE DRAIN EXTENSION WITH (1) #6-32 x 3/8" PAN HEAD TAPPING SCREW #51754-S2

1¾"

¾"

¾"

3/8"

5/16"

7/16" DIA. HOLE

FABRICATE (1) L.H. & R.H. DRAIN EXTENSION FROM .030 CRS. NOTE: ROUND CORNER AS SHOWN TO MATCH CONTOUR OF THE COWL TOP EXTENSION. R.H. SHOWN – L.H. OPPOSITE

Fig. 7 – Water Leaks – 1966 Bronco – (Article 588)

LOOSEN (8) BOLTS SUFFICIENTLY TO PERMIT APPLICATION OF SEALER

VIEW SHOWING UPPER CORNER OF WINDSHIELD AND ROOF

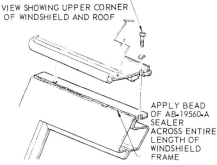

APPLY BEAD OF AB-19560-A SEALER ACROSS ENTIRE LENGTH OF WINDSHIELD FRAME

Fig. 8 – Water Leaks – 1966 Bronco – (Article 588)

VIEW SHOWING BRAKE PEDAL SUPPORT

LOOSEN (9) BOLTS SECURING BRAKE PEDAL SUPPORT, APPLY AB-19560-A SEALER AROUND EACH ATTACHING HOLE AND RETIGHTEN BOLTS.

Fig. 9 – Water Leaks – 1966 Bronco – (Article 588)

APPLY A BEAD OF SEALER AB-19560-A AROUND ENTIRE PERIMETER OF AIR INLET DUCT OPENING AS SHOWN

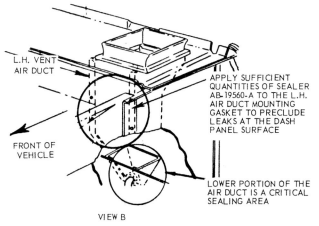

VIEW A

HEATER AIR INLET DUCT

L.H. VENT AIR DUCT

APPLY SUFFICIENT QUANTITIES OF SEALER AB-19560-A TO THE L.H. AIR DUCT MOUNTING GASKET TO PRECLUDE LEAKS AT THE DASH PANEL SURFACE

FRONT OF VEHICLE

LOWER PORTION OF THE AIR DUCT IS A CRITICAL SEALING AREA

VIEW B

Fig. 10 – Water Leaks – 1966 Bronco – (Article 588)

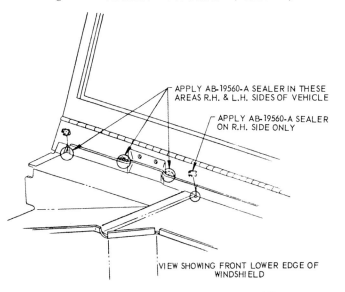

APPLY AB-19560-A SEALER IN THESE AREAS R.H. & L.H. SIDES OF VEHICLE

APPLY AB-19560-A SEALER ON R.H. SIDE ONLY

VIEW SHOWING FRONT LOWER EDGE OF WINDSHIELD

Fig. 11 – Water Leaks – 1966 Bronco – (Article 588)

606 WATER ENTRAPMENT IN THE REINFORCING BEADS IN THE FRONT FLOOR PAN UNDER THE RUBBER FLOOR MAT

(1966 Bronco Model 96 (Roadster))

Water may become trapped under the rubber floor mat and collect in the reinforcing beads in the front floor pan of early production Model 96 Bronco vehicles. This condition could result in premature rusting of the floor pan and cause customer dissatisfaction.

This problem was corrected in production on November 15, 1965, by drilling (15) 3/16 in. diameter holes, one each in the center of each reinforcing bead in the front floor pan to allow the water to drain out of the reinforcing beads.

Dealers encountering customer complaints of water collecting in the floor pan beads of the Bronco should employ the following corrective procedure:

1. Remove the rubber front floor mat.
2. Drill or punch (15) 3/16 in. diameter holes, one in the center of each reinforcing bead as indicated in Fig. 36.

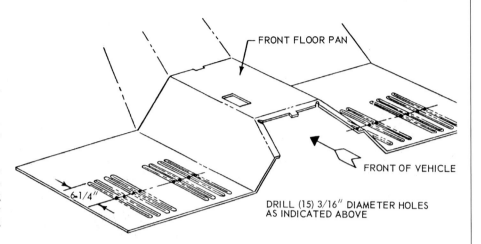

Fig. 35 – Improper Installation of Dimmer Switch – (Article 605)

FRONT FLOOR PAN

FRONT OF VEHICLE

6-1/4"

DRILL (15) 3/16" DIAMETER HOLES AS INDICATED ABOVE

Fig. 36 – Water Entrapment in the Reinforcing Beads in the Front Floor Pan under the Rubber Floor Mat – 1966 Bronco – Model 96 (Article 606)

3. Repaint around the holes to prevent rusting.
4. Replace the front floor mat.

WARRANTY STATUS – REIMBURSABLE
Oper: SP-11135-B-66
Time: 0.2 hrs.

609 WATER LEAK – ANTENNA LEAD GROMMET – COWL SIDE AREA

(1966 Fairlane, Falcon, All Models)

Noticeable water leaks in the right side of the cowl panel are sometimes caused by the improper seating of the radio antenna lead grommet. The antenna lead grommet is located in a critical water drain off area. As shown in Fig. 38, the antenna lead grommet should be checked for a tight seal when customer complaints of water leaks in the right hand cowl side area are encountered.

WARRANTY STATUS – INFORMATION ONLY

610 POTENTIAL WATER LEAKS AROUND THE COVER PLATE ON THE REAR CORNER PILLARS

(1966 Bronco – Model 98)

It has been noted on units equipped with the long roof, that water enters into the vehicle at the top of the rear corner body pillars and flows into the stake pockets. This water has a tendency to leak into the passenger compartment in the area where the rear corner cover plate attaches to the pillar. This problem was corrected in production on September 21, 1965. (Ref. Fig. 39).

Dealers encountering customer complaints relative to this problem should perform the following corrective procedure:

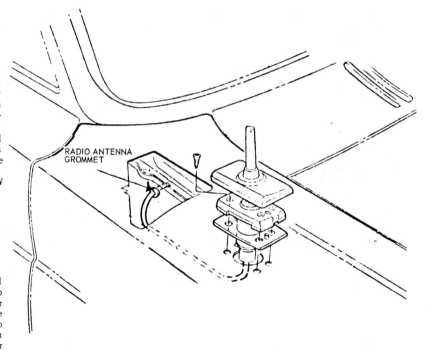

RADIO ANTENNA GROMMET

Fig. 38 – Radio Antenna Lead Grommet – (Article 609)

1. Remove the Body Rear Corner Panel Reinforcement Cover Plate (C4TB-9928038-9) by removing one attaching screw (52721-S8).
2. Apply a bead of AB-19560-A Sealer around the perimeter of the cover plate and the attaching screw hole as shown on the attached sketch.
3. Reinstall the cover plate to the rear corner pillar.
WARRANTY STATUS — REIMBURSABLE

611 GASOLINE LEAKS AND/OR FUEL ODORS IN THE PASSENGER COMPARTMENT

(1966 Fairlane — Sedans and Convertibles)

Some 1966 sedans and convertibles built prior to November 15, 1965, may experience a problem of gasoline leakage because of a fractured weld at the juncture of the fuel tank filler neck and the fuel tank at the top side. This fracture results from the filler neck interfering with the back panel at the top of the filler neck access hole.

Production correction consisted of decreasing the height of the filler neck at the back panel opening and thus eliminating the metal to metal interference.

When customer complaints of a gasoline leak or odors are encountered, the following steps should be taken to correct the problem.

1. Examine the filler neck to fuel tank soldered joint to determine if there is a break in the weld.
2. If there is a break in the weld examine the back panel to determine if an interference condition exists between the fuel tank filler neck and the back panel at the top side.

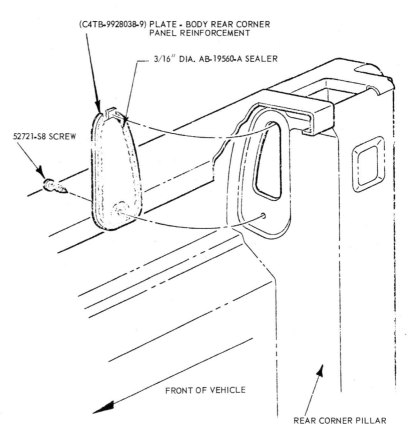

Fig. 39 — Potential Water Leaks Around the Cover Plate on the Rear Corner Pillars — 1966 Bronco — Model 98 (Article 610)

The pieces in the corners of the frame rails and the front crossmember on the Bronco frame are called K-braces. Budd Company's initial testing of prototype Bronco frames showed that they did not meet requirements for torsional rigidity, so these braces were added. (Photo Courtesy Tim Hulick)

it extremely strong and stiff. The combination of the Bronco's unitized body and strong frame made it about three to four times torsionally stiffer than a pickup truck of the same era. Adding a roof increased the torsion and bending stiffness and adding doors increased the bending stiffness. The front and rear bumpers also provided a substantial contribution to the torsional stiffness.

The Budd Company conducted testing on a bare frame and a body-on-frame before the first mechanical prototype was built. After gathering input from the monobeam-equipped feasibility vehicle and another truck run on some durability courses, Budd subjected the frame to 70,000 pothole cycles at each wheel and 308 lateral loads for each 1,000 pothole cycles.

Based on the results of this testing, Ford modified the design of the transmission/transfer case crossmember and added K-braces to the front and rear crossmembers, which after additional testing, proved to be successful and were incorporated into the production frame design.

The first frame design also had all the body mount brackets and suspension hangers welded to the frame rails. After some additional fatigue analysis, several of these members were

These metal tags are known as buck tags. They were wired to the firewalls of 1966 and 1967 Broncos and indicated to assembly-line workers what was supposed to be on the Bronco. The black tag is from an early truck and spells out what should be installed. By the time of the teal tag, the words were shortened to abbreviations. Trying to decipher these tags can be a challenge. (Photo Courtesy Tim Hulick)

instead bolted or riveted to the frame and the radius arm brackets were both bolted and welded to the frame. Further body testing brought about some changes, including relocation of cross sills, tunnel and front floor surface changes, mounting flange revisions, and additional material to strengthen panels.

The body was mounted to the frame with eight rubber mounts, offering excellent frame-to-body isolation. In addition, the mounts were designed for ease of assembly. All of the mounts were installed on the frame line and when the body was installed, an assembly-line pit was not needed and one operator could handle the joining of the two assemblies.

Interior

By today's standards, the Bronco's interior was stark, but in 1966, Ford proudly bragged about its standard features, including a vinyl rubber floor mat, front seat belts, lockable glove compartment, dual vacuum windshield wipers, ashtray, and the aforementioned column-mounted transmission shifter and single transfer case shifter. The instrument cluster, mounted in the dash to the left of the steering column, housed a speedometer, fuel gauge, temperature gauge, and ammeter. A heater and

The interior of this survivor 1966 roadster shows off the 1966-only silver upholstery on the front and rear seats and the black 1966-only armrests on the rear seat. (Photo Courtesy Tim Hulick)

This roadster is equipped with a set of the mirrors commonly referred to as "roadster mirrors," so called because they were standard on roadsters. They were seen in 1966 on wagons, sport utilities, and roadsters alike. (Photo Courtesy Freeze Frame Image LLC, Al Rogers)

The standard spare-tire mount for Broncos equipped with a bulkhead behind the front seat was the mount shown on this roadster. An optional mount put the spare tire on the inside of the tailgate, which made it hard to raise and lower due to the added weight. (Photo Courtesy Freeze Frame Image LLC, Al Rogers)

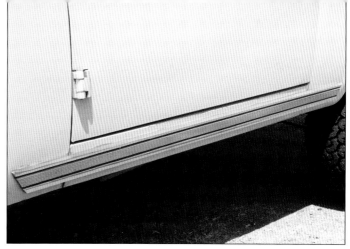

This roadster is equipped with a heater and defroster, a $60.55 option for 1966. The 1966-only knobs were pulled from the Ford truck parts bin. The ashtray was placed near the driver in 1966–1967 and moved closer to the passenger in 1968. The screw-on cover at the right covers the radio speaker; it is found only in roadsters because many of them did not have tops. (Photo Courtesy Freeze Frame Image LLC, Al Rogers)

Rocker trim was introduced in 1966 along with the red and white rocker stripes that were available for that year only. Obviously, you could only have one or the other. (Photo Courtesy Tim Hulick)

THE PONY UPHOLSTERY MYSTERY

The top-of-the-line upholstery available in 1965–1966 Mustangs became known as the Pony upholstery, consisting of sections of horizontal and vertical stitching bisected by a horizontal panel embossed with pony images running toward a small, rectangular badge in the center. Offered in both single and two-tone color combinations, the patterns were definitely a step up from the standard Mustang upholstery.

As the Bronco market heated up, collectors found that a number of the 1966 trucks (6 of 10) have original Pony upholstery on the front and rear seats, even though no official documentation exists to indicate it was ever an option. Because the 1966 Bronco's front bucket seats are Mustang seats, retrofitting Pony upholstery to them is a fairly straightforward proposition. However, the Bronco's model-specific rear seat is a bit more

challenging to upholster in the Pony pattern.

Because no documentation exists that it was ever a factory option, but several original owners have sworn their trucks came that way from the factory, some historians believe it may have been a dealer-installed option or an aftermarket item available from dealers. Bronco historian Tim Hulick has noted that the body code on the data plate on these trucks is a "9," which corresponds to the "parchment rosette" code from later years. Hulick also notes that the inset portion of the upholstery that includes the embossed horses is a color that appears to be exclusive to the Broncos.

The Pony upholstery mystery continues to provoke debate and discussion among owners and historians alike.

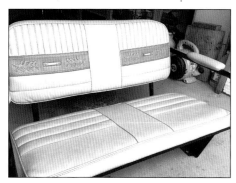

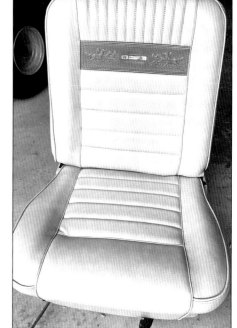

This 1966 Bronco rear seat is upholstered with the Pony upholstery; the subject of many spirited discussions among Bronco aficionados. Factory or not? The jury is still out. (Photo Courtesy Tim Hulick)

This is a close-up view of the horses in the Pony panel on the front seat. Experts on the 1966 Bronco note that the colors in the upholstery found in the late 1966 examples are Bronco-unique colors not found on any Mustang upholstery. (Photo Courtesy Tim Hulick)

Because 1966 Bronco seats were early Mustang seats, the Pony upholstery fit well on these buckets. The number of trucks upholstered with this pattern is unknown, but a handful of trucks, including those from original owners, have the unique pattern on their seats. (Photo Courtesy Tim Hulick)

defroster were optional. A full-width bench seat in front was the standard seat with a metal bulkhead behind it.

Optional was a single (driver's) or double front bucket seats with a bulkhead behind them. With the buckets, a rear bench was also optional. If the rear bench was selected, the bulkhead was deleted so access to the rear seat was possible. For 1966, the seats were upholstered in a silver-gray vinyl fabric. The rear seat's armrests were black in color.

For customers wanting more flash, 1966 Broncos could be ordered with the Custom Equipment package. It included front and rear chrome bumpers, bright-metal taillight bezels, hubcaps (on the 15-inch wheels), armrests on the models with doors, a cigarette lighter, bright-metal horn ring, and sun visors on both sides of the windshield frame. These items could also be ordered individually from the factory.

Tires and Wheels

Standard rolling stock on 1966 Broncos were 15x5.5–inch steel wheels carrying 7.35x15 bias-ply tubeless tires. Although this size seems extremely narrow today, period testers praised the choice as the competition offered 6-inch-wide tires as standard equipment. The 15-inch wheels could be equipped with 1966-only hubcaps if the Custom Equipment package was checked on the option list. Other tubeless tire options for 1966 were 7.75x15, 8.15x15, and 9.15x15 high-flotation tires. Ford also offered tube-type tires in the 6.50x16 size on 5-inch wide wheels. Of the two, the 15-inch wheels were much more common, with the 16-inch wheels highly prized by collectors today.

On the roadster, sports utility, and wagon models with bulkheads, the spare tire was mounted on the back of the bulkhead on the passenger's side. On wagons and roadsters with the optional rear seat, it was centrally mounted on the inside of the tailgate.

Colors

The 1966 Bronco boasted an impressive palette of 11 colors. The metal roofs were painted Wimbledon White to give a two-tone paint combination. Red and white rocker panel stripes were an option as well.

Options

In addition to the options that Ford installed at the factory, the Bronco also offered a number of accessories that were Ford sanctioned. They had Ford part numbers but were manufactured by aftermarket suppliers and installed at the local dealer. These options included a convertible top with vinyl doors and plastic windows, a dash or windshield-mounted compass,

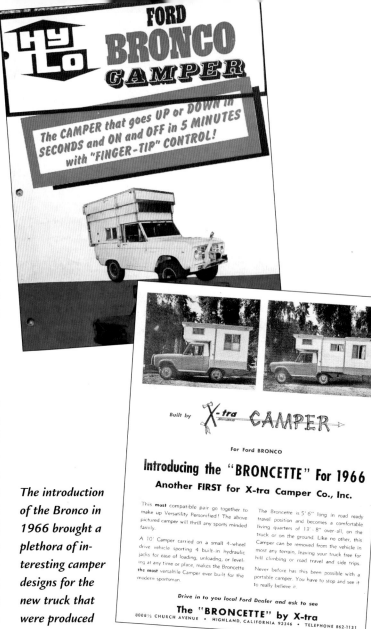

The introduction of the Bronco in 1966 brought a plethora of interesting camper designs for the new truck that were produced in very small numbers. Taking some of these designs out on the open road, or the trail, was often a test of even the hardiest driver's nerves.

dash-mounted handrail, Warn locking hubs, PTO, CB radio, snowplow, winch, tachometer, air bags for the coil springs, and a trailer hitch. Ford also listed such rarely seen options as a backhoe, boom, firefighting equipment, grass mower, posthole digger, rotary broom, spray equipment, trencher, and wrecker attachments.

Production and Collectibility

Total production for the 1966 model year was 23,776 units. Based on Ford sales data, Bronco sales momentum took a while to build, with only about 6,600 units sold through January 31, 1966. To put the annual total sales in perspective, this number represented approximately 50 percent of the total market sales of the prior model year, spread across four manufacturers.

Although these sales numbers were small compared to the rest of Ford's line, they represented a strong number in the segment, accounting for 40 percent of the sport utility sales for the 1966 model year. Predictably, the largest seller was the wagon with 12,756 examples going to customers. The sports utility pickup achieved just under half that amount with 6,930 units. The roadster logged an impressive 4,090 sales. Stories have surfaced telling how roadsters languished on dealers' lots for a year or more without selling. Many also had hardtops and doors added to them to make them more palatable for

This father and son are enjoying their 1966 Broncos on Arizona trails. These Broncos are both show and go, equally at home at a Goodguys car show and crawling down an Arizona trail. (Photo Courtesy Mark Gangsei)

This recently unearthed 1966 roadster is a true survivor. Bearing a VIN that places it on the first or second day of production in August 1965, and with the odometer registering only about 40,000 original miles, it carries many unique parts that were seen on the earliest trucks only.

A study in contrasts: The bone-stock Springtime Yellow 1966 U14 half cab looks downright dainty compared to the 1969 Super Swamper–shod trail rig. A majority of first-generation Broncos have received many modifications over the years that reflect their owners' tastes and preferences. (Photo Courtesy Tim Hulick)

This 1966 roadster calls Elizabeth, Colorado, home. Sporting a set of the 1966-only wheel covers, it sees plenty of use exploring Colorado mountain trails. The pup seems to like roadster rides as well. (Photo Courtesy Scott Barnes)

Bronco enthusiasts over the years created some interesting names for unique features on the trucks. For example, the small metal creases outboard of the headlight ring on the early 1966s are called eyebrows; thus, the early grilles (the first four to five months of production) with this feature have become known as eyebrow grilles. (Photo Courtesy Tim Hulick)

customers wanting more amenities than the sparsely equipped trucks offered.

The desirability and collectability of the 1966 models has ebbed and flowed over the years. In some states with strict emissions laws, such as Arizona, the 1966s have always been popular because they fall outside the required testing years.

In other cases, 1966s have not been as popular because most of them were fairly rudimentary in terms of options, and the 6-cylinder engine was not desirable. In more recent times, as the value of stock vehicles has risen, the 1966s have gained in value as collectors search out early or first-year production vehicles to add to their collections.

PROTOTYPE BRONCO

One of the first prototypes. The first production Bronco. The "Shelby Bronco." It's been known by a number of names over the years, and its story and whereabouts were a mystery to many and a subject of much speculation for many years. Noted historian Jim Allen said it best when he called it "the earliest known surviving Bronco."

The vehicle identification number (VIN) plate, which is mounted on the driver-side doorjamb instead of the kick panel on production trucks, decodes as a U14 Sports Utility painted Rangoon Red. In a field of trucks that have great stories behind them, this blue half cab has one of the most interesting ones of all.

The fifth character in the VIN, "S," indicates this is a very special Bronco. The S denotes that it was built at the Allen Park, Michigan, assembly plant, known as the "Pilot Plant" for new Ford cars and trucks.

After production, the whereabouts of the prototype truck were unknown. It was known that in July 1967, it was loaded onto a car hauler in Dearborn and taken west to Carroll Shel-

by's Shelby American facility in Los Angeles, California. There, the Bronco was registered for a time to Lew Spencer's High Performance Motors dealership in El Segundo, California, before making a move to the Christmas Land and Cattle Company, a ranch co-owned by Carroll Shelby and D. A. Witts, near Terlingua, Texas.

Living on the ranch for many years, the Bronco lived a hard life, with repairs made by ranch hands or occasionally by the nearby dealership, Big Bend Ford. In 1978, ranch hand Harold Wynn decided that he had had enough of paying for repairs on the old Bronco and inquired at the dealership about trading it for a new 1978 model. After some wrangling with one of the dealership's co-owners, Vincent "Vinnie" Yakubanski, Wynn got a new Bronco and Vinnie got the prototype for $100.

Vinnie soon repainted the red Bronco a fresh shade of 1979 Ford metallic blue on the body with gray covering the half cab. Vinnie used the little Bronco as a family recreational rig and a motorcycle hauler. He even used it to haul a dignitary

This familiar press release photo reveals itself to be the prototype Bronco in one of its iterations. Key identifying factors include the non-standard Ford letters on the grille, 289 badge placement on the fender, lack of locking hubs, and the unique rocker trim that has only been seen on this truck. (Photo Courtesy Motor Trend Group, LLC)

Today, the prototype Bronco wears a half cab top and has retained many of its unique features and parts from more than 50 years ago. It is the elder statesman of the Bronco line, spending its days at Gateway Bronco in Hamel, Illinois. (Photo Courtesy Terry Marvel)

in a small Texas town parade one year. That dignitary was none other than Carroll Shelby, who remarked to Vinny that perhaps he shouldn't have sold that Bronco after all.

Eventually, Vinnie parked the Bronco in a pole barn on his property and bought another 1966 Bronco to drive.

In 2016, Seth Burgett, owner of Gateway Bronco in Hamel, Illinois, learned that Vinnie was interested in selling his beloved Bronco. Burgett traveled to Texas, struck a deal, and became the next caretaker of the special little Bronco. Under Burgett's ownership, the Bronco has received extensive media coverage along with auto show appearances that have allowed many enthusiasts to view the truck.

Inspections by knowledgeable Bronco historians have provided more insight into the origins of this truck and the details of its life before its shipment to Shelby's facility in 1967. A closer look at the engine compartment and its exterior and interior features determined that the Bronco had a significant role in two defining moments in the first two model years of the Bronco: the introduction of the 289 V-8 engine in March 1966 and the introduction of the Sport Bronco package for the 1967 model year.

The key pieces of evidence to confirm that this truck was the prototype for the 289 engine installation in the Bronco were two photos from the collection of noted 1966 Bronco collector Terry Marvel. The photos are of Ford General Manager Donald Frey posing with the engine compartment of a Bronco with an obviously nonproduction 289 and another showing the engine compartment.

This Ford photo shows the first 289 V-8 installation into the prototype Bronco. Note the downflow radiator and the air filter from a passenger car application. Both items are still with the truck today. (Photo Courtesy Ford Motor Company)

Some key elements of the Bronco engine compartment in the photos match up exactly with Burgett's Bronco. The unique air cleaner and radiator in the period photo are still with the truck today. On the cowl, the passenger-side air intake is of a unique construction; it appears to be handmade and is covered by a wire mesh with a small square pattern. The mesh is clearly seen in the Frey photo. The engine compartment still

PROTOTYPE BRONCO CONTINUED

Ford Division General Manager Donald Frey stands proudly next to the prototype Bronco holding the 289 V-8 between its flanks. The unique screen on the passenger-side fresh-air intake housing is one of the key elements that helped identify Burgett's Bronco as this truck. More than 50 years later, 1966 Bronco expert Terry Marvel recreates the pose at Burgett's Gateway Bronco shop. (Photo Courtesy Terry Marvel)

shows traces of the original Rangoon Red color.

The hood prop retaining tab is a small piece of formed metal on top of the core support that answered a long-running question for historians. Ford apparently made a last-minute switch from that tab to a drilled hole in the core support for the prop rod and removed the formed pieces of the tabs on the bodies during production.

The engine mounts on the frame are definitely not factory but are constructed like something you would expect to see in a prototype engine installation at an original equipment man-

ufacturer (OEM). The engine's timing cover and dipstick are from a car; the oil pan is custom fabricated. There are 289 emblems adorning the front fenders, as they did on production Broncos after March 1966, but the emblems here are located lower and closer to the front fender opening than on production trucks.

The exterior inspection of the prototype Bronco also yielded a bumper crop of unusual pieces that added to the story of this truck. The Sport package was not available on Broncos until the 1967 model year, but the little half cab contains several

These photos are from early sales literature that used the prototype Bronco, one obviously more retouched than the other. The prototype was used in Ford marketing literature as late as 1974, often with some airbrushing. The key indicators are the 289 emblem placement on the front fender and the rocker trim extending from one fender opening to the other.

BRONCO'S EXTRA POWER (V-8 AND SIX) lets you storm up hills, pull big trailers, plow deep drifts, blaze new trails.

One of the key pieces on the prototype Bronco that helps identify it in various advertising photos in subsequent years is the full-length rocker trim. Where production pieces ended short of the fender openings, the prototype piece extended to the edge of the fender opening.

The cobbled-together hood release along with the prototype Sport grille lettering is visible here. The hood-release lever is a crude two-piece affair that doesn't have a latch extending past the grille-like production pieces. The letters were borrowed from the Ford car parts bin.

items that point to it being the Sport package prototype. One of the most interesting items is the Sport badging on the front fenders. At first glance, the badges appear to be identical to production pieces, but a closer look reveals the "Sport" portions of the badges are actually separate pieces that are carefully cut to fit around the "B" in the Bronco script. On top, the castle turrets are cut through the badging; they are only small reliefs on the production pieces. The chrome and red grille letters, picked from the Ford parts bin, resemble but are not identical to those found on the Sport package.

The Bronco's flanks carry two items of interest: the rocker panel and beltline trim. The beltline trim wasn't available on 1966 Broncos, but it was part of the 1967 Sport package, lending credence to the theory of this being a Sport package development prototype. The rocker panel trim is more interesting, as it resembles the rocker panel trim found on Sport Broncos, but with one notable difference: it covers the entire length of the rockers between the front and rear fender openings. The production trim stopped several inches short of the fender openings on either end.

The prototype Sport portion of the Bronco emblem was also a one-off piece. The emblem is a separate piece from the "B" in the Bronco script and there are separations between the stanchions at the top of the emblem. On the production piece, the Sport badge is part of the emblem casting; no separations at the top of the emblem.

Marketing materials from 1967 and later have revealed a number of photos that featured this truck; the rocker panel trim and the 289 emblem location on the front fender were dead giveaways. Thanks to the magic of airbrushing and other touchups in the pre-Photoshop area, photos of the truck were found in Ford marketing materials as late as 1974. Various holes in the body show that it wore a full hardtop, softtop, and fiberglass door inserts in addition to the cur-

One of the key identifying factors on this truck that confirms it to be the 289 prototype rig is this passenger-side fresh-air inlet box. As shown in the period photo with Ford executive Don Frey, this box is a rough fiberglass unit with molded-in hardware cloth as a screen. Production pieces were plastic.

PROTOTYPE BRONCO CONTINUED

rent half cab.

A few other oddities also reside inside the cab, including missing locks on the doors and glove box, 1967 horn button, 1967 Sport bucket seats with chrome trim, and an early 1966 transfer case shifter modified to resemble a late 1966/early 1967 shifter.

There will likely continue to be other oddities and unusual features discovered on this truck as Burgett and the crew at Gateway Bronco continue to peel back the layers of the onion and discover exactly what they have on their hands.

This small fabric tab snap hiding beneath the drip rail of the half cab top on the prototype Bronco hints at the numerous configurations of this truck. This truck saw use as a roadster, sports utility (half cab), and wagon by Ford. (Photo Courtesy Tim Hulick)

DUNE BUSTER

As part of the introduction of the Bronco in 1966, Ford debuted its Bronco show truck, known as *Dune Buster*, in auto shows around the country beginning in November 1965. It was designed in Ford's Styling Center in Dearborn, with customization work by Barris Customs of North Hollywood, California.

Many exterior and interior modifications were made to a Bronco roadster to give it a unique look inside and out. The exterior color was Golden Saddle Pearl, and it covered a custom roll bar approved by the National Hot Rod Association (NHRA) with integral headrests behind the front seats. The windshield frame featured a custom, bright-metal frame with rounded corners. The rear flanks were covered by a wood-grain applique, and chrome exhaust side pipes ran along the rocker panels. A race-style fuel filler replaced the stock cap, and the Bronco emblems were moved from the front fenders to the rear corners of the rear quarter panels.

Customized fiberglass half doors filled the door openings. Riders climbed into the truck via custom inset steps above the aluminum heat shielding behind the exhaust pipes.

Wheels were custom-machined steel alloy units with knock-off hubs.

In front, the hood had a scoop, and the front and rear bumpers had rubber bumpers to help keep dents and dings to a minimum.

Inside, *Dune Buster* retained its column shifter, but the steering wheel was replaced with a walnut-rimmed model. The seats were upholstered in suede and perforated leather on the cushions and seatbacks. The instrument panel was also trimmed with suede and the stock plastic control knobs were jettisoned for walnut versions that matched the steering wheel. A tonneau cover appeared over the rear compartment. The sides of the bed were topped with a stainless steel rail.

Dune Buster disappeared from public view after 1966,

only to emerge again on the show circuit in the fall of 1970 and renamed *Wildflower*. Although obviously the same truck, the pearl paint from five years prior had been replaced with a paint scheme highlighted by a "psychedelic design of blues, yellow, and reds topped off by a pink grille." The upholstery was changed to match this era-correct paint scheme, and the beige carpet was changed out for red carpet.

After the second round of auto shows, the *Dune Buster/ Wildflower* Bronco disappeared for good, and its whereabouts remain a mystery to this day. During our 2007 conversation, George Barris remembered building the Bronco but had no idea what happened to it.

Two young models show off Dune Buster, *a Ford styling exercise executed by famed car customer George Barris in Hollywood, California.* Dune Buster *featured a host of custom features that played well on the 1966 auto show circuit. (Photo Courtesy Ford Motor Company)*

1967–1969: BUILDING ON A GOOD THING AND REFINING THE BREED

Following all the hard work and hype surrounding the Bronco's launch in 1966, it's understandable that Ford took a deep breath for the following several model years and made only evolutionary changes to keep the truck fresh and ahead of the competition. With the strong sales numbers from 1966, word was out that the little bobtail was a strong performer both on and off the trail.

The Bronco continued to be a worthy competitor to the Jeep CJ-5 and International Scout for the 1967 and 1968 model years. In 1969, another competitor, Chevrolet's K5 Blazer, appeared on the scene. The Blazer represented another perspective on the SUV, sacrificing small size and maneuverability for increased interior room and better highway manners.

Although the Blazer sold less than 25 percent of the Bronco's sales totals during its inaugural year, in a few years it surpassed the totals of all other SUVs and eventually drove the design of the second-generation Bronco. Unlike its competitors, the Blazer was based on an existing half-ton pickup chassis, which helped shorten the design cycle and allow increased commonality of parts with its pickup cousins.

> " Compared to the Jeep, Land Rover or Toyota, the Bronco is a dandified rig. It looks like a suburban car perched over its wheels on over-sized springs. On the highway it rides like any other high-powered Detroit product, so you have the feeling that it is just another mass-produced production gimmick. But it literally leaped over those mountain trails . . . The Bronco was a top performer on both highway and trail. "

Broncos saw duty with law enforcement personnel, particularly in the early production years. In this photo from 1969, an officer of the Ontario Provincial Police buckles on his skis as he leaves his faithful bobtail. (Reproduced with permission of the OPP Museum)

Reviews

In a comparison test published in *Popular Science* (May 1967), the reviewers effusively praised the Bronco: "Compared to the Jeep, Land Rover or Toyota, the Bronco is a dandified rig. It looks like a suburban car perched over its wheels on over-sized springs. On the highway it rides like any other high-powered Detroit product, so you have the feeling that it is just another mass-produced production gimmick. But it literally leaped over those mountain trails . . . The most surprising of the three was the Bronco . . . The Bronco was a top performer on both highway and trail."

By 1969, reviews were still positive, although testers were more blunt about the Bronco's shortcomings. In its June 1969 issue, *Four Wheeler* mentioned the issue of wheel hop that many owners had complained about.

Autodriver magazine, writing in the October 1969 issue, complained that the steering wheel was too small, probably the only drivers to ever register such a complaint. Their complaints about the slow steering ratio, however, were echoed by others. Fuel range (their test rig only had one tank), vacuum wipers, and a spare mounted on the inside of the tailgate rounded out their list of quibbles. In general, they were quite pleased with the Bronco, heaping praise on its off-road abilities, the power of its 302 V-8 engine, and its relative comfort compared to its competitors.

Powertrain

Ford made a big splash in 1967 when it advertised the Bronco as part of the "3 Point Warranty Plan." The 24-month/24,000-mile warranty was on the complete vehicle. The 5-year/50,000-mile warranty was on the powertrain. The third component

Before a Bronco was delivered to a customer, it received the extensive list of pre-checks as specified on this Pre-Delivery Service Sheet. Many of the items took very little time but some, such as checking ignition timing, distributor dwell, and toe-in, were not quick tasks.

was only one dealer certification per year regardless of the miles driven. With increasing competition among manufacturers as to warranties, Ford believed its year-old vehicle was mature enough to offer such coverage. Curiously, it was never mentioned again in any of the Bronco sales literature in following years.

Engine

The engine list for 1967 and 1968 continued the 1966 offerings with, in Ford's words, the "responsive 170 ci six" as the base engine and the "extra-spirited 289 ci V-8" as the popular option.

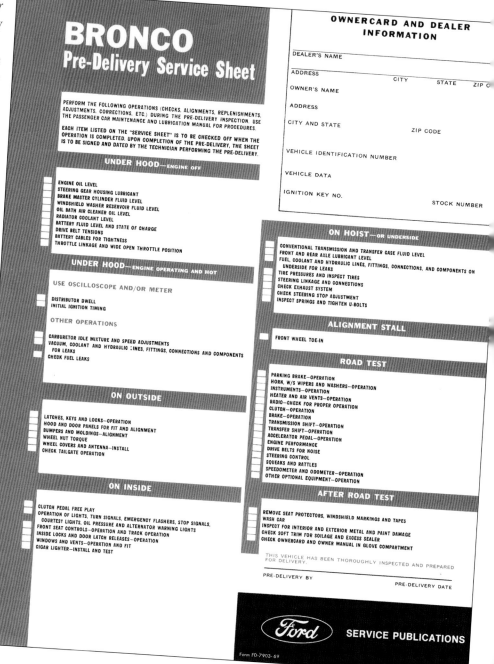

170

An oddity in the records for 170-ci 6-cylinder engines in 1967 was the production of 328 "low-compression" engines (installed in U13 Roadsters) that ended up in South America. These trucks, and their accompanying Marti Reports, have started appearing in recent years. Why and how the trucks ended up in South America with the unique engines remains a mystery. In 1968, the 170 lost its oil-bath cleaner and gained a paper filter element with a thermostatically controlled hot and cold air-intake system and some emissions-control equipment.

In 1968, Ford discontinued the oil-bath air cleaner on the 170-ci 6-cylinder and replaced it with a more modern paper filter element air cleaner mounted directly on top of the carburetor. The filter housing color was changed from black to blue. (Photo Courtesy Tim Hulick)

289

In 1968, the 289 also gained the thermostatically controlled engine air intake management similar to the 6-cylinder along with emissions control equipment. The system managed the airflow to decrease engine warmup times and generate fewer emissions. The familiar vinyl washer fluid bag that had been used for many years in nearly every Ford (including the 1966 and 1967 Broncos) was replaced for 1968 with a hard plastic reservoir mounted on the front of the driver-side inner fenderwell.

A badge of pride on the 1966–1968 trucks was this 289 V-8 emblem on the leading edge of the front fender. It told the world that you had a 200-hp V-8 under the hood, which was the most powerful V-8 offered in a recreational 4WD vehicle at the time.

302

In 1968, after five years of production, Ford ceased production of the 289 and introduced the 302 V-8 in its passenger car line. Externally identical to the 289, the 302 displacement was gained by increasing the stroke by 0.125 inch, to 3 inches, and shortening the connecting rods slightly. The bore skirt was extended slightly to eliminate piston slap.

The Bronco had to wait until the 1969 model year to have the 302 under its hood. Compared to the 289, it offered slightly increased horsepower (205 versus 200) and more torque (300 versus 282) with both ratings generated at 200 rpm higher than its predecessor. The compression ratio was lowered from the 289's 9.3 to 8.6:1 in the 302.

The 302, with a few exceptions, was offered for the remainder of the Bronco's lifetime. Like the 289, it had a thermostatically controlled hot- and cold-air intake system with a closed positive crankcase ventilation (PCV) system, exhaust emissions controls, and a dry-type air filter. An oil-bath air filter (1 pint capacity) was optional.

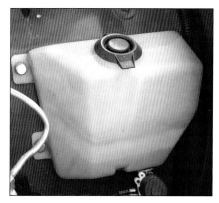

For 1968, the vinyl washer bag was discontinued and replaced by a plastic tank with the washer motor mounted at the bottom. This style of tank continued to be used through the 1970 model year. (Photo Courtesy Randy Harral)

Transmission

Ford continued to emphasize its fully synchronized gears and additional passenger room thanks to the column-mounted shifter of the 3-speed manual transmission.

Transfer Case

With the Dana 20 transfer case unchanged, Ford continued the use of the T-handle shifter introduced in March 1966 but changed from a shifter boot to a plastic cover with a white gear indicator to help the driver determine the transfer case gear setting. The shifter pattern decal on the dash was discontinued.

Axles and Suspension

Ford continued the use of the Dana 30 front axle and 9-inch rear axle in the Bronco. For 1968, Ford revised the

68-T8L9   JUNE, 1968   DEARBORN, MICHIGAN

FORD

1968 FORD TRU... NEWS FL...

NEW EQUIPMENT WILL MAKE ... MORE RUGGED THAN EV...

Since its introduction in late 1965, the rugged 4-wheel drive Ford Bronco has proven its reliability and durability for rough and tumble action at work or play.

In view of the ever growing use of the Bronco for "off-the-road" travel, especially in competitive events, Ford is making available a new heavy-duty front axle with "beefed-up" differential parts to improve its reputation for ruggedness. This new DSO option will be available on early 1969 models.

However, a special Kit, for 1968 or earlier models, is being made available right now through the

Autolite Ford Parts Depot... Bronco owners to adapt t... to their present vehicle. ... either "locking" or "non-l...

This will be good news ... do a great deal of tra... where the country gets ... gets rougher.

The new Bronco fro... Running Hubs with th... engine and front driv... life.

EASIER STEERING, TOO!

A special Steering Kit, consisting of a hydraulic shock absorber mounted between the drag link and frame gives the "off-the-road" traveler easier handling. By damping out most of the shock from the rough terrain it minimizes driver fatigue. The Kit Part No. C6TZ-3E-650A is available at Autolite Ford Parts Depot.

How to order Kit with Part Numbers

The Part No. for ordering the heavy-duty front axle parts from Autolite Ford Parts Depots is 840-9030 designating either locking or non-locking type. The Kit will include:

1 — Non-Locking Differential, Part No. C8TA-3002-EU   or

1 — Locking Differ... Part No. C8T...

Each will include ...

1 — Drive Shaft, ... Part No. C8...
2 — Front Axle F... Part No. C8...
2 — Front Axle ... Part No. C...
1 — Front Whe... Part No. C...
1 — Front Wh... Part No. C...

These parts are ... Depots; therefo... parts allow a... Fall this equipment can b... Bronco under the Part No. DSO 840-90...

... run it in the country where the snow gets deepest and he needs a Bronco to plow his way out.

... uses his Bronco for those rough-riding, off-the-road Rallye competitions that tax the stamina of car and driver. Since the Broncos have been

entering competitive events they have gained an enviable reputation for reliability and dependability.

... likes to do his hunting and fishing far from the beaten paths of civilization — and needs transportation that will stand the gaff.

... does his Bronco riding in rugged mountainous country where the travel can get mighty rough.

Stroppe team driver Ray Harvick aloft in his racing Bronco is the perfect graphic to accompany this 1968 Ford document detailing the introduction of a kit for a heavy-duty front axle in the Bronco. It consisted of a locking or non-locking differential, new driveshaft, new bump stops and spacers, and new brake lines. (Photo Courtesy Terry Marvel)

1967

The 1967 Bronco bodies are nearly identical to the 1966 models in that other than a 289 emblem on the front fender, if so equipped, the side body panels are devoid of any reflectors or lights. To accommodate the beltline trim for the Sport Bronco package, the door locks were moved up slightly in the doors (just below the door handles) for 1967.

Ford also added reverse backup lights, and the taillights gained small white lenses in the process. The 1967 trucks also had one-year-only smaller exterior mirrors. The 1967 tailgates were the first produced with the raised feature

Dana 30 kingpin assemblies and added polyurethane-filled bearing caps that compensated for wear and increased the life of the bearings.

The 9-inch rear was again offered in two capacity ratings: 2,780 and 3,300 pounds. They were known as the "small bearing" and "large bearing" axles, respectively, due to the difference in sizes of the axle bearings on the outboard ends of the axles. The fill plug in the axle housing was eliminated, and a fill plug was added to the third member casting instead.

The two rear axle sizes corresponded to the two GVW packages available: 3,900 and 4,700 pounds. With the higher GVW package came an increase in the rear brake size from 10x2.5– to 11x1.75–inch drums. Rear springs were also uprated from the standard 930-pound progressive leafs (five-leaf pack) to the 1,280-pound pack (six-leaf pack).

As an obvious nod to safety, Ford also introduced a dual hydraulic brake system with dash-mounted warning light for 1967, replacing the single-reservoir master cylinder.

Body

From 1967 to 1969, Ford made enough changes to the exterior of the Bronco so it's usually possible for enthusiasts to identify the specific year of the truck if enough of the original pieces are still in place.

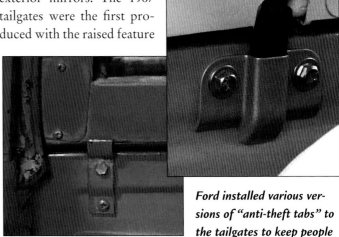

Ford installed various versions of "anti-theft tabs" to the tailgates to keep people from opening the tailgate without first opening the liftgate. The version on the blue tailgate is found on the 1966–1967 trucks, which had one at each corner of the tailgate. In later years, Ford changed to one tab close to the center of the tailgate, shown here on a yellow tailgate. (Photo Courtesy Tim Hulick)

in the top section just below the top of the tailgate. Tire-carrier options continued to be a bulkhead mount (for wagons with a bench seat and the half cab) and on the inside of the tailgate (wagons with a rear seat). The 1967 trucks had a unique one-year-only jack mounting configuration where the jack was mounted inside the spare tire to save space in the rear passenger compartment.

1968

For 1968, Ford added reflectors mounted low at the edges of the front fender and rear quarter panel (sides and rear). The door locks were moved below the beltline on the door where they stayed for the remainder of the first generation's lifetime. The door latches and strikers were changed slightly and moved about an inch lower on the door and doorjamb.

As a nod to owners' backs and biceps, a swing-away outside spare tire carrier became an option for Bronco wagons. In addition to making the tailgate much easier to operate, the move of the

spare tire from the tailgate to the external carrier freed up valuable interior space. The spare-tire carrier became so common that most people did not realize it was an option. Once it became an option, the spare tire jack mount was moved to the inner fender on the driver's side under the hood where it remained through 1977. The bumpers also gained curved ends this year.

1969

In 1969, Ford enlarged the front turn-signal lenses to replace the 1966–1968 versions. The lens color was also changed from clear to orange. In recent years, the earlier lenses have become popular again, so many owners have switched to them.

For the first three years of production, the front turn-signal lamps featured these clear lenses with a small inset into the grille. In 1969, the lenses grew in size and changed to orange.

An unknown number of 1967 Broncos were exported to Colombia, where some of them were modified with barn doors to replace the liftgate and tailgate. An enthusiast purchased a number of these trucks and sold them to new owners in the United States nearly 50 years later. (Photo Courtesy Joe Cardi)

A new feature for mid-year 1969 Broncos was 2-speed electric windshield wipers, replacing the previously used vacuum units. Note that Ford marketing made special note that the competition was still using vacuum wipers. The electric system used a single motor with a linkage to drive both wipers. (Photo Courtesy Terry Marvel, Randy Harral)

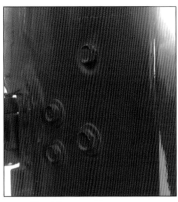

The 1966–1968 Broncos had doors with removable window frames. A telltale way to identify the removable frames is to look for the bolts shown in these photos. For 1969, Ford switched to welded frames, which eased assembly and helped with frame rigidity. The removable frames are aesthetically more pleasing on trucks with their tops removed.

With the demise of the roadster model after the 1968 model year, Ford made some changes to the body that made it a tighter, more integrated structure. Designers added reinforcements in the rocker panels, door hinge area, and the top. Insulation was added in the cowl and firewall area. Although the top was still removable, Ford made some changes to make it less obviously so. Starting in late 1968, the vacuum windshield motors were finally replaced with a single electric motor and linkage.

Although the windshield still folded down, Ford removed the large chrome knobs at each inside lower corner and replaced them with regular bolts. At the same time, the fold-down latch mechanism at the top of the windshield frame and on the hood was eliminated. Another change was the elimination of the bolt-on door window frames that had been used in the 1966–1968 trucks.

Interior

For 1967, the Bronco's interior was evolutionary, rather than revolutionary, with several of the 1966-only items disappearing for good.

1967

For 1967, Ford once again offered the base Bronco package, which included standard convenience features such as a padded dash, seat belts, driver-side outside rearview mirror, turn signals, dual vacuum windshield wiper motors, windshield washers, and a vinyl-covered floor mat.

Replacing 1966's Custom Equipment package was the new Sport Bronco package, which proved to be one of the most enduring sporting trim packages in the model's history and, in

The 1967 Bronco seats are a one-year-only item featuring horizontal pleats in the upholstery. Because this is a Sport Bronco, the seats also have the 1967-only chrome hinge covers that extend up the sides of the backrests. Also visible are horizontal door pleats along with one-year-only window cranks and door handles. (Photo Courtesy Tim Hulick)

The radio knobs identify this dash as a 1967 Bronco. Also visible is the 1967-only chrome strip along the bottom of the dash. Ford didn't find production stability until 1968 because of the many unique features found on the 1966 and 1967 models. (Photo Courtesy Tim Hulick)

the words of Ford's marketing department at the time, "a real winner with the young crowd." The package was available on the wagon and pickup (renamed from Sports Utility for 1967) models only.

On the outside of the truck, the Sport Bronco package included an argent-painted grille with bright aluminum trim surround, FORD letters in the grille, chrome headlight rings, chrome windshield and window trim, chrome drip-rail molding, chrome taillight bezels, chrome taillight release handle, chrome bumpers front and rear, and chrome bumper guards on the front bumpers. Bright-metal hubcaps and "Sport Bronco" emblems on the fenders rounded out beautification.

The optional bucket seats had full-length chrome pivot arm covers (1967 only), a chrome horn ring, pleated door trim panels with bright-metal moldings, bright-metal instrument panel molding at the top and bottom of the instrument panel (1967 only), hardboard headliner with bright retainer moldings (wagon), parchment-colored vinyl front floor mat with bright retainer moldings, driver and passenger armrests, and a cigar/cigarette lighter.

Proving that Ford was still figuring things out with the 1967 trucks, the standard Broncos and Sport Broncos had different armrests on the doors. The standard models were a smaller and slimmer shape; the Sport armrests more closely resembled the larger 1968-newer armrests. In addition, the 1967 trucks featured a one-year-only upholstery pattern on the bucket seats (rosette parchment color with horizontal pleats) and one-year-only dash knobs.

Many of the options that were standard on the Sport Bronco package were also available separately if the buyer didn't want the expense of the entire package. Beginning in 1968, Ford offered the optional Convenience package, which included a cigarette lighter, horn ring, and map light.

In 1956, Ford had blazed the path toward greater automotive safety with its Lifeguard Design program, the most memorable aspect of which was the addition of seat belts to passenger cars. The program was widely regarded as a flop in terms of generating additional sales, and Ford stopped promoting it after a short time.

In the wake of additional automotive safety concerns raised in the mid-1960s by the likes of Ralph Nader, Ford once again revived the "Lifeguard" term for its 1967 cars and trucks. For the Bronco, it resulted in a paragraph in the second edition sales brochure touting such features as a dual hydraulic brake system with warning light, seat belts, a padded instrument panel, an outside mirror, windshield washers, variable-speed windshield wipers, padded sun visors, a thick-laminate safety glass windshield, turn signals, backup lights, emergency flashers, corrosion-resistant brake lines, a T-handle transfer case shifter with positive lock, and safety-designed instrument panel controls.

Although several of these items were new for 1967 (most notably the dual hydraulic braking system), Ford's marketing for the 1967 model year highlighted existing items on the Bronco. There were not many additions or changes to the trucks as a result of safety concerns. Lifeguard Design was again mentioned in the 1968 sales brochure and then disappeared for the rest of the model's life.

1968

For the 1968 model year, Bronco interiors changed slightly. The previously optional fresh-air heater and defroster became standard. The dash pad changed to a different shape with significantly more padding on about two-thirds of it. The dash changed with a narrower speaker grille, and the ashtray moved to the passenger side of the dash. The dash knob shape changed for the third time in three years to a shape that remained through 1977 production.

For 1968, Ford changed the armrests yet again for the final time in first-generation trucks, shown here from a later-year Ranger model. While changing the armrests, Ford also changed the door-release handles and recessed them into the door panel for greater safety. (Photo Courtesy Jack Niederkorn)

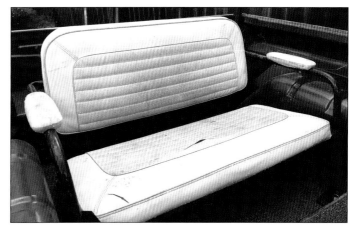

The 1967 Bronco rear seat was a one-year-only version, featuring parchment upholstery with horizontal stitching. The armrests are the same shape as the 1966 version with a white cover instead of the 1966's black cover.

The data plate was moved from the driver-side kick panel to the inside of the glove box door. The inside door releases were changed to a paddle lever mechanism recessed into the door panel behind a larger, thicker armrest pad that also remained for the rest of the first generation's life. The window cranks changed to a softer plastic knob. The upholstery was changed to a parchment color with vertical pleats.

1969

In 1969, Ford increased the safety equipment again by listing optional shoulder harnesses for the front and rear seats (if so equipped) and an optional center passenger seat belt if equipped with the bench seat.

This gorgeous blue 1969 Sport Bronco is ready to play in the snow. The lack of a windshield latching bracket on the hood and windshield frame indicate that it's a truck made during the second half of the model year. (Photo Courtesy Stace Reich)

The parchment floor mat and bright applique on the door panel are dead giveaways that these two men are discussing a 1968 Bronco Sport. Also visible are the new-for-1968 dash pad and dashboard. (Photo Courtesy Ford Motor Company)

Tires and Wheels

For 1967–1969, Ford continued offering a variety of tire sizes on the standard 15x5.5–inch wheels, including 7.35, 7.75, 8.25, and 9.15 widths. The 15-inch wheels were equipped with wheel covers if the Sport package option box was checked. Ford also continued the option of tube-type 6.50x16–inch tires on 16x5–inch wheels.

Colors

From late 1966 through 1968, the color palette remained largely unchanged with 12 or 13 offerings. In 1969, Ford highlighted that 8 of the 15 colors offered were new "lively" colors: Candy Apple Red, Royal Maroon, Reef Aqua, Light Ivy Yellow, Norway Green, Empire Yellow, Cordova Copper, and Boxwood Green. Changing tastes in greens and blues along with a move toward a few more vivid colors were in keeping with the tastes of the day.

Collectability

Like all first-generation Broncos, the 1967–1969 models are extremely collectible and desirable. Historically, these models have not been as desirable as 1973-later models due to their Dana 30 front axles and lack of more popular amenities such as power steering, automatic transmissions, or disc brakes. With parts more readily available to upgrade these trucks, the desirability deficits have been greatly reduced in the past several decades.

For 1967, Ford switched to these optional wheel covers, which were sourced from the Ford passenger car parts bin. Ford continued to use this same cover through the 1977 model year. (Photo Courtesy Freeze Frame Image LLC, Al Rogers)

First-year Sport Broncos have been particularly popular in collector circles due to some of the unique trim pieces found only on the 1967 models. Because of their low production numbers, the 1967 and 1968 roadsters have also become popular, particularly those with a 289 V-8. Very few examples of these trucks have survived into the 21st century.

Production

The roadster model production declined precipitously for 1967 with a total of 698 trucks produced, which was only 17 percent of the previous year's total. Of those, 199 were equipped with the 289 V-8, 171 with the standard 170 6-cylinder, and 328 with the "low-compression" export 170 6-cylinder. Interestingly, 519 of those 698 roadsters are listed in the 1967 Marti report as having "glassed and framed doors." (Copyright Marti Auto Works, martiauto.com, and used with permission.)

Sales stories from the 1966 model year indicate that many 1966 roadsters languished on the sales lots, so it's no wonder Ford put real doors on so many of the 1967s to get them off the lot and onto the road.

In 1968, production again dropped, down 69 percent to only 212 units. Of those, 136 had a 289 V-8 under the hood, 74 units had a 170 6-cylinder, and 2, according to Kevin Marti, are a question mark but were most likely equipped with the export 170.

This white 1969 wagon's owners explored many remote locations with the Early Bronco Registry based in Poway, California. Overlanding before overlanding was "cool," they allegedly did have the kitchen sink among their belongings on the back of their Bronco. (Photo Courtesy Bruce Bolander)

In the late 1960s, two four-wheeling friends, John Karp and Hal Sealund, began installing aftermarket parts on Broncos in the San Diego area as part of their El Gitano package, and K Bar S Bronco Parts was born. They sometimes unintentionally tested the integrity of the parts in their trucks. Here's Hal hauling the mail in his "demo truck" after an obvious rollover. (Photo Courtesy Hal Sealund)

A quintessential "sleeper" Bronco with high-performance goodies under a stock body, this is a 1968 Bronco. Retaining its uncut fenders, it has a 1999 Explorer 5.0 engine with EFI under the hood. An NP435 4-speed manual transmission transfers the torque to a Dana 44 front axle and big-bearing 9-inch rear end, which both have disc brakes on each end. (Photo Courtesy Aron Payne)

It's a snowy day in January 1968 and a Bronco wagon is in the middle of helping an overturned truck. Through the years, Broncos have performed acts of mercy, helping stranded motorists stuck in snow, mud, and other treacherous situations. (Photo Courtesy Tim Hulick)

This owner-modified 1967 Bronco has plenty of goodies to make scaling high elevations such as Mosquito Pass a piece of cake, including a 5.0 Explorer electronic fuel injected (EFI) engine, a ZF-2 5-speed transmission from a Ford F250, and an Atlas 2-speed transfer case. (Photo Courtesy Erik Hazelhurst)

This well-preserved 1968 Bronco is an excellent time capsule of what an enthusiast-modified Bronco looked like in the late 1960s and early 1970s. A Stroppe padded steering wheel and roll bar adorn the interior; the exterior features fender flares and oversized tires on vintage slot mags. A PTO winch on a custom bumper rides up front. (Photo Courtesy Tom Carper)

Don't try this with every Bronco! This 1969 Sport has been upgraded with a mix of half- and three-quarter-ton running gear and sports a brake controller for the 16-foot 3,200-pound trailer. The owner, an automotive engineer, has incorporated many thoughtful upgrades into his truck. (Photo Courtesy Jesse Weifenbach)

Based on these disappointing sales, it's no surprise that Ford discontinued the roadster model after 1968. Its low sales bore out the fact that consumers were demanding more comfort and protection from their 4WD vehicles than ever before.

For 1967, production totaled 14,230 units, a 40-percent drop from 1966 totals. Most of that reduction was in the roadster and pickup totals, as Ford clearly saw where sales would come from in the future. As roadster sales plummeted, pickup sales stabilized during the three years, with 2,000 to 2,600 annual sales.

Wagon sales picked up a bit again for 1968 for a total of 16,629 sales.

For 1969, Ford was pleased that sales climbed again to 20,956, with 18,639 wagons.

Located in the Jemez Mountains north of Albuquerque, the Gilman Tunnels once served as part of the Sante Fe Northwestern Railway. Opened in 1924 and closed in 1941, the tunnels form a stunning backdrop for this Albuquerque-based 1968 Ford Bronco. (Photo Courtesy Adam Buckner)

MILITARY BRONCOS

This vintage post card is of particular interest to Bronco owners because it shows the "military Bronco" still in use at the Citadel military school today.

This 1967 Bronco wagon started life as a military Bronco and still retains the data plaque on the dash and the bars over the headlights. After its military stint, it was repainted and became part of a search-and-rescue fleet for a sheriff's department in northern Washington. (Photo Courtesy Tim Hulick)

In 1967, Ford briefly entered the government supply business with the Bronco line. The US government ordered 120, painted in a military green color, according to the trucks' Marti Reports, and assigned a six-digit DSO number beginning with "83." These trucks were distributed among the four service branches and repainted per the directives of each branch. Based on the number of surviving trucks, the navy was probably the largest customer. Other survivors painted in air force blue have been found as well as a number of trucks used in civil defense and other government entities.

All of the Broncos supplied under the government contract were U15 Wagons powered by the 170-ci 6-cylinder engine. According to interviews conducted by Dustin and Anne Olson and published in a *Bronco Driver* article, the military was not terribly impressed by the Broncos and felt that they were underpowered. The Olsons noted that the Broncos were used for administrative and transport duties but saw no combat action. Although records do not exist on their length of service, the Olsons' research found them in use until the 1980s.

Most of the trucks that have survived are characterized by unique metal headlight covers, a data plate affixed to the dashboard, and a custom rear bumper. Although the military Broncos are a very small, unique subset of the first-generation trucks, they have yet to generate a large amount of interest among collectors.

SPORTSMAN SPECIAL

Through the years, Ford's Denver District put together some unique Ford special editions to sell in the Colorado region. In 1966–1967, Ford sold High Country Special Mustangs, which were similar to the popular California Special Mustangs. For 1968–1970, it assembled and promoted the Rocky Mountain Sportsman Special Bronco (also known as the Sportsman Edition) in three colors: Boulder Bronze, Mountain Green, and Sky Blue. The primary means of truck identification was a badge (some triangular and some a script) attached to the front fenders below the Bronco emblem.

The exact contents of the package are unknown but were purported to be a gun rack/fishing rod holder, roof rack, extra chrome trim, and the aforementioned badging.

Some Sportsman Special Broncos have survived, although the numbers are small enough to make this Bronco Edition unknown to many.

These badges were destined for the fenders of a Bronco with a Sportsman Special package. Little is known about the package, which was offered on 1968–1970 Broncos sold through the Denver DSO. (Photo Courtesy Tim Hulick)

The Marti Report for this 1970 Rocky Mountain Sportsman Special lists a custom metallic blue color, but the owner believes the truck was originally Boulder Bronze based on his inspection. (Photo Courtesy Landon Flynn)

On this 1970 Bronco, the Rocky Mountain Sportsman Special badging is a script rather than the triangular badges found on the 1968–1969 examples of the truck and has "Rocky Mountain" added to the name. (Photo Courtesy Landon Flynn)

BOSS BRONCO

By 1969, the Bronco was in its fourth year of production without any high-performance variants in the stable. That all changed in 1969 when Ford performance giants Kar-Kraft and Bill Stroppe got together for just over a week in the spring of 1969 to assemble a high-performance Bronco that Stroppe had proposed to Ford management. Called a "Special Bronco" in a year-end "summary of accomplishments" document from Kar-Kraft in 1969, this Bronco was unknown to Ford and Bronco enthusiasts for years.

In place of the stock 302, a high-performance 351W (1969 Shelby GT350 210S code) with a 4-barrel carburetor was installed, topped by a hood scoop from

Colin Comer has recreated the stripe and lettering on the front fender of the Boss Bronco. The 302 emblem on the fender was removed during the initial build process because a 351 Windsor is under the hood. Comer also added period-correct chrome steel wheels. (Photo Courtesy Colin Comer)

Ford's high-performance car parts bin. Behind the 351, the Kar-Kraft crew installed a C4 automatic transmission, shifted by a well-integrated Mustang floor shifter in the cab. Of note to Bronco enthusiasts, this installation may have been the first C4 installed in a Bronco; the transmission-to-transfer case adapter is unique and unlike any other previously seen units.

With 4.11:1 gears and limited-slip differentials front- and rear-driving wide chrome wheels and Gates Commando tires, the truck could move quickly through rough terrain and use the race-proven Stroppe dual shocks installed front and rear. In the rear, a pair of Stroppe's fender flares were added to the cut rear quarter panels for tire clearance.

The interior was also given some subtle additions, including a Stroppe roll bar and custom vinyl-covered panels on the inside of the quarter panels. It was a foreshadowing of higher trim-level details found on Broncos in the 1970s. Repurposed rocker panel trim served as trim strips for the quarter panel covers.

A large, black, hockey stick–shaped stripe was applied to the Empire Yellow body, resembling the future 1971 Boss 351 Mustang. Based on two historical photos of the truck, there were apparently two versions of the stripe; the first edition was a plain stripe and the second had "Boss Bronco" inserted into the stripe near the door edge. The grille was painted black with chrome headlight rings and had bright grille trim and Ford letters, identical to the Special Décor trim seen seven years later on production Broncos.

The Boss Bronco's black grille coupled with red Sport letters, bright grille trim, and headlight rings is a foreshadowing of the 1976–1977 Special Décor Bronco colors. The aftermarket front stabilizer bar and the Mercury Cougar hood scoop are also visible. (Photo Courtesy Colin Comer)

This crude metal piece is likely the first C4-to-Dana 20 adapter. Flanges for the transmission, transfer case, and crossmember mounting ears were welded on the housing. This artifact was found in the Kar-Kraft Boss Bronco when Colin Comer and his crew refurbished the truck. (Photo Courtesy Colin Comer)

Parked in front of the Ford Design Center, the Boss Bronco is shown with Boss Bronco lettering on its front flanks, the design Colin Comer chose to duplicate in his refreshment of the truck. (Photo Courtesy Colin Comer)

The Bronco was built while Semon E. "Bunkie" Knudsen was Ford's president and his favorite designer, Larry Shinoda, was running the Ford design studio and producing Boss 302 Mustangs. Several of Knudsen's favorite cars were painted pale yellow. Apparently Kar-Kraft and Stroppe weren't shy in trying to please their bosses with their vehicle name and color/stripe selections. In the end, it was all for naught, as Knudsen was fired by Ford in the fall of 1969.

Most concept cars and project vehicles are crushed, but this Bronco somehow escaped that fate and remained intact when Kar-Kraft closed for good in December 1970. For the next 46 years, it disappeared from enthusiasts' radar.

In 2016, *Lost Muscle Cars* author Wes Eisenschenk came across a Kar-Kraft inventory list, which listed the Bronco and its VIN. A quick internet search revealed that the Bronco had recently been a no-sale on eBay. Eisenschenk contacted the owner and a deal was made. Apparently no one who had owned the truck since 1970 knew of its pedigree.

Eisenschenk discovered a factory power steering box from a 1973-later Bronco had been added at some point along with a power brake booster. A 1976–1977 factory-style front sway bar had been added also. The truck's flanks had lost the "Boss Bronco" logo and the chromed, steel wheels and Gates Commando tires had been replaced with stock-sized wheels and some modest tires with narrow white sidewalls. The Boss had lost its bite.

As the truck was introduced to the enthusiast world via several online forums and social media, it soon caught the eye of noted car collector and author Colin Comer. For the second time in just a few months, the Kar-Kraft Boss Bronco went to a new home.

Comer and his crew quickly refurbished the mechanical powertrain components of the Bronco to get it into drivable condition and replicate the 1969 configuration. They discovered that the engine had been balanced and blueprinted during its initial build and included a few other high-performance tricks. As a finishing touch, they repainted the original stripe, added "Boss Bronco" decals to the fenders, and installed a new set of wheels that closely resemble the originals.

Chapter THREE

> " 1972 FORD Bronco Explorer—Sure-Footed Adventurer in the Great Outdoors. "

1970–1972: MIDDLE AGE

The dawn of a new decade brought with it a new era of changes for the Bronco along with new competitors in its marketplace. Changes to the Bronco were evolutionary, rather than revolutionary, and reflected increased governmental influence in the automotive industry in the areas of emissions and safety.

The Chevy Blazer's stablemate, the GMC Jimmy, was introduced in 1969 and gave the Bronco additional competition. Like the Blazer, Ford emphasized Bronco's unique styling (the Blazer and Jimmy shared styling with "regular" Chevy pickups), coil-spring suspension, superior ground clearance, better approach and departure angles, tighter turning circle, more brake lining area, and an all-steel top. Ford emphasized that the GM top was fiberglass and extremely heavy.

Ford continued to point out the Bronco's strong points compared to traditional competition, such as the Jeep Universal (CJ-5) and International Scout. Ford also took aim at some non-traditional competitors including the Jeep Wagoneer, Jeepster Commando, and International Travelall in 1970. The primary differentiator was cost, as most of these competitors were in a different market segment than the Bronco.

Reviews

By 1970, the Bronco had been on the market for more than four years, and with increasing competition, a few of the bobtail's shortcomings were starting to show in road tests and reviews. For example, in the June 1971 issue of *Pickup, Van and Four Wheel Drive* magazine, the tester wrote, "Our test Bronco turned out to be a pickup version and we have to start by saying that we can't imagine why anyone would buy a pickup with such a small cargo area. It may exactly fill somebody's needs but honestly we can't imagine any application that couldn't be better filled by either the wagon version or a standard-size 4wd pickup." The article went on to mention that the editor's Bronco had traveled 60,000 miles and never left him stranded, although it had a healthy appetite for CV joints in the driveshafts, something that still plagues first-generation owners today. The ubiquitous tailgate rattle was also mentioned.

In the June 1971 issue, *Motor Trend* also was thinking of updates. "We like to pon-

This is an early 1970 example of the blatant photo retouching in the pre-computer era. In this photo, the new-for-1970 marker lights are obviously painted on and in a much higher location and of a smaller shape than the actual lights. This photo was likely modified before 1970 production examples were available for photographs. (Photo Courtesy Ford Motor Company)

This 1971 Bronco would command top dollar in the collector market today. Not only is it a stock, uncut Bronco, but it's also a Bronco Sport with the highly desirable, and rare, rocker panel trim and the chrome drip-rail trim on the hardtop that only appeared on the Bronco Sports from 1967 to 1971. (Photo Courtesy Ford Motor Company)

der how good this machine would be with an automatic transmission and power steering. Ford should offer these two items as options; they are well worth the extra money . . . In our little contest the Blazer wins hands down with the Bronco a distant second."

Pickup, Van and 4WD also conducted a survey of more than 100 first-generation Bronco owners in 1971 and came away with the conclusion that "It isn't perfect, but it has never let me down." The magazine found the engine to be incredibly durable and reliable and owners impressed with the Bronco's maneuverability and power. Again, choppy ride, U-joint issues, rattles, poor brakes, and lack of amenities such as an automatic transmission, power steering and brakes, and air-conditioning were mentioned.

Engine

The 170-ci 6-cylinder and 302-ci V-8 continued as the available engines for 1970–1972 with very few changes. Historically, many enthusiasts lamented the drop in horsepower in the early 1970s as the death knell of the performance era, and the Bronco was no different. Between 1971 and 1972, horsepower ratings on the 302 V-8 dropped by more than 25 percent.

Although the engines experienced decreases in power as emissions equipment was added and compression ratios dropped, the majority of the horsepower "loss" was only on paper thanks to the way horsepower and torque measurements were taken.

In 1972, Ford was still advertising the Bronco as a nimble and maneuverable off-roader, but it could also take your polyester-clad children with you to the grocery store where Mom apparently parked anywhere she wanted while doing her grocery shopping. (Photo Courtesy Ford Motor Company)

In addition to their more sporting pretentions, Broncos were also used as utility vehicles, particularly in the early years. One of the more unusual uses was as a "gas sniffer" rig to check for gas leaks in city streets. This particular Bronco is shown in Illinois, but similar rigs were also used to patrol Arizona city streets. (Photo Courtesy Jack Niederkorn)

Starting in 1972, manufacturers switched from a gross to a net measurement, governed by SAE standards J1349 and J2723. The net system still measured the engine's output on a test stand, but it also included all the accessories on a normal engine, production ignition timing and carburetor settings, and a full exhaust system. The gross rating did not.

170

In the Bronco's case, the 170 6-cylinder's output dropped from 100 to 81 hp and the 302 V-8's output dropped from 205 to 148 hp. Torque ratings also dropped: the 6-cylinder registered 133 ft-lbs, down from 148.

302

The V-8 put out 260 ft-lbs, down from 300. For 1972, the 302's output dropped even further to a rating of 139 hp and a torque rating of 237 ft-lbs.

The oil-bath air cleaner for the 302 V-8 ceased to be available after 1971, as oil-bath air cleaners had lost their luster by the early 1970s.

Emissions

The Bronco gained several emissions control items starting in 1970 to help its engine burn cleaner. First, the manual carburetor choke gained automatic control in 1970. In addition, as part of new emissions control requirements, an optional evaporative emissions system was offered for 1970 (standard for California). It consisted of breather lines on each tank that fed a plastic tank behind a sheet metal panel behind the driver-side front seat. This container fed a charcoal canister mounted on the passenger-side frame rail behind the driver-side front wheel. The canister was attached to the engine's intake system, so engine vacuum sucked the vapors into the engine upon startup to limit emissions to the atmosphere.

Gas tank sizes were also reduced as part of this package with the main tank dropping from 14.5 to 12.7 gallons, and the auxiliary's capacity registering at 10.3 gallons, down 1.2 gallons from the earlier version. In 1971, the evaporative emissions system became standard for all models.

In 1972, the Bronco gained an interesting item to help with emissions called the ambient air thermal sense switch. Visible as a diamond-shaped metal plate screwed into the doorjamb near the top hinge, the switch controlled emissions by disabling the distributor's vacuum advance unless the vehicle was moving faster than 25 mph or the ambient air temperature was below 50 degrees. This oddity was also seen on some 1973 models.

For 1971, the Extra Cooling radiator for the V-8 was listed as an option for the first time, and in 1972, it was joined by the reduced sound level exhaust system, which was a requirement in California and New York. The reduced sound level system was simply an extra 90-degree bend in the tailpipe so it pointed to the rear of the vehicle instead of out the side behind the rear tire.

In the engine compartment, the windshield washer reservoir grew larger in 1971.

The biggest powerplant news for the period was that 1971 was the last year of the 6-cylinder engine in California. Beginning in 1972, the 302 was the standard, and only, engine available in the Golden State.

Axles and Suspension

For 1970, Ford continued the use of the Dana 30 front axle and 9-inch rear axle in the Bronco.

For 1971, Ford enlarged the size of the windshield washer reservoir slightly. It remained this shape and size through the end of the generation's run in 1977. (Photo Courtesy Larry Crumpler)

For 1970, Ford changed the shape of the air filter slightly, making it larger and blue (replacing the previously used black color). (Photo Courtesy Eric Dill)

In 1970, Ford introduced a vapor recovery system for the fuel tanks to help keep fuel vapors out of the cab. One of the key items in this system was this charcoal canister mounted behind the passenger-side front wheel.

Dana 44-1

Soon after the start of the 1971 model year, Ford upgraded the front axle in the Bronco from the Dana 30AF to the Dana 44-1F. In doing so, the front axle's capacity was increased from 2,500 to 3,000 pounds. Upgrades from the Dana 30 to the 44 included an increase in the ring gear diameter from 7.2 to 8.5 inches and an upgrade in the size of the axle tubing from a 2.5- to 2.75-inch diameter while keeping the axle tubing thickness constant at 0.3125 inch. The increase in the ring gear size necessitated a larger center section, and the steering knuckles were now attached to the axle housing by ball joints instead of kingpins.

As with the Dana 30, the Dana 44 was available with a limited-slip differential as an option (rear limited-slip required when ordering). The Dana 44 was an upgrade that can be attributed to Ford's testing in the brutal environments found in racing off road in desert races such as the Baja 500, Baja 1000, and Mint 400. Bill Stroppe and others had been testing a version of the Dana 44 front axle for several years prior to its introduction in production vehicles. With the Bronco, racing really did improve the breed.

The 9-inch rear axle was again offered in two capacity ratings: 2,780 and 3,300 pounds, as in previous years, with a limited-slip once again offered as an option. Axle ratios were again 3.50, 4.11, and 4.57:1 with the lighter-duty axle and 3.50 and 4.11:1 with the 3,300-pound unit. The 11x2–inch front drums were standard with all GVW packages. On the rear, the lighter-duty axle was equipped with 10x2.5–inch brakes; the 3,300-pound unit was shod with 11x1.75–inch shoes.

In 1972, the GVW ratings of the Bronco were increased from two packages rated at 3,900 pounds and 4,700 to 4,300 pounds and optional packages of 4,500 and 4,900 pounds. The increase in GVWR was due to higher capacity ratings for the front and rear springs and higher capacity belted tires.

Body

The 1970 Broncos were immediately distinguishable from their predecessors by the addition of side-marker lights

New heavy-duty Dana 44

Now standard...the heavy-duty front axle that helped BRONCO win at Baja!

How good is Bronco with the new Dana 44 heavy-duty front axle? Good enough to take first place in the production 4x4 class in the 1970 Baja 500. Which is pretty darn good. In fact, the Bronco-Dana 44 combination is just too good to be an extra-cost option—so, beginning with production September 27, we made it standard. Bronco's other goodies are so good we wouldn't want to change them. That 33.6-ft. turning diameter, for instance . . . tightest of any 4-wheeler. Or that 11.3-inch ground clearance. Or that approach angle of 40.2 degrees and departure angle of 26.9 degrees. Or that 28.6-degree ramp breakover angle. Or those identical front and rear tracks of 57.4 inches. These are the kinds of numbers that make you a winner in the desert and the hills. That's what Broncos are all about. Give one a try. Your Ford Dealer will be happy to put you in the saddle.

A better idea for safety: Buckle up   FORD BRONCO

At the end of September 1970 (or October 1 according to other sources), Ford introduced the Dana 44 front axle in the Bronco. Boasting 500 pounds more capacity than the Dana 30 it replaced, the Dana 44 addressed the shortcomings that owners found in the Dana 30 and matched the front axle found in the Blazer (a wider version of the Dana 44). (Photo Courtesy Ford Motor Company and Larry Crumpler)

to the front and rear corners of the body sides, replacing the previously used reflectors from the 1968–1969 years. The side-marker lights were mounted approximately mid-height on the body panels, just under the 302 emblem on the front fenders, with an amber-colored lens in front and a red lens in the rear lights.

The addition of the lights was mandated by Federal Motor Vehicle Safety Standard (FMVSS) 108, which went into effect on January 1, 1969. The purpose of the side-marker lights was to allow a driver to see other vehicles approaching at an angle at night, or to see vehicles stopped straight ahead in the driver's line of vision, hopefully helping to avoid collisions.

At the same time, a slight change was introduced to the operation of the turn signals in the grille. In their previous configuration, they went off when the headlights were turned on. In 1970, they stayed on when the headlights were turned on to give additional lighting to the front end.

In 1972, when the 302 became the only available engine in California, the 302 engine emblem was dropped from the front fenders of V-8–equipped models.

The only other change to the body during these years was the addition of an optional driver-side remote mirror starting in 1971. This is highly prized by collectors today.

Bright body side and tailgate models and rocker panel moldings continued as options as with previous years.

Interior

For 1970, the Bronco continued with the two trim levels that had been available since 1967: standard Bronco and Sport Bronco.

Ford touted the standard features of the Bronco with a level of detail that seems absurd today, but when one considers that competition such as the Jeep CJ-5 and International Scout may not have had such items available, the context becomes more acceptable. Items making the list included: driver-side chrome exterior mirror, roll-up glass windows, padded instrument panel, black vinyl floor mat, electric windshield wipers, and a locking glove box. The Sport Bronco, with its bright trim and more lavish interior accoutrements, continued unchanged through these years.

For 1970, Ford added these build stickers to Bronco doorjambs. It allows interested parties to quickly check the build date and VIN number of the vehicle. These door stickers today are reproduced by Marti Auto Works in Peoria, Arizona.

This immaculate 1971 Sport is one of the rare Broncos with a top painted to match the body as a factory option. The Albuquerque owner has used this truck for much backcountry travel over the years, belying its immaculate appearance. It's a close match to the red truck that Ford used in numerous brochures and advertisements in the early 1970s. As in many of the ads, this one shows one particular character who insisted on carrying his bedroll on his back instead of leaving it in the truck. (Photo Courtesy Ford Motor Company and Larry Crumpler)

In 1972, the standard bench seat was discontinued and two buckets seats became standard, regardless of whether the truck was ordered with a wagon or pickup top.

Explorer

For the first time since the introduction of the Sport Bronco package in 1967, Ford ventured into new territory in 1972 by introducing a new trim package called the Explorer. Although it was offered for several years, 1972 was the only year that it was offered as an add-on to the Sport package. Ford announced it as the "1972 FORD Bronco Explorer—Sure-Footed Adventurer in the Great Outdoors."

In practical terms, Ford's sales brochure listed it as being available only in a Durango Tan exterior color, although Marti Reports have since proved that it was available in several other hues.

On the interior, Ford for the first time deviated from its parchment upholstery and introduced a special Ginger Random–striped cloth pattern for the seating surfaces on the front and rear seats with a light brown vinyl material on the bolsters, armrests, and perimeters of the seats. The door panels resembled the Sport panels but had brown accents below the bright retainers, replacing the parchment-colored pieces of the Sport panels. The full-length floor mat resembled the Sport mat's texture but was brown in color.

Bright body side and tailgate moldings were also standard. The rest of the truck received the standard Sport package treatment. The glove box received a special "Explorer" badge to denote the special trim level. (Copyright Marti Auto Works, martiauto.com, and used with permission.)

Although never mentioned in any Ford documentation, Ford offered an option of this bracket on the passenger-side rear quarter panel, allowing the tire carrier to be swung around as shown in the picture with the tire mounted on the outside. Particularly useful for easier access to the tailgate and advantageous for towing, the bracket has become known among enthusiasts as the "ranch hand" bracket. They are most prevalent on 1969 models but appear on 1968–1972 models also. (Left Photo Courtesy Chuck Binder)

Tires and Wheels

For 1972, Ford introduced bias-belted tires in the new letter sizing system. The standard size became E78x15 tires with G78x15 tires used on the 4500 and 4900 GVW packages. The letter-size tires were slightly smaller than their comparable predecessors and as a consequence, the ground clearance at the differentials decreased a bit. High flotation tires up to 9.15 were still available for owners who desired them. The 16-inch wheels were discontinued and 7x15 tube-type tires replaced them for 1972 as well.

Colors

For 1970–1972, the color choices offered totaled 17 for each year. In 1970, new exterior colors were Diamond Blue, Pinto Yellow, Acapulco Blue, and Carmel Bronze Metallic. By 1972, there were 9 new exterior colors, including a total of 5 metallics.

Owners have wondered for years about this plate on the driver-side doorjamb, found usually on 1972 Broncos. It's part of a mechanism called the ambient air thermal sense switch and helps with emissions by disabling the distributor's vacuum advance under certain conditions. (Photo Courtesy Andy Pecota)

Somewhere in Mexico, this longtime early Bronco owner demonstrated just how far 4WD gets you in a mud hole (i.e., farther than if you had 2WD). This 1970 model, known as Mombasa has carried the owner and his family on many adventures through the years. (Photo Courtesy Steve Sampson)

This 1970 Bronco bears the license plate VIVA OLY (not shown) and a wing on top as homage to the famous racer. With a highly modified suspension system underneath it, this truck serves as a rolling showcase for the talents of Elite Broncos, located in El Cajon, California. (Photo Courtesy Boyd Jaynes)

Production and Collectibility

Bronco production totals for 1970 dropped 12 percent from their 1969 levels to a total of 18,450 units. Of that total, 1,700 were pickups and 16,750 were wagons.

In 1971, production climbed to 21,056 units, while the total pickup production dropped to 1,503. For the year, 4,739 were Sport Broncos, 22.5 percent of the total.

For 1972, pickup production dropped even more to 1,307 units while total production climbed to 21,115 with 7,732 of those being Sport Broncos, 36.6 percent of the total. And of those 7,732 Sport Broncos, 3,006 were also equipped with the Explorer package. (Copyright Marti Auto Works, martiauto.com, and used with permission.)

Of the trucks in this era, the 1971s equipped with the Dana 44 and the 1972 models have always been the most desirable, particularly the late 1972s, which started to see some of the options including power steering, an automatic transmission, and the Ranger package that technically weren't available until the 1973 model year. The 1972 Explorer Sports have become more popular with collectors due to some of the one-year-only features of those trucks. The most valuable of the 1971 and 1972 models, however, was a version that first traveled to Long Beach, California, for a makeover before being released to Ford dealers and customers.

Stroppe Baja Bronco

It is perhaps easiest to understand the Stroppe Baja Bronco's place in the history of the Ford Bronco by comparing it to

This 1970 Bronco wagon takes a break on top of Engineer Pass in the San Juan Mountains in southern Colorado. It breathes easy, even at the high elevations in the San Juans thanks to a Ford SEFI system transplanted on the 302 engine. The owner performed a frame-off restoration on the truck over several years. (Photo Courtesy Casey Nicholas)

another special model that occurred a few years earlier in Ford Motor Company's history: the Shelby Mustang.

Bill Stroppe and Carroll Shelby were both racers and motorsports enthusiasts of the highest order. Shelby earned his fame and notoriety through sports car racing in Europe and the subsequent conversion of AC Aces into Cobras before turning his attention to Mustangs.

Stroppe followed a longer and less glamourous path, starting with modifications to a Ford-powered racing boat in the late 1940s that caught the eye of Benson Ford. From there, he dabbled in nearly everything Ford-powered, from Lincolns in the La Carrera Panamericana races in the 1950s to stock cars, sprint cars, and fuel economy run vehicles.

Silhouetted against the striking central Arizona skyline, a 1970 Bronco travels a high desert trail near Prescott. Equipped with an NP435 4-speed transmission and a 351 V-8 topped with fuel injection, the truck is used for a variety of outdoor activities in the central Arizona backcountry. (Photo Courtesy Sam Berg)

Built as a father-and-son project, this red 1972 half cab is a standout in any crowd. Sporting 38-inch tires, the center of gravity has been kept as low as possible so the rig has minimal lift with larger fender cutouts. Reliability has been increased with the addition of a transplanted late-model fuel-injected Explorer V-8 engine backed by a C4 automatic transmission. The Bronco sees trail time and also makes appearances at local car shows. (Photo Courtesy Mike Bautista)

This Bronco's owner has owned this Bronco since his teen years in the 1980s. Like many longtime owners, the Bronco has evolved over the years to suit his tastes and needs for the trails he traverses. Today it's 13 inches longer than stock, riding on 40-inch tires, with coil-over suspension, and powered by a 351W V-8 backed by a 700R4 transmission and STaK 3-speed transfer case. (Photo Courtesy Mike Bautista)

A late September snowfall covers the ground at the Ophir Summit in the Toiyabe Range in central Nevada. Cresting at nearly 11,000 feet in elevation, this 1970 Bronco summited the pass with ease on a 2013 expedition; the same cannot be said for others in the group. (Photo Courtesy Lars Pedersen)

Both took vehicles that were capable, but not extraordinary, in their stock form, and greatly expanded their capabilities based on their experiences in racing. For Shelby, it was the Mustang. Stroppe's palette was the Bronco, which was a capable vehicle off the showroom floor, but one that could be improved and Stroppe knew how to do it after thousands of bone-crushing miles in Baja. As the initial Baja Bronco press release stated, "the name Stroppe is near magic in off-road racing circles."

Baja Bronco Modifications

Each Baja Bronco started life as a Sport Bronco Wagon equipped with regular-production options such as the higher

Poppy Red, flat black, Wimbledon White, and Astra Blue Metallic are to first-generation Bronco owners as Wimbledon White and Guardsman Blue stripes are to first-generation Mustang owners. Bill Stroppe has often been referred to as the Carroll Shelby of the Bronco world. (Photo Courtesy Eric Rumpf)

This 1971 Stroppe Baja Bronco is one of the finest restored Baja Broncos in existence. The multi-year restoration involved the use of many rare and new old stock (NOS) parts for its completion. It rides on a beautiful pair of chromed steel wheels shod with an original pair of Gates Commando XT tires. Originally sold in California, it now resides in the Chicago area. (Photo Courtesy Jack Niederkorn)

Ford News Release
Public Relations, Ford Division
P.O. Box 1509, Dearborn, Mich. 48121
Telephone: (313) 322-4474

BAJA BRONCO
FOR RELEASE JANUARY 28, 1971

SAN JUAN CAPISTRANO, Calif. -- A new version of the race-proven Ford Bronco, designed to put into one package all the features off-roaders want and need, will be built by Bill Stroppe and Associates, Long Beach, Calif., and sold through Ford dealers.

The "Baja Bronco" will feature Ford's powerful 302-cubic-inch-displacement V-8 and smooth three-speed transmission, plus Stroppe-supplied special paint, roll bar, wide wheels and tires and extra-shock absorbers. Optional equipment will include an automatic transmission installed by Stroppe.

The base vehicle for the Baja Bronco will be the Sport Bronco Wagon, which includes such items as pleated parchment vinyl front seats, vinyl door trim panels, bright metal grille, bumpers and window moldings plus horn ring and cigarette lighter. The vehicle features a red, white and blue paint treatment and flat, black paint will be used on the hood.

The name Stroppe is near magic in off-road racing circles. Stroppe-prepared Broncos won the tortuous Baja 1000 off-road rally in 1969 and the 500-mile version of the race in 1970. Stroppe himself is Off-Road racing advisor to the Ford Motorsports Association.

Special Baja Bronco equipment to be installed, sold and serviced by Bill Stroppe, Inc., includes roll bar, eight-inch wide wheels and Gates XT 10.00 x 15 off-road tires, double shock absorbers front and rear, frame mounted Class II trailer hitch and a rubber dipped steering wheel. Other Stroppe-prepared features include rear fender flares and modified front fender openings, outboard braces to the front bumper and Stroppe's own Baja Bronco nameplates.

BAJA BRONCO
FOR RELEASE JANUARY 28

CONQUISTADOR -- Developed from the winning Ford Broncos of Baja California off-road races, Bill Stroppe's Baja Bronco features heavy duty equipment, wide wheels and tires, a roll bar and an optional automatic transmission. Decked in the colors of the Stroppe Racing Team, the Baja Bronco will be sold exclusively through selected Ford dealers by Bill Stroppe and Associates, Long Beach, Calif.

#

Ford
Public Relations, Ford Division
P.O. Box 1509, Dearborn, Mich. 48121
Telephone: (313) 322-4474

On January 28, 1971, these documents and photo announced the Stroppe Baja Bronco to the automotive world at a press conference held in Tucson, Arizona. Shown wearing Firestone tires rather than the production Gates Commando XT tires, the Baja Bronco proved to be a hit with the motoring press.

GVW package, swing-away tire carrier, 302 V-8, Extra Cooling package, reduced sound level exhaust system, chrome passenger mirror, and auxiliary fuel tank with skid plate.

Ford painted the Broncos a combination of Astra Blue, Wimbledon White, and Poppy Red with a non-glare black hood to mimic the colors used on Stroppe's racing Broncos. A Baja decal replaced the Sport emblem on the Bronco badge on each front fender, and a tire cover with the Baja Bronco logo covered the spare tire on the back.

Once the Broncos were built in Detroit, they were shipped to Stroppe's facility in Long Beach, California, where Stroppe performed additional modifications to the trucks before shipping them to the ordering dealer.

Rick Williamson has wonderful memories of working at Stroppe's shop as a college student nearly 50 years ago. Williamson helped perform the Baja modifications under the watchful eye of Whitey Clayton, the Stroppe foreman in charge of Baja conversions. Williamson recalls that Clayton "showed you how to do it once, and you'd better pay attention because he didn't want to show you again."

Certain tasks, such as rolling the front fenders and changing the speedometer gear for the larger tires, stick in Williamson's mind today. He recalls that trucks were usually modified in batches of two or three at a time, with the various modifications carried out in parallel on the trucks. After all the modifications were completed, the trucks received some paint touchups and then a final inspection and road test before shipment to dealers.

Like Shelby's Mustangs, the Baja Broncos were a combination of custom modifications and judicious use of existing Ford parts repurposed to increase the vehicle's performance. The suggested retail price of the Baja package on top of the Bronco's purchase price was $2,031.67.

In 1971, a Stroppe Baja Bronco package was the only way to buy a Bronco with power steering and an automatic transmission. Contrary to popular belief, these two items were not standard on the early Bajas but were popular options.

For the power steering conversion, Stroppe notched and plated the frame and installed a heavy-duty four-bolt Saginaw power steering box. He dipped into the Ford parts bin to source the C4 automatic transmission, automatic steering column, and transmission cooler for his transmission conversion. Behind the transmission, he used a custom adapter with the word "STROPPE" cast into it to adapt the transmission to the Dana 20 transfer case.

Although the Bajas already had the stiffest springs available from Ford, Stroppe's experience convinced him of the beefing needed in the suspension, so dual shock brackets were welded to each corner of the truck. Additional shocks helped dampen the Bronco's body roll and bouncy ride.

Because larger tires were installed, Stroppe cut the rear fenders of each Baja Bronco and installed fiberglass fender flares

Ford designer Kenneth Dowd was responsible for the Baja Bronco logo found on Baja Bronco tire covers and used in other Baja marketing. The cactus was also used on the Baja Bronco fender decals installed behind the Bronco emblem on the front fenders. (Photo Courtesy Eric Rumpf)

This immaculate undercarriage belies the tough heritage of the Bill Stroppe Baja Broncos. In 1971 and 1972, Stroppe's automatic transmission conversion included a Ford accessory transmission cooler mounted underneath the radiator, protected by an expanded metal shield. Also visible is the pitman arm on the custom-mounted Saginaw power steering box. (Photo Courtesy Jack Niederkorn)

One desirable option of the Stroppe Baja Bronco conversion in 1971 and 1972 was power steering. Stroppe modified the frame (including the front body mount) to install the four-bolt Saginaw steering box. On this immaculately restored truck, the trimmed inner fender with black welting is visible along with the Stroppe bumper brace, period-correct dual gold shock absorbers, and original Gates Commando tires. (Photo Courtesy Jack Niederkorn)

White steel wheels were optional on Stroppe Baja Broncos, but they are not nearly as common or well-known as the slot mags that most associate with the trucks. This truck has fender flares on the front fenders in addition to the rears, which were installed at Stroppe's shop. (Photo Courtesy Eric Rumpf)

In 1971 and 1972, before the availability of the C4 automatic transmission as a factory option, Bill Stroppe offered the 3-speed automatic as an option in his Baja Broncos and as a kit in his catalog. The cast adapters that connected the transmission to the transfer case had the word STROPPE cast into them. Today, the adapters are highly prized items. (Photo Courtesy Cliff Cox)

The interior of this 1975 Baja is a well-preserved example. Visible are the Sport floor mat, Baja Bronco key ring, and padded Baja Bronco steering wheel. The black hood was intended to minimize glare for the driver. (Photo Courtesy Eric Rumpf)

painted red to match the body. At the front, the leading edge of each fender was subtly cut and rolled to give enough clearance for the 10x15 tires. For the 1971 and 1972 model years, the Gates Commando tires were mounted on 8-inch-wide steel wheels that were available in white, blue, black, or chrome.

Behind the front bumper, Stroppe added a diagonal brace at each corner that extended to the frame rail, strengthening

a part that was often damaged during extreme off-road conditions. He also offered a Class II trailer hitch, which had the capability of towing a 3,500-pound trailer with a tongue weight of up to 500 pounds.

The interior also received several items gleaned from Stroppe's off-road experience. The driver's hands gripped a handsome, foam-dipped steering wheel, which proved to be much more comfortable than the thin, stock unit. Passengers were given a higher degree of protection with the addition of a sturdy roll bar that had foam on the upper half of its hoop and was tied into the bedsides and multiple planes of the body and inner fenderwells for additional rigidity. The shape of the

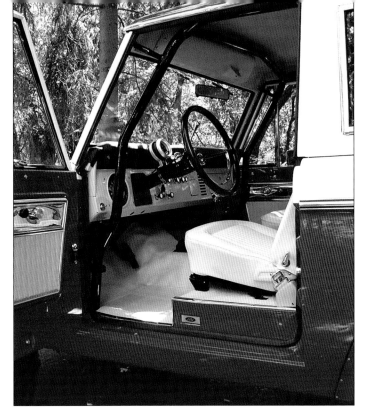

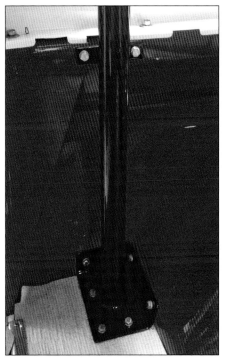

The roll bar used in the Stroppe Baja Broncos reflected Stroppe's racing vehicle roots. A total of 26 bolts secured it to the vehicle. The main mounting pads connected to three body panels and tabs on the vertical bars attached to the inner quarter panels, adding rigidity to the body structure. (Photo Courtesy Jack Niederkorn)

This Baja features a period-correct Autometer tachometer mounted on the steering column along with a Stroppe-built roll cage added to the standard Baja Bronco roll bar. The parchment floor mats that were part of the Sport package and used in the Baja Broncos are not reproduced. The owner found his mint-condition example in a junkyard Bronco. (Photo Courtesy Jack Niederkorn)

bar also meant it could serve as a handrail for rear passengers in rough terrain.

According to the Baja Bronco sales brochure, for "the off roader eager for country that would make a burro think twice . . . or who wants to be ready for competitive runs," Stroppe offered some additional high-performance items including a 4-speed toploader conversion with Hurst shifter, 4-barrel carburetor, Detroit Locker locking differential, tachometer, air-conditioning, dual exhaust, competition seat belts, and shoulder harnesses. Baja Bronco historian and restorer Andrew Norton has documented these and other interesting additions to certain Bajas including roll cages, 351 Windsor engines, and Cibie lights that were processed through Stroppe's shop.

Bronco owners could also bring their personal trucks to Stroppe's shop and have the entire Baja package installed, which was now known among Stroppe enthusiasts as kit Bajas. Stroppe's parts was also available via mail order and from dealership parts departments.

1973–1975

With the introduction of factory power steering and an automatic transmission for 1973, the Baja Bronco lost a bit of its distinctiveness compared to standard production Broncos. However, it gained two items that many enthusiasts have come

This is a Tampico Yellow Stroppe-modified Bronco. The original owner took it to Stroppe's shop and had many of Stroppe's Baja Bronco components installed. Now owned by Baja Bronco expert Andrew Norton, it is used for everything from a parts runner to a family desert cruiser.

to associate with all Baja Broncos: the option of 15x8.5–inch U.S. Indy "slot mags" (aluminum wheels) and the classically styled Cactus Smasher front push bar.

The highest production year for the Baja Bronco was 1973 with 120 rolling out the doors of Stroppe's Long Beach shop. Production plummeted to just 30 units per year for the following two years, with production ending during the 1975 model year.

Various reasons for the decline in sales have been given: erosion of Bronco sales due to stronger market competition, the high cost of the Baja conversion, the downturn in the US economy following the 1973 oil embargo, and the closing of Stroppe's shop in 1974.

LAW ENFORCEMENT BRONCO

Broncos were used in a variety of law enforcement roles throughout the model's life span. The earliest models were used to patrol Central Park in New York City while the last generation of trucks patrolled the southwestern United States as part of the US Border Patrol Fleet.

One of the more unique law enforcement Broncos was a 1972 model owned by the Dover Township Police Department (now the Toms River Police Department) in Toms River, New Jersey. With a purchase price of approximately $4,000, the police department added additional lighting, rescue equipment, and wider wheels and tires for greater flotation on the sandy beaches it patrolled. When it wasn't used for patrol and rescue on the nine beaches under the department's jurisdiction, it was parked in front of the Surf Club, a local beach bar/nightclub, as a deterrent at closing time.

This Bronco, like so many others, succumbed to rust with parts of its body and drivetrain showing up in a Delaware Bronco shop's inventory more than 40 years later.

The late patrolman Thomas Dugan prepares rescue equipment on his 1972 Ford Bronco. The Bronco was a beach patrol and rescue vehicle used by the Dover Township Police in Toms River, New Jersey. (Photo Courtesy Tom's River Police Department)

Patrolman Dugan cuts an impressive figure as he prepares to enter his beach patrol Bronco unit. When not on patrol, the Bronco was parked as a deterrent in front of a local beach bar/nightclub. (Photo Courtesy Tom's River Police Department)

The patrol Bronco used wider than stock steel wheels and high flotation tires to aid in its travels on the beach. Also visible in this shot is the optional transfer case skidplate. (Photo Courtesy Tom's River Police Department)

THE EIGER SANCTION   LITHO. IN U.S.A. Ⓤ   75/130

The Cactus Smasher push bar is one of the more recognizable features of the Stroppe Baja Broncos, but like the slot mags, they didn't appear on the trucks until 1973. Although the name may no longer be considered politically correct, its classic shape has an enduring quality that still looks great today. A pair of period-correct Cibie lights complete the look. (Photo Courtesy Eric Rumpf)

Many Early Bronco enthusiasts know of The Eiger Sanction for one simple reason: it features several scenes with a Stroppe Baja Bronco. The 1975 thriller starred Clint Eastwood and George Kennedy. Their four-wheeled costar appeared in several scenes filmed in Monument Valley, Arizona.

With a total production of fewer than 400 units (per Marti production numbers) and an unknown number of trucks converted to Baja Broncos at Stroppe's shop, the Baja Bronco has always been guaranteed a high level of exclusivity in the Bronco world. With the feverish increase of Bronco prices during the second decade of the 21st century, prices of the Stroppes increased as well. In 2018, the first two $100,000+ Baja Broncos sold at auction. (Copyright Marti Auto Works, martiauto.com, and used with permission.)

Stroppe Baja Bronco Production	
Year	Total
1971	100
1972	80
1973	120
1974	30
1975	30

(Copyright Marti Auto Works, martiauto.com, and used with permission.)

This 1972 Baja was a custom order that was originally painted Poppy Red. Now painted a slightly darker color, the truck sports a Cactus Smasher and slot mags and is equipped with nearly every option available on Baja Broncos in 1972. (Photo Courtesy Tom Carper)

1973–1975: IMPROVEMENTS FINALLY ARRIVE

Amid dismal events such as the Arab oil embargo and Watergate dominating the headlines, the Bronco received some good news in the form of long-overdue upgrades to its powertrain and trim packages. Power steering and an automatic transmission, the top two requests on most enthusiasts' wish lists, were finally offered as options. An upgraded interior trim package, the Ranger package, also became available, offering previously unavailable luxury in the Bronco.

Reviews

By 1973, the Bronco had been on the market for seven years with very few changes. As such, the mainstream automotive media rarely featured it in print, so the task of testing fell on the 4WD enthusiast publications including *Four Wheeler*, *Off Road*, and *Pickup, Van and Four Wheel Drive*.

"Bronco Revolution!" proclaimed *Four Wheeler* in its May 1973 issue, heralding the arrival of the long-awaited automatic transmission and power steering; "Ford engineers have finally caught up with the guys at Chevrolet and International . . . Four wheeling doesn't have to mean a crash box and muscle man steering anymore— and that fact is finally sinking in. No one would consider the Model A or Model T the epitome of pavement driving in 1973 and the same philosophy applies off road."

This 1974 Bronco Ranger is a true survivor truck. Painted in 1974-only Bold Orange, it has about 70,000 original miles and was purchased from the original Nebraska owner in 1988. Other than a few minor repairs and normal maintenance, this is as close to original as you get. (Photo Courtesy Freeze Frame Image LLC, Al Rogers)

Looking oh-so-cool in his mid-1970s' sunglasses and hair style, the unknown gentleman behind the wheel of this 1973 Bronco Ranger in a 1973 Bronco publicity photo is probably having a pretty good time driving such a cool truck off pavement. (Photo Courtesy Ford Motor Company)

For 1973, Ford launched its most aggressive marketing campaign for the Bronco since its introduction in 1966, including taking aim at the female buyer. The news of an automatic transmission, power steering, and the new Ranger trim package was worth spending advertising dollars on, even as Ford recycled a seven-year-old racing Bronco photo and the grocery shopping photo from the previous year in the ad. (Photo Courtesy Ford Motor Company)

Four Wheeler noted that with the automatic "it is easy to walk or ease over relatively large rocks with no strain." But the publication wasn't as happy with the small brake pedal, which was the same one used when a clutch pedal resided beside it, not allowing a driver to easily modulate the brake pedal and accelerator pedal while easing over rough terrain. It also found the new power steering to be over boosted on paved surfaces. *Four Wheeler* concluded, "Maybe the Ford engineers have their minds in the right direction after all."

Pickup, Van and Four Wheel Drive, always a bit more direct in its reviews, summarized the new model as a "sparkly new 1973 model still hampered by 1965 thinking." It liked the power steering but felt that the steering was still far from ideal with non-linear behavior in its range of motion. As with most testers in the 1970s, the deficiencies in the braking system were: high pedal effort and the tendency to skid sideways in panic stops. The publication praised its off-pavement performance but felt that the front limited-slip differential option, a rarity in 4WDs, should be ordered only in rare circumstances. Surprisingly, the summary was fairly sunny, praising its size, off-road performance, automatic transmission, and power steering. Reservations were the steering and to "avoid situations where you need a lot of brakes."

Engine

The big news in the engine department for 1973 was the introduction of the 200-ci 6-cylinder engine as the standard engine, replacing the 170-ci 6-cylinder used since the Bronco's introduction in 1966. Although the engines were in the engine family and had many similarities, there were some key differences.

The most notable, and very desirable from a durability standpoint, was that the 200 had seven main bearings instead of the 170's four, increasing the crankshaft's rigidity and support. The 200 also had hydraulic lifters instead of the mechanical ones in the 170, resulting in a quieter engine. The 200 featured both a slightly larger bore and longer stroke than the 170, which resulted in slightly higher horsepower (89 versus 82 hp) and torque (156 versus 131 ft-lbs) ratings.

As with the 170 Six in 1972, the 200-ci Six was not available in California, where the 302 remained the sole engine offering. Although the 200 was definitely an improvement, the majority of buyers checked the V-8 option box, and the 200 only lasted two years in the Bronco. By 1975, it was gone, and the 302 was the only engine available for the rest of the first generation's run.

1973

The 302 received a few minor changes in 1973–1975. During the 1973 model year, the valve covers changed from having

For 1973, Ford added a radiator overflow bottle on the passenger-side inner fender. Prior to the bottle, the overflow tube went down the side of the radiator to the ground. (Photo Courtesy Eric Dill)

"Power by Ford" lettering to a simple Ford oval near the back. The front dress on the engine changed slightly with the addition of the power-steering pump.

1974

In 1974, solid-state breakerless (electronic) ignition became available as an option on 49-state trucks and mandatory on California rigs as part of a special engine emissions package. In 1975, the solid-state ignition became standard on all trucks, greatly reducing the maintenance headaches long associated with points and condensers. The standard alternator continued to be a 38-amp unit with a 55-amp-unit option.

The air filter was also changed, adjusting the snorkel shape and gaining a cold-air induction hose that pulled air from the core support next to the battery instead of pulling hot air from the engine compartment as with previous versions.

1975 Northland Special Package

For 1975, Ford introduced the Northland Special package for improved cold-weather starting. It included a 400-watt engine block heater, 50/50 antifreeze, Traction-Lok (limited-slip) rear axle, 70 amp-hour battery, and a 55-amp alternator. The engine block heater was also available as a separate option.

The biggest news was the use of unleaded fuel to meet new emissions requirements. This meant the addition of a catalytic converter to the exhaust system, hardened valve seats in the engine's heads, and restrictors in the fuel filler necks to preclude the use of regular-fuel nozzles at service stations.

Ford downgraded the power and horsepower ratings to a measly 122 hp and 218 ft-lbs of torque from the previous year's ratings of 135 hp and 228 ft-lbs. A reported 4-degree retardation in cam timing may have been partially responsible for the poor output.

Transmission

As with every other year of Bronco offered to date, the standard transmission offered was the column-shifted, 3-speed manual.

For the first time, however, the 1973 Bronco order form included an optional transmission. Bronco owners were finally able to order an automatic transmission as long as the 302 V-8 was also chosen: the SelectShift Cruise-O-Matic C4 3-speed transmission, a $236 option. "SelectShift" was a marketing term coined by Ford to denote that the transmission could be started in second gear and would remain in second gear at all RPM until shifted. Thankfully for off-roaders, the transmission could also be manually shifted from drive into second or first gears and remain in those gears for situations where a bit of engine compression braking was desired.

By the time of its introduction in the Bronco in 1972, a few months before the official start of the 1973 model year in August, the C4 had been in use for nine years as a medium-duty transmission in many Ford products, most notably the Mustang, and enjoyed a good reputation for durability and simplicity. The transmission had an aluminum case, removable aluminum bellhousing, and in the Bronco, a removable cast-iron tailhousing adapter that mated it to the Dana 20 transfer case. Cooling was handled by a small heat exchanger located in the passenger-side tank of the radiator.

When installed in the Bronco, the transmission was equipped with a heavy-duty servo (cover denoted with an "H") and a deep oil pan with a dimple in it where the fluid pickup resided to eliminate fluid starvation on steep climbs. Similar to the units used in Ford's other light trucks, the Bronco's C4 was a pan-fill unit whereas the car units were case-fill models. Transmission ratios were 2.46, 1.46, and 1:1.

Transfer Case

For 1973, the Dana 20 transfer case received two significant changes that were not considered upgrades by many enthusiasts. A slight change to the gearing lowered the low-range ratio from 2.46:1 to 2.34:1, lowering the overall crawl ratio.

Gone was the unique T-handle transfer-case shifter that had been in use since late in the 1966 model year, replaced by a more conventional-looking shifter with a round black knob engraved with the shift pattern. The shifter now resembled those found in Ford's pickups and competitors such as the Chevy Blazer. The new shift pattern resembled a backward letter J; the shifter has become known as the J-shifter. According to research by Bronco enthusiast Phil Lindenmuth, the J-shifter was phased in during the 1973 model year in the late fall of 1972, so early examples of the 1973 model still had the familiar T-handle shifter.

Although the front output shaft retention method was changed and shaft bearings upgraded, consumers complained about the difficulty in shifting the early versions of the J-shifter. *Four Wheeler* noted in its test of the 1974 model that "this new shifter is one of the most difficult to operate that we've encountered . . . it is almost impossible to get to 4-Lo. Once it is in 4-Lo, it won't go back to 4-Hi." Ford engineers listened to *Four Wheeler* (according to a 1975 road test a year later) and redesigned the linkage, making it easier to shift.

Axles and Suspension

During the 1973–1975 model years, Ford changed the GVW ratings several times to offer consumers more choices depending on the planned use of the vehicle.

In 1973, Ford added a 4,450-pound GVW package, which included the same tires, axles, and front springs as the standard 4,300 GVW package, but included slightly higher-rated rear leaf springs (1,475-pound rating at the ground). The addition of the 4,450-pound package brought the total GVW choices available to four.

Load ratings and spring ratings changed several times during these years as Ford transitioned to a computer-selection process for matching springs to the GVW packages. The GVW rating was calculated using a new worksheet beginning in 1975. For 1975, the standard rear axle capacity rose from 2,780 to 2,900 pounds, the 4,450-pound GVW package disappeared, and a new 4,600-pound GVW package appeared.

In 1974 and 1975, Ford produced a third rear-axle assembly, the so-called "medium-duty" rear axle that married the 9-inch housing with "late model" big-bearing ends and the smaller 10-inch-diameter drum brakes found on small-bearing rear-axle assemblies. Used on mid-range GVW trucks, the "late model" housing ends foreshadowed the introduction of that housing end across the Bronco lineup for the 1978 model year.

The year 1975 also brought a change to revised ride heights for the Bronco. The floor measurement for an unloaded truck rose from 25.5 to 26.9 inches.

Manual steering continued to be offered as the standard steering setup during these years with the supplier of the steering box changing from Ross to Gemmer for 1974.

Power steering was part of the big changes for the 1973 model year, and it was available only with the V-8. Ford chose to use a recirculating ball integral power steering box manufactured by Saginaw. The Bronco-specific unit had 5.3 turns lock-to-lock and was attached to the frame using three bolts. To complete the installation, Ford added a rag joint at the end of the steering column; a universal joint coupled the other end of the shaft to the steering box's input shaft. A Thompson

This profile of a Bronco power steering box was always a welcome sight when an enthusiast stuck his nose in a Bronco's fenderwell to see whether it had power steering. The Bronco box had one bolt on the leading flange and two bolts on the trailing flange. The box used on the International Scout was almost identical except it had two bolts on the leading flange and one on the trailing flange. (Photo Courtesy Larry Crumpler)

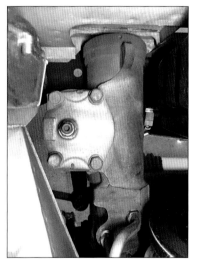

The Bronco's steering box, manufactured by GM's Saginaw gear division, has always been desirable, particularly in the days before power steering conversions became popular. It was designed specifically for the Bronco and fit in a tight space between the body core support, radiator, and inner fender. (Photo Courtesy Larry Crumper)

When Ford added power steering to the options list in 1973, the core support required a slight modification for the added size of the power steering box. Ford added this pushout to accommodate the larger box.

power steering box bolted to the front of the 302 V-8 on the driver's side provided the hydraulic assist to the worm and sector gears in the steering box.

Body

The exterior appearance of the Bronco did not change during the 1973–1975 model years with the exception of the various decal and stripe features associated with the introduction of the new Ranger package for 1973.

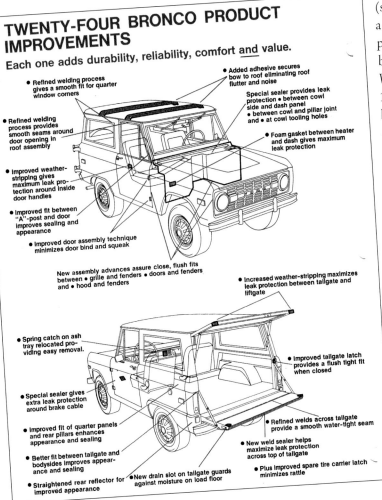

TWENTY-FOUR BRONCO PRODUCT IMPROVEMENTS
Each one adds durability, reliability, comfort and value.

- Refined welding process gives a smooth fit for quarter window corners
- Added adhesive secures bow to roof eliminating roof flutter and noise
- Special sealer provides leak protection • between cowl side and dash panel • between cowl and pillar joint and • at cowl tooling holes
- Refined welding process provides smooth seams around door opening in roof assembly
- Foam gasket between heater and dash gives maximum leak protection
- Improved weather-stripping gives maximum leak protection around inside door handles
- Improved fit between "A"-post and door improves sealing and appearance
- Improved door assembly technique minimizes door bind and squeak
- New assembly advances assure close, flush fits between • grille and fenders • doors and fenders and • hood and fenders
- Increased weather-stripping maximizes leak protection between tailgate and liftgate
- Spring catch on ash tray relocated providing easy removal.
- Improved tailgate latch provides a flush tight fit when closed
- Special sealer gives extra leak protection around brake cable
- Improved fit of quarter panels and rear pillars enhances appearance and sealing
- Refined welds across tailgate provide a smooth water-tight seam
- New weld sealer helps maximize leak protection across top of tailgate
- Better fit between tailgate and bodysides improves appearance and sealing
- Straightened rear reflector for improved appearance
- New drain slot on tailgate guards against moisture on load floor
- Plus improved spare tire carrier latch minimizes rattle

Ford's data book in 1975 detailed 24 Bronco product improvements, many consisting of increased sealing and better assembly techniques. Most of these are minor items, and it is difficult to note the differences between comparable 1974 and 1975 Broncos. (Photo Courtesy Ford Motor Company)

Interior

The interior of the 1973 Bronco brought several changes that visually separated it from its earlier brethren. With the introduction of the automatic transmission for the 1973 model year, the steering column gained an automatic shifter (slightly shorter than the 3-speed manual shifter) along with a gear indicator. In 1973, the indicator was simply a clear piece of plastic with PRND2L markings on it without any backlighting. The test results of the 1973 model in *Four Wheeler* complained about the lack of lighting, and so in 1974, Ford added a shrouded cover to the indicator and also backlighting so the driver could see the gear in low-light conditions.

In 1974, the hazard light switch was moved from the dash to the steering column just behind the steering wheel. And in 1975, the Bronco's steering wheel was changed to the same steering wheel used in F-Series and Econoline trucks.

Temperature controls, lights, wipers, and hazard controls on the dash also gained lighted indicators on the dash for 1973. In 1974, the previously standard map light was replaced with a dome light as the standard interior lighting. A subtle change to the instrument cluster occurred for the 1975 model year when "Unleaded Gasoline Only" was added under the speedometer.

The standard Bronco trim package continued to offer such basic amenities as a heater/defroster, lockable glove compartment, padded instrument panel, 2-speed electric windshield wipers, sun visors, vinyl rubber floor mat (black), and white-painted steel bumpers as standard equipment.

The Convenience Group was an optional package that offered a day/night mirror and map light to all Broncos plus the cigarette lighter and horn ring when they were not otherwise included (without the Sport Bronco or Ranger trim packages).

A number of the standard items from the Sport and Ranger packages could be ordered as options to the standard Bronco trim package if the buyer wanted to customize the truck or perhaps save some money by not purchasing the entire package.

In the 1970s, it was difficult to find replacement tops for Broncos. An aftermarket top made by Kelly Manufacturing in Springfield, Ohio, was a replacement that is still occasionally seen today on some Broncos. The similarity to early Scout tops is more than coincidental, as Kelly was the OEM supplier for the International Scout as well.

Sport

The Sport package added vinyl door-trim panels with bright moldings, a hardboard headliner with bright retainers, a vinyl parchment simulated carpet front floor mat with bright retainers (matching rear mat with optional rear seat), cigar lighting, horn ring, chrome metal windshield and window frames, bright grille surround and tailgate-release handle, bright headlights, side-markers and rear reflector bezels, an argent-painted grille, chrome bumpers front and rear with bright front bumper guards, and bright wheel covers.

Explorer

The Explorer package returned for 1973 with a few changes from 1972. For 1973, it was only available as an upgrade to the standard Bronco package, not the Sport package of the previous year. To the standard Bronco, the Explorer added bright bumpers, taillight bezels, wheel covers, and body side and tailgate moldings.

Exterior color choices were Grabber Blue or Burnt Orange. Inside, it added a bit of unique luxury with special Orange or Blue random-striped cloth seat trim that matched the exterior colors. The door panels were also color-keyed to the interior color and the dash was painted body color. The rear quarter panels had vinyl covers that were color-keyed to the upholstery, and the glove box door sported an Explorer instrument panel plaque.

In 1974, the Explorer package was similar to the 1973 offering but changed the color choices to Brook Blue Metallic or Viking Red. Inside, the seats were offered in either Blue or Red Stirling cloth to match the exterior colors. The door panels were once again color-keyed to the interior colors, and this year also included rubber floor mats of a matching color. The Explorer floor mats are highly prized by today's collectors and are not reproduced.

The Explorer trim package was not offered for 1975.

Ranger

Found on some late 1972 models, and officially introduced for the 1973 model year, the Ranger trim package was the ultimate in luxury for first-generation Broncos. A step above the Sport and Explorer packages, the Ranger offered previously unheard-of features in the Bronco including color-keyed full carpeting (including the tailgate and wheel housings); color-keyed vinyl door trim panels with wood-tone accents; color-keyed vinyl trim on rear quarter panels; cloth and vinyl seat trim in ginger, blue, or avocado; color-keyed instrument panel paint; and a black plastic coat hook mounted at the roofline behind the passenger's front seat. The optional rear

Sharp-eyed Bronco enthusiasts note that this interior belongs to a 1974 model by its one-year-only combination of the emergency flasher switch on the steering column, shrouded and backlit gear indicator for the transmission shifter, and 1966–1974-style steering wheel. (Photo Courtesy Freeze Frame Image LLC, Al Rogers)

This one-year-only upholstery color was found in 1973 Explorer Broncos. In Ford-parlance, it was known as burnt orange. Enthusiasts today refer to it as the "tequila sunrise" upholstery pattern. (Photo Courtesy Tim Hulick)

seat was required with the Ranger package.

On the exterior, the swing-away tire carrier was standard, and the spare tire was covered with a white vinyl cover with "Bronco Ranger" lettering, the bucking-horse logo, and orange accent piping at the seams. The hood and lower body sides had white vinyl stripes with an orange accent stripe. If the optional bright-metal rocker panel molding was ordered as an option, the tape stripes were deleted.

Despite the Ranger package's rather hefty cost of $405, about 25 percent (5,666) of the year's total Bronco production was equipped with this top-of-the-line package. Similar production percentages also applied to the 1974 and 1975 Bronco

This is Bronco luxury, circa 1974: On the interior, the $405 Ranger package gave you color-keyed carpeting on the floors, fenderwells, and tailgate, with matching panels in the rear quarters to match the upholstery (shown here in Ginger in this 1974 survivor). (Photo Courtesy Freeze Frame Image LLC, Al Rogers)

For the 1974 Explorer, Ford offered red floor mats along with the red upholstery. Finding one today is extremely rare and finding one in good condition is like finding the proverbial hens' teeth. (Photo Courtesy Eric Dill)

models. With the exception of a change from Avocado to Green as one of the interior colors for 1975, the Ranger package remained essentially unchanged from 1973 to 1975.

Tires and Wheels

For 1973, the wheel color changed from white to argent according to official Ford documentation. Evidence seems to indicate that *argent* in these years really meant gray. Wheel size remained 15x5.5 for the duration of this period. Tire sizes were E78x15, G78x15, or L78x15, depending on GVW and desired load capacity. For old-school types, 7x15 tube-type truck tires were still an option across all models.

Bright wheel covers were an option on the standard Bronco model and standard equipment on the Sport, Explorer, and Ranger models.

Colors

The Bronco was offered with 17 exterior color choices for 1973–1974 with 4 of those new for the 1973 model year: Raven Black, Midnight Blue Metallic, Bright Lime, and Hot Ginger Metallic.

For 1974, Ford boasted 9 new colors, including 2 new so-called glamour colors: Gold Glow and Ivy Glow. Bold Orange was an exclusive Bronco color for 1974.

For 1975, the color count increased to 18 with Ford again boasting 9 new exterior colors, including an exclusive Dark Jade Metallic.

Production and Collectability

Despite the introduction of power steering, the automatic transmission, and the Ranger package, 1973 Bronco production did not rise significantly as compared to the 1972 model year: 21,894 versus 21,115. Of those sold, 3,407 were Sport models, 2,949 were Explorers, and 5,666 were the new Ranger model.

Surprisingly, despite the downturn in the US economy during the model year, 1974 proved to be the best year for sales of the first-generation Bronco with 25,824 units leaving showroom floors. Perhaps it took a while for the good news of the 1973 upgrades to spread. Rangers continued to be strong sellers with 5,940 units produced and the Explorer package trucks found 3,163 new homes. (Copyright Marti Auto Works, martiauto.com, and used with permission.)

The growing popularity of the larger, truck-based Chevy Blazer, and GMC Jimmy; the introduction of the Dodge Ramcharger/Plymouth Trailduster twins in 1974; and the effects of the economic downturn finally sinking in were to blame for

This 1973 Bronco has run trails on both coasts. In the early 2000s, it lived in North Carolina and enjoyed the muddy, lush trails of the Southeast. After a move to Arizona a few years later, it enjoys stretching its legs in places such as the red rocks of Sedona, Arizona. (Photo Courtesy Brian Blaylock)

Sporting Special Décor stripes from the 1976–1977 Bronco, this 1974 example crawls the John Bull Trail in the mountains near Big Bear, California. In addition to extensive trail use, Wanda, as the truck is known, has appeared in American Express and Sears ads in recent years. (Photo Courtesy Mike Bautista)

Not all Stroppe Baja Broncos sit stationary in large collections or hermetically sealed garages. This 1974 Baja (one of only 30 made that year) is still used in the dirt the way God and Bill Stroppe intended. In 2018, the owner and his wife led a group of Bronco enthusiasts on a trip down the Baja Peninsula, traveling nearly 2,500 miles in the process. The Baja is pictured here with a beautiful sunset along the Pacific coast during that trip. (Photo Courtesy Scott Barnes)

the precipitous decline in Bronco sales for 1975. The effects of the economy finally took hold for the 1975 model year with only 13,125 sold, a 49-percent reduction in sales from the previous year, and the worst year of sales for the first-generation Bronco. Of those 13,125 produced, 3,964 were the Ranger model. (Copyright Marti Auto Works, martiauto.com, and used with permission.)

The 1973–1975 models have traditionally been among the most desirable of the first-generation Broncos, behind only the 1976–1977 models, due to the availability of power steering, the automatic transmission, and the Explorer and Ranger trim packages. This was particularly true in the years when automatic transmission swaps and power-steering conversions were not as commonly available in the aftermarket. As the value of the first-generation trucks has skyrocketed, these models have led the way in terms of collectability and value. Original condition and restored Ranger models bring the highest returns at auctions and other sales compared to other stock models from other years.

This 1973 Bronco Ranger is a familiar sight at East Coast Bronco events and cruises, its owner behind the wheel and her dog Enzo riding shotgun. A small lift, fender flares, and a roll cage add some flair to the well-maintained ride, which still sports its original Ranger interior. (Photo Courtesy Melissa Magness)

Broncos were also popular vehicles for railroad use. The Bronco's track width fit well on standard-gauge railroad tracks. In the 1980s, drivers sometimes put their Bronco on the tracks, aired down the tires so they formed around the rails, put the Bronco's transfer case in low range, and sat on the hood looking for game to hunt.

Legendary rocker Ted Nugent has owned examples from at least three generations of Broncos in his lifetime, during a period of more than 40 years. Here, Ted and wife Shemane pose with his 1974 Bronco wagon that was rebuilt with the help of Bronco Graveyard and many other vendors. (Photo Courtesy Ted Nugent and tednugent.com)

A herd of Broncos poses in front of imposing red rock spires near Sedona, Arizona, on the Broken Arrow Trail. The Arizona Classic Bronco Club has led runs from mild to wild throughout the state since 1991. (Photo Courtesy Tom Alexander)

By 1973, the Bronco was considered by many to be getting long in the tooth. Features that had been innovations at the time of its introduction seven years earlier were now common; the Bronco had been surpassed by the competition.

As part of the planning for future upgrades to the existing Bronco platform, Ford Light Truck Engineering performed a package study in 1973 to prepare assumptions for an improved Bronco in 1976. Cost information from the studies was to be used in determining whether the full-size Bronco should be introduced in 1976 or deferred a few more years in favor of a modernized first-generation Bronco.

Bearing the project number TAL 06 and funded at $35,000, the study looked at layout investigations intensive enough to determine cost assumptions for the following studies: improved instrument panel (lighted controls only), windshield wipers mounted on the bottom of the windshield, full-time 4WD (using a NP208 transfer case), 10x15 tires, and new disc brakes. Secondary investigations looked at the 351-ci engine and improved fuel tank capacity (an additional 5 gallons).

Studies of the 351-ci engine package, full-time 4WD, improved instrument panel, and low-mounted windshield wipers were discontinued due to either low feasibility confidence and/ or excessive vehicle tear-up (too invasive and requiring significant redesign of existing structures). Following are the feasibility confidence level and vehicle tear-up rating for each study:

1976 "Upgraded Bronco" Studies		
Study	Feasibility Confidence Level	Vehicle Tear-up
10x15 LT tire profile	95 percent	Moderate
Full-time 4WD	50 percent	Moderate
Improved instrument panel	95 percent	Minor
Low-mounted windshield wipers	70 percent	Major
Increased fuel tank capacity	70 percent	Minor
351-ci engine	50 percent	Major
New front disc brakes	100 percent	Moderate

Light Truck Engineering moved forward with the planning, which resulted in the adoption of disc brakes for the 1976 model year Bronco.

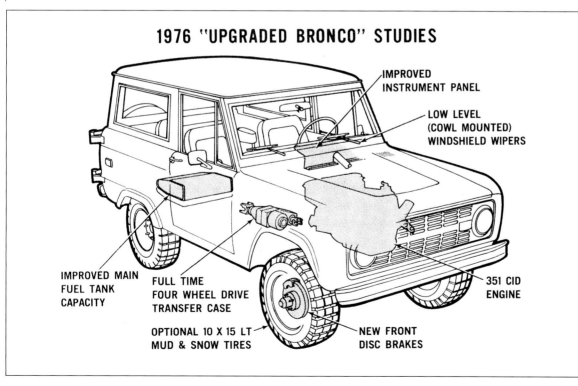

1976 "UPGRADED BRONCO" STUDIES

IMPROVED INSTRUMENT PANEL

LOW LEVEL (COWL MOUNTED) WINDSHIELD WIPERS

351 CID ENGINE

NEW FRONT DISC BRAKES

OPTIONAL 10 X 15 LT MUD & SNOW TIRES

FULL TIME FOUR WHEEL DRIVE TRANSFER CASE

IMPROVED MAIN FUEL TANK CAPACITY

This graphic from a 1973 design status presentation is a peek into the minds of Ford truck engineers that year. Although a number of these items were addressed by the aftermarket, the only one that came to fruition from the factory in the first-generation trucks was disc brakes, which came along in 1976, as this graphic predicted. (Photo Courtesy Don Wheatley)

SILVER FOX

Many Broncos on the road today have been modified, restored, and possibly totally rebuilt from their original showroom configuration many years ago. However, there are very few that have been rebuilt numerous times and, in the process, found themselves featured in print media spanning several decades. The *Silver Fox*, as it is known, is one of those rare rigs, having first appeared in *Four Wheeler* more than four decades ago.

The *Fox* began life as a well-equipped 1967 Bronco Sport ordered in Thunderbird gray color offered that year. The owner, Duane Kennedy, began modifying the Bronco and venturing into the backcountry on 4WD exploration trips. Kennedy, a cowboy at heart, treated his vehicle like a favorite horse; the attention lavished on the Bronco meant it was virtually a member of the family. Today, Kennedy and his children have fond memories of desert trips in the Bronco.

A few years later on a Broncos West Club outing near Borrego, California, the front axle housing broke. A few months later on a trip to Texas Canyon in Southern California, the unthinkable happened when Kennedy rolled the Bronco. Thankfully he was unhurt, and after a thorough analysis, he discovered that the steering shaft of the steering box had broken due to a small hairline fracture caused by that previous incident in Borrego.

Now the real decision time came: Should he fix his crumpled 1967 Bronco or should he head to the dealership and buy a brand-new Bronco? It's a decision faced all the time by enthusiasts looking at large repair bills on a damaged, aging friend that, despite the wrinkles and wear, tugs at our heartstrings.

Kennedy ultimately kept his Bronco and bought a new 1974 body from a local Ford dealer. The resulting rebuild process took eight months and cost more than $2,000 (in 1974) but in the end Kennedy certainly felt that it was worth it. A machinist by trade, he cleaned and painted every nook and cranny of the truck and replaced the original 289 V-8 with a freshly rebuilt 351 Windsor from a 1969 Mustang.

In later years, he swapped the original 3-speed transmission for a 4-speed toploader transmission and also added power steering. To ensure that he wouldn't have any more front-end problems, he had James Duff install a Dana 44 front end. To top it off, he installed a fiberglass hood from Duffy's Bronco Service and had a local top shop add a custom sunroof (it was the 1970s, after all). He added a number of custom features that he built himself including custom coil-spring spacers, front and rear axle trusses, shift knobs, and various latches and mechanisms that could only come from the mind of a brilliant machinist. To top it all off, he had a local paint shop lay down a beautiful silver base coat topped with a colorful blue, red, and gold pattern that seemed to embody the 1970s. The rebuild process

The vibrant sunburst pattern on the Silver Fox Bronco is accentuated in this desert backdrop near Borrego, California. Continuing the tradition of the truck's original owner, Duane Kennedy, the truck today explores the trails of Southern California with an undercarriage so clean you could eat off it. (Photo Courtesy Terry Marvel)

Duane Kennedy, the original owner and builder of the Silver Fox exercises his Bronco at Pismo Beach as part of a photo shoot for Four Wheeler in the mid-1970s. At the time, Kennedy had just completed an extensive rebuild of the truck, combining the original 1967 frame and drivetrain with a 1974 body. (Photo Courtesy Terry Marvel)

was documented in the August 1975 issue of *Four Wheeler*.

Fast-forward six years and Kennedy was still enjoying his beautiful Bronco when *Petersen's 4 Wheel & Off Road* magazine came calling for another photo shoot that included his truck and James and Judy Duff's iconic Broncos. The Duffs had the article reprinted into a poster, which was mailed with their catalogs for many years.

Kennedy sold the Bronco in the late 1990s and it disappeared until September 2008, when another longtime Bronco enthusiast, Terry Marvel, was browsing Craigslist and noticed what seemed to be a familiar truck listed for sale in the Los Angeles area. Marvel was familiar with the *Silver Fox*, having once met Kennedy in the early 1990s, and noticed a few key items on the Bronco for sale that jogged a memory for him. An inspection confirmed that it indeed was the *Fox* and Marvel quickly made the purchase. He was thrilled that such an iconic Bronco was now his!

Having already built and restored several Broncos, Marvel immediately made plans to revive the *Silver Fox*. He met Kennedy and his family and learned about the history of his new purchase. Marvel decided to restore the Bronco to its original configuration with a few modern upgrades added.

He went over every piece of the chassis, carefully cleaning and refurbishing the parts that didn't need replacing. When needed, he replaced worn parts with NOS pieces from his collection. The body received a fresh coat of paint, along with the 1970s graphics, from Mark Atherton at Beach City Broncos in El Cajon, California. The Bronco had worn several styles of wheels over the years and Marvel sourced a set of custom-made units from Stockton Wheel to duplicate his favorites. Armstrong TRU-TRAC tires were no longer available, so Marvel found a modern set of Wild Country tires that closely replicate the classic tread pattern.

The engine is still a 351W with the classic Mach 1 shaker hood. Along the way, the Dana 44 had received a disc brake conversion and Marvel added a power brake booster to make braking activities a little easier in modern Los Angeles traffic. The truck still has the 1967 dash, and it's easy to see that this truck is the real deal by checking out all the vintage event plaques plastered across the dash; many of them are more than 50 years old.

Years ago, fellow Bronco owners assumed Kennedy didn't actually use his Bronco off-road because it was always clean. It was *used*. He was just fastidious about its cleaning and maintenance, and Marvel has continued that tradition. Although you could eat off the undercarriage and the *Silver Fox* has won the coveted Bill Stroppe Trophy at the annual Fabulous Fords Forever show in California, it has also seen off-road use at Early Bronco Registry events in the Southern California desert; the Arizona Classic Bronco Stampede; camping trips in Big Bear, California; and Southern California locales. The *Silver Fox* has lived an incredible life with multiple owners, and it's a story that has not yet ended.

This is one of the earliest pictures of the Silver Fox taken in the late 1960s. Duane Kennedy had already added flares to the rear wheels and added larger tires on chrome steel wheels, which were popular at the time. Fifty years later, the truck still has the same license plates that are shown in this photo. (Photo Courtesy Terry Marvel)

Although any kid in the 1980s could have a poster of a Lamborghini or Porsche on their bedroom walls, those with an extra bit of class and perhaps machismo had one of these posters from James Duff Enterprises above their pillow. The reprint of a 1981 Petersen's 4 Wheel & Off Road article featured Duane Kennedy's Silver Fox and the Duffs' Pony Express and Mrs. Duff's trucks. (Photo Courtesy James Duff)

DENVER BRONCO

After four years of production, the sales of the Stroppe Baja Bronco had declined to where only a few dozen of the model were being sold each year (30 in 1974), and times were changing at Bill Stroppe's shop in Long Beach, California. A combination of economic pressures within his business and the overall economy forced him to close his doors in the fall of 1974 and cease production of the Baja Broncos.

According to popular lore, Ford already had a number of the Broncos produced, painted, and waiting to become Baja Broncos when Stroppe ceased operations. According to the Denver Bronco Registry webpage, Golden Motors Ford in Golden, Colorado, purchased the Broncos from Ford (DSO 763000), realizing they could be turned into Denver Bronco Editions quite easily because the Baja Bronco colors were very similar to the Denver Broncos football team colors. Seventy-seven units were purchased and taken to Colorado, where the dealership installed fender flares and a Denver Broncos spare tire cover.

Although this all makes for a good story, it seems impossible to verify the exact circumstances under which the Denver Bronco Edition was conceived and executed because some outlying questions still remain. Kevin Marti's records indicate that Ford built 214 Denver Broncos for the 1975 model year. (Copyright Marti Auto Works, martiauto.com, and used with permission.) That's more than the previous three years' production of Baja Broncos combined. Why would Ford have that many Broncos waiting in the wings for Baja production? Marti's reports also reveal that at least some of the Baja Broncos were produced after the Denver Broncos were built in the fall of 1974. And would Ford have changed the warranty tags on those dormant Bajas-to-be to have the Denver DSO instead of the Los Angeles DSO?

Although they have white hoods instead of the black units found on Baja Broncos, Denver Broncos at first glance resemble Baja Broncos enough so that to the casual observer, they appear to be identical. They have also been a source of confusion within the enthusiast community over the years. Because the trucks did not go through Stroppe's shop, they lack the performance modifications such as dual shocks, roll bar, push bar, and lights that were often found on Baja Broncos. A few Denver Broncos did not receive the rear fender flares and remained uncut.

Denver Bronco Editions have lagged

This 1975 Denver Bronco is one of the cleanest examples of the limited-edition Broncos. The red, white, and blue paint scheme mimics that of the Stroppe Baja Bronco, minus the black hood. On this particular example, the roll bar, wheels, and front fender flares are not original. (Photo Courtesy Greg Overton)

behind Baja Broncos in value, with the highest sale price of $75,000 recorded by 2018. However, their low production numbers and unique development story has ensured a special place for them in the history of the Bronco.

The Denver Bronco Edition is often mistaken for a Baja Bronco. The Marti Report lists that 212 of these trucks were built and sold as a regional special through the Denver District Ford dealers. Denver Broncos lacked the roll bar, dual shocks, padded steering wheel, and bumper braces that were installed on the Bajas. (Photo Courtesy Greg Overton)

1976–1977:
GOING OUT ON TOP

> "Due to improvements in suspension, steering, and braking, the 1976–1977 Broncos have long enjoyed the highest collectability value of the 12 years of first-generation Bronco production."

As the country anticipated its 200th birthday celebrations, Ford decided to add some fairly significant upgrades to the Bronco. This was surprising considering that the current bodystyle was old and more than ready for its platform change and updates in the eyes of most enthusiasts.

In its sales materials, Ford continued to focus on the advantages of its smaller size with the phrases "lean and nimble," "the sporty little four-wheeler without the bulk of many large units," "it's designed to go places many of the larger vehicles can't," and in a direct shot at Blazer, Jimmy, and Ramcharger, the Trailduster "Bronco is not a modified four-wheel drive pickup, it's designed specifically for off-road use where trim size and an extra margin of maneuverability are important."

To focus on nimbleness and maneuverability, most of the upgrades were in the drivetrain, where they were needed most to make the vehicle more enjoyable to drive.

Marketing

For 1976–1977, Ford's marketing department made a special advertising push to the youth marketplace through its Free Wheelin' promotional materials. Employing a catchphrase of the mid-1970s, print ads and a specific Free Wheelin' brochure show the younger set engaged in activities such as cruising, surfing, riding dirt bikes, camping, working on hot rods, boating, attending musical concerts, and hanging out at the beach; all the while smiling and having way too much fun hanging out around their shiny, parked cars. No doubt, as the brochure stated in its title, "Ford Wheelin' and 'Free Wheelin'" were synonymous!

For this marketing effort, Ford commented, "Lean machines for twisting around trees or barging across boulder-strewn streams. Drive away from it all in a fully-equipped Sport Bronco . . ."

The Broncos featured most prominently in both year's brochures were the new Special Décor Editions.

The first-generation Broncos have a reputation as excellent snow machines, which made them invaluable on the snow-covered plains of Montana.

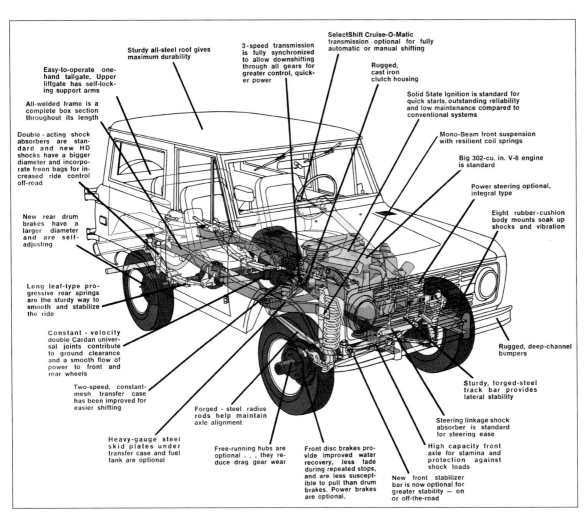

Easy-to-operate one-hand tailgate. Upper liftgate has self-locking support arms

Sturdy all-steel roof gives maximum durability

3-speed transmission is fully synchronized to allow downshifting through all gears for greater control, quicker power

SelectShift Cruise-O-Matic transmission optional for fully automatic or manual shifting

Rugged, cast iron clutch housing

Solid State Ignition is standard for quick starts, outstanding reliability and low maintenance compared to conventional systems

All-welded frame is a complete box section throughout its length

Double-acting shock absorbers are standard and new HD shocks have a bigger diameter and incorporate freon bags for increased ride control off-road

Mono-Beam front suspension with resilient coil springs

Big 302-cu. in. V-8 engine is standard

Power steering optional, integral type

Eight rubber-cushion body mounts soak up shocks and vibration

New rear drum brakes have a larger diameter and are self-adjusting

Long leaf-type progressive rear springs are the sturdy way to smooth and stabilize the ride

Constant-velocity double Cardan universal joints contribute to ground clearance and a smooth flow of power to front and rear wheels

Two-speed, constant-mesh transfer case has been improved for easier shifting

Heavy-gauge steel skid plates under transfer case and fuel tank are optional

Forged-steel radius rods help maintain axle alignment

Free-running hubs are optional . . . they reduce drag gear wear

Front disc brakes provide improved water recovery, less fade during repeated stops, and are less susceptible to pull than drum brakes. Power brakes are optional.

New front stabilizer bar is now optional for greater stability — on or off-the-road

High capacity front axle for stamina and protection against shock loads

Steering linkage shock absorber is standard for steering ease

Sturdy, forged-steel track bar provides lateral stability

Rugged, deep-channel bumpers

This cutaway of the Bronco appeared in the 1976 and 1977 factory Bronco brochures. It highlights the features available during those years, including power disc brakes and the front sway bar. This illustration also gives a good sense of how tall and narrow the early Bronco is in its stock configuration. (Photo Courtesy Ford Motor Company)

The implication is clear. Buy yourself a new Bronco and you might just fall in love and find yourself a new partner. And you'll get to hang out together at the beach at sunset, leaning back on some hot sheet metal that's been in the sun all day, while wearing very little clothing. This photo, part of Ford's Free Wheelin' advertising brochure, was probably the raciest Bronco advertisement in the vehicle's 30-year history. (Photo Courtesy Ford Motor Company)

Baja-prepared Bronco

This photo of a group of young people enjoying their Baja Bronco on a camping trip appeared in the 1976 Free Wheelin' brochure, which aimed to make Fords more appealing to young people. Ironically, Baja Broncos had gone out of production a year earlier when Bill Stroppe closed his business. So, either this brochure was prepared long before the 1976 model year commenced or Ford's marketing department was woefully out of touch with what vehicles they were actually selling. (Photo Courtesy Ford Motor Company)

Engine

Ford redesigned the cylinder heads on the 302 for 1977, raising the compression ratio from 8.0 to 8.4:1. This change, according to Ford, resulted in better cooling and easier emissions compliance. The net effect on dyno results was that the 1977 Ford 302 had 12 additional horsepower and 19 ft-lbs more torque than 1976 versions.

More noticeable than the head redesign was the introduction of the Ford Duraspark II ignition system. Easily identifiable by its larger-diameter distributor cap, the Duraspark ignition system was used with great success in many Ford vehicles until the advent of fuel-injected engines in the late 1980s.

Other changes for the year were limited to a slightly higher alternator output rating (38 versus 40 amp) and 55 versus 60 amp on the optional higher-capacity unit.

The unique angled bracket with power brake booster was optional in 1976–1977 Broncos only. The booster was an 8-inch dual-diaphragm unit, actuating a 1-inch-bore master cylinder. The 1976–1977 fender had a crease for steering shaft clearance and was also lowered on the rear edge to allow for clearance for the booster assembly. The jack for the vehicle is stored in the black vinyl bag on the inner fender. (Photo Courtesy Freeze Frame Image LLC, Al Rogers)

The most visible feature on this 1977 302 engine is the large cap of the Duraspark II electronic ignition distributor. The Duraspark system proved to be reliable and transformed the amount of ignition maintenance necessary for the typical Bronco owner, making replacement of points and condensers and setting dwell a thing of the past. (Photo Courtesy Freeze Frame Image LLC, Al Rogers)

Transmission

The standard transmission continued to be the 3.03 Ford 3-speed, column-shifted unit. Since its introduction in 1973, the optional C4 3-speed automatic became more popular, and the majority of the Broncos sold during these years were equipped with automatic transmissions: 68 percent in 1976 and 70 percent in 1977. (Copyright Marti Auto Works, martiauto.com, and used with permission.)

Brakes

Bronco owners were finally granted their long-desired wish for better brakes; Ford added brakes from the F-150

Not every 1976 and 1977 Bronco came with power brakes. Those that did not had a manual master cylinder mounted with a custom aluminum bracket sandwiched between it and the firewall. (Photo Courtesy Andrew Norton)

4WD truck comprised of 11.75-inch-diameter front rotors squeezed by single-piston calipers and 11-1/32x2.25-inch rear drums. The rotors were bolted onto new steering knuckles with a revised Ackerman angle and a larger opening for the axle shafts to pass through.

Power assist for the brakes was optional and a popular accessory as evidenced by the fact that most of the 1976–1977

Broncos have the vacuum booster in place. The 8-inch dual-diaphragm booster was angled away from the firewall for clearance and to allow the proper pedal ratio for the boosted setup through the use of a pivot bracket with two lever arms of varying lengths.

The extra bulk of the vacuum booster and its mounting bracket required additional massaging of the driver-side inner fenderwell. In addition to the crease added in 1973 for the steering shaft, the top of the fenderwell was lowered slightly for clearance. Manual-brake master cylinders had an aluminum block approximately 1 inch thick between the master cylinder and the firewall.

Steering

For 1976, a manual steering box was still standard and with a Saginaw-sourced steering box optional as in prior years. However, the power steering box turned lock-to-lock was reduced from 5.3 to 3.8, ensuring as Ford stated, "improved 'close quarter' maneuverability."

In addition to the quicker steering ratio, a collapsible steering shaft with a U-joint at the box end replaced the one-piece shaft with the bell coupler used in previous years. The collapsible shaft ensured a greater measure of safety in the event of a front-end collision.

Haltenberger Linkage

In addition to the steering box, Ford introduced what has proven to be one of the more controversial items on the early Bronco platform: the inverted-Y steering linkage. Known in technical circles as the Haltenberger linkage, it added some compliance to the connection between the two front wheels and was generally believed to be more resistant to the violent front-end shimmy known as death wobble. It was also used on Ford's Twin I-Beam 2WD front suspension systems and 4WD Twin-Traction Beam front ends as the movement of the linkage closely matched the wheel-travel arcs of the front beams, minimizing bump steer.

On the Bronco and F-150, the linkage functioned as designed when used with stock and slightly larger-than-stock tires and wheels and stock suspension components. *Pickup, Van and Four Wheel Drive*, in a contemporary road test, noted, "The tendency of the older Broncos to self-steer over bumps is gone."

Once a lift kit was installed and front-wheel travel increased, the shortcomings of the Haltenberger linkage became apparent as the wheels experienced large amounts of toe change as the suspension extended and the tie-rod effectively became shorter. The compliance of the system became a liability with hard use and bent tie-rods were the result. Ford used the Haltenberger linkage for only two years on the

The 1976–1977 steering linkage is known as the Haltenberger linkage, or inverted-Y setup. It offered greater tie-rod clearance compared to the 1966–1975 linkage, greater resistance to the infamous death wobble, and better road manners with stock, or nearly stock, tires. The thick rod underneath the axle is the optional front sway bar, available as an option on 1976–1977 Broncos only. (Photo Courtesy Drew Peroni)

Bronco before returning to the T-style cross-steer linkage. The drawbacks apparently outweighed the benefits.

Behind the steering linkage, Ford modified the track bar (panhard bar) shape and reshaped the upper bushing to give it more lateral compliance.

Chassis

The Bronco chassis changed very little for the years 1966–1977, and it received one of its few changes for the 1976 model year. In addition to the modified track bar, Ford redesigned

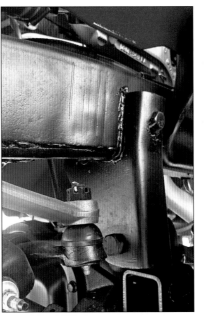

The track bar bracket (the large U-shaped piece hanging off the frame directly in front of the coil-spring cup) was longer for 1976–1977, coinciding with the change in the steering linkage for those years as well. The optional power steering box, changed to a quicker ratio for 1976, is barely visible in the extreme left. A 1976–1977–specific pitman arm is shown as well. (Photo Courtesy Drew Peroni)

the track bar mount on the frame. The attachment point was lowered 2 inches and the bracket on the frame was moved back slightly so it gave more clearance for the suspension's compression travel. The net effect of these changes was that the track bar and passenger-side tie-rod traveled in the same plane, reducing chassis oversteer and producing more neutral handling.

In previous years, the track bar was above the drag link, producing a more pronounced oversteer condition. Lowering the track bar bracket lowered the roll center of the front suspension and produced a higher roll-moment couple (making the vehicle have a greater tendency to sway in turns), which Ford countered by offering an optional front sway bar for the first time.

Axles and Suspension

For 1976, Ford eliminated the 4,300-pound Gross Vehicle Weight Rating (GVWR). In concert with the adoption of the larger rear drum brakes, it also reduced the number of rear axle bearing types from three offered in 1974–1975 to only one for 1976. The big-bearing axle carried a rating of 2,900 pounds, down from the 3,300-pound rating of earlier years. The 4,400-pound GVW rating became standard with 4,600 and 4,900 optional. If you wanted a rear seat, the 4,600-pound GVW was mandatory.

The actual changes to accommodate the optional ratings were limited to a larger tire size (G78-15 versus E78-15) and higher capacity springs. Towing recommendations remained Class 1 trailers with a trailer weight up to 2,000 pounds with the 4,900-pound GVW package. The Extra Cooling radiator and 3-speed C4 automatic transmission were also recommendations for best towing capacity.

The front coil-spring ratings, both standard and optional, were increased slightly as well, from 1,075 and 1,130 pounds to 1,140 and 1,190, respectively. Bill Sanders, writing in the August 1976 issue of *Four Wheeler*, noted that the spring rates made a difference: "Even on the street, the front end seemed much stronger, with firmer control. When we took the Bronco off-road into some really choppy terrain, the suspension changes got even noticeably better. In places where we had taken Broncos previously on road test and had the front end bottom out, all that was gone. Ride was still not harsh, yet the bottoming was gone. For a bobtail, the Bronco corners quite flat and smooth."

For 1976, Ford also limited the axle ratio choice to 3.50:1/3.54:1 for California residents (due to emissions regulations), while the rest of the country could still specify 4.11:1 ratios. Unfortunately for off-roading enthusiasts, the limited-slip front axle option was discontinued.

The 1977 Broncos used this one-year-only rear axle housing, which is stronger than any of the other housings used. A wider version was used on the full-size Broncos that followed. Its strength comes from larger axle tubes and the larger center section. Before they were available in the aftermarket, 1977 housings commanded a healthy premium as used parts. The plastic gas tank shown was used on 1977 Broncos only. (Photo Courtesy Drew Peroni)

Proving once again that what is tried first in California usually ends up implemented later in the remaining 49 states, Ford reduced the only available axle ratio option to one in 1977: 3.50:1. Those gears were housed in a one-year-only axle housing, which is generally considered to be stronger than those offered in previous years. Although it was narrower, its overall shape resembles the housing used in the 1978-newer full-size Broncos with the housing having thicker tubes and 1/4-inch-larger diameter than previous years' housings.

Body

Visually, the 1977 Bronco is one of the easiest years for enthusiasts to identify thanks to their fuel filler doors on the

Here's one of the most recognizable features of the 1977 Broncos: the gas cap door. The introduction of the door coincided with the introduction of this feature in the 1977 Ford pickup line. Because the door is dimensionally larger than the gas cap it replaced, the rear side-marker lights had to be flipped from a horizontal to a vertical mounting position. (Photo Courtesy Terry Marvel)

The body structure in the first-generation Broncos had few changes in its 12-year run. One of them was the addition of this triangular brace for the 1976 model year. It added rigidity between the inner fender and the core support.

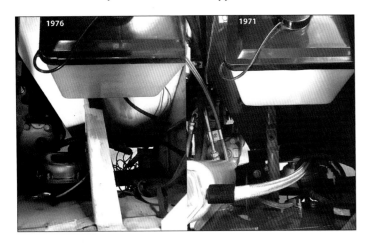

With the introduction of the Duraspark electronic ignition system in 1977 Broncos, Ford ignition distributors gained a wider and slightly taller ignition cap. The cap interfered with the main crossmember in the hood, so for 1977 only, the hoods have a slight depression in the crossmember for distributor-cap clearance. (Photo Courtesy Dave Kunz)

driver-side quarter panel. The change to fuel doors on the Bronco coincided with the same change integrated into Ford's light-duty pickups.

Coincident with the fuel filler changes, Ford also discarded the previously used 12.2-gallon steel main fuel tank and installed a 14-gallon plastic tank. The optional auxiliary fuel tank was increased in size from 7.5 to 8 gallons while retaining its skid plate. To keep tooling costs low, 1977 Broncos were only produced with two fuel filler doors in the quarter panel. If the auxiliary tank was not ordered, the front fuel door was nonfunctional and screwed shut on the backside of the quarter panel.

The change to fuel doors also necessitated a change to the mounting configuration of the rear corner marker lights. For 1977 only, they were moved to a vertical orientation to allow additional space for the rear filler door.

Colors

The 1976 Explorers were available in two colors: Copper and Blue Metallic. The Copper trucks were available with tan or white tape stripes and tan vinyl interiors. The Blue Metallic trucks had white stripes and blue vinyl interiors.

For 1976, Ford added six new exterior colors: Castillo Red, Bali Blue, Indio Tan, Mecca Gold, Cayan Red, and Silver Metallic (available after February 2, 1976). It also classified the Ginger Glow and Medium Green Glow colors as glamour colors, available only as an extra-cost option.

In 1977, Ford added several new colors including Light Blue, Vista Orange, Medium Silver Metallic, Bright Emerald, Light Jade, and Medium Copper. Jade Glow and Dark Cinnamon were optional colors for the model year.

Interior and Trim Levels

Ford again offered three trim levels for 1976–1977 Broncos: base, Sport, and Ranger, plus the Explorer package and the Special Décor Group.

Base

The base model was de-contented and offered even fewer standard features with the passenger-side seat, instrument panel pad, and locking hubs moving from the standard features column to options. All 1977 models switched from rubber black floor mats to parchment-colored mats.

Sport

The intermediate Sport model, as in prior years, added more splash to the exterior with plenty of chrome and bright accents on the exterior and upgraded door panels and other trim inside.

Ranger

The Ranger package was again the top-level trim package for 1976–1977 with few changes other than the green interior being changed to a jade color for 1977.

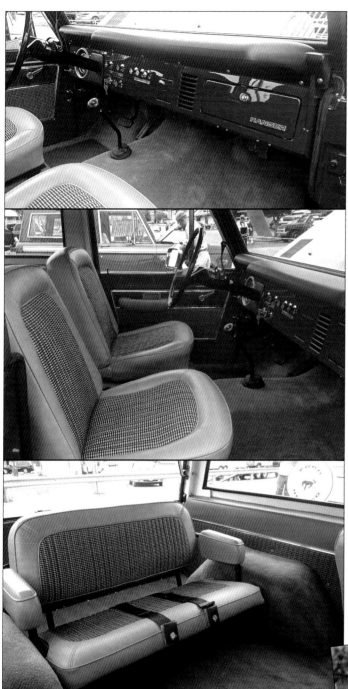

This tan Ranger interior, sumptuous by early Bronco standards, was one of three Ranger interior colors (the others were blue and jade) offered in 1977. Color-keyed seats, door panels, rear quarter panel covers, and full carpeting were a far cry from the bare-metal, utilitarian interiors of the early base models. The dash is unusual in that it's a radio-delete dash, which is uncommon for an otherwise highly optioned truck. (Photo Courtesy Drew Peroni)

Explorer

The model year 1976 saw the return of the Explorer package to the Bronco after a year's absence from the option sheet. It remained for the 1976 model year only. As in previous years, the Explorer package ($160) was a less expensive option compared to the Sport ($432) and Ranger ($634) packages. The Explorer was an add-on to the base Bronco with some parts from the Sport and Ranger packages and a few items of its own. The 1976 Explorer was the only year with an Explorer-specific stripe on its flanks.

The Explorer glove box door badge displays the compass emblem that was used on all the Ford Explorer packages in the 1970s. A similar compass was also mounted on camper shells of Ford F-Series trucks in the 1970s. (Photo Courtesy Dennis Bragg)

This 1976 Bronco Explorer (identified by the stripe running the length of the vehicle) was the first Bronco purchased by a prominent Bronco collector in 1990. Nearly all the paint and striping, including the Explorer-unique tan stripes down the side of the vehicle, are original. The exterior color is Medium Copper, which has an orange-ish hue. Note that Explorers came with the standard Bronco grille with black-painted letters. (Photo Courtesy Dennis Bragg)

The tire covers on the Explorer trucks are unique to that model with the same stylized compass from the glove box door displayed on the cover. Explorer tire covers are not available as a reproduction item at the present time, making them an extremely rare item. (Photo Courtesy Dennis Bragg)

Special Décor Group

The Bronco highlighted in the Free Wheelin' brochure had an exciting trim addition for the year called the Special Décor Group. Available on base and Sport Bronco models only, this package added bright windshield and side and rear window frames (also included in the Sport package). All exterior colors were available except Silver Metallic with the body and top being a single color standard, although a Wimbledon White top was available as an option.

The tape stripe, available in white, black, or yellow, depending on the exterior color, ran laterally across the hood and dipped onto the body flanks just ahead of the Bronco

The Special Décor package was available on both standard and Sport Broncos. Because this is a Sport model, it is equipped with the Sport door panels. Normally it would also have the Parchment floor mat, but this particular vehicle has a black vinyl floor mat from the standard Bronco package. (Photo Courtesy Tim Hulick)

Sport Bronco with Special Decor Group.

This artwork is definitely in the 1970s style, as are the mustaches and hats on the Bronco's passengers. The color, though, is timeless (perhaps Bright Medium Blue), particularly when paired with the Special Décor stripes. A truck like this, splashing through a stream in the outback, would definitely get an enthusiast's juices flowing. (Photo Courtesy Ford Motor Company)

emblem on the front fenders and ran the length of the body, ending at the junction of the rear quarter panels and the taillight housings.

In front, the grille and headlight rings were painted black (marketing brochures show chrome headlight rings) and were offset by bright Ford letters on the grille and a chrome grille surround. Bumpers were chrome and hubcaps were included with the package. An optional rocker panel molding was available with the Special Décor option.

For 1977, many of the Special Décor–equipped trucks had an optional argent silver and black wheel cover sometimes referred to as a "mag cap." This particular wheel cover had been used in previous years on Ford's F100s with the Explorer package.

This 1977 Special Décor Bronco (with the Sport Bronco package) is high on many enthusiasts' wish lists today. This particular example wears the 1977-only hubcaps borrowed from the Explorer package F-Series pickups. One of the key identifying features of the Special Décor package was the black grille, a color selection that has aged well. Although the sales materials at the time showed the Special Décor trucks with chrome headlight rings, most of the production models were delivered with black headlight rings. (Photo Courtesy Tim Hulick)

Tires and Wheels

The Bronco continued its offerings of 15x 5.5–inch wheels for 1976 and 1977. For 1977, the wheels listed in documentation as an argent color since 1973 finally switched to a true argent (silver).

Tubeless tires continued to be offered in E78x15, G78x15, and H78x15 sizes depending on GVW. The 7x15 tube tires were also an option.

Collectability and Value

Due to improvements in suspension, steering, and braking, the 1976–1977 Broncos have long enjoyed the highest collectability value of the 12 years of first-generation Bronco production. The disc brake axles, tighter ratio power steering box, power brake booster, and other refinements make these trucks a more enjoyable driving experience than their older counterparts. As many as four levels of trim ensure a wide variety of refinement in these years as well.

In 1976, Bronco sales increased by 16 percent over 1975 for a total of 15,256 units sold. Of those, 2,408 were Sport Broncos, 1,610 were Explorers, and 2,971 were Rangers. Whether their push toward the younger generation via the Free Wheelin' promotions helped contribute to the higher sales is not known. Slipping a bit from 1976 totals, production for the 1977 Broncos ended at 14, 546 units. Of that total, 3,243 were Sport Broncos and 3,199 were Rangers. (Copyright Marti Auto Works, martiauto.com, and used with permission.)

Stroppe Ambulance Bronco

During the 1970s, a prominent element in Ford's advertising arsenal was a yellow light bulb, symbolizing Ford's "Better Idea" slogan (i.e., a light bulb going off in someone's head when they had a great idea). In 1976, Ford Motor Company embarked on a grand scheme to fly a yellow hot-air balloon across the United States. At night, the lit balloon looked like a giant version of that familiar Ford light bulb.

According to a chapter entitled "The Great Balloon Chase" in Tom Madigan's biography of Bill Stroppe entitled *Boss: The Bill Stroppe Story*, the idea to fly a yellow hot-air balloon across the United States was the brainchild of Wally Clayton of J. Walter Thompson, Ford's longtime advertising agency. The Thompson agency was responsible for many of Ford's more memorable advertisements over the years and something like a weeks-long balloon trip across the country was not out of the ordinary. Ford Motor Company bought into the idea and provided not only a great deal of financial support but also the full resources of its media department to provide materials to be shared in magazines, newspapers, radio, and TV.

Entitled the "Great American Sail," playing off "sale" and "sail," the proposed trip had several purposes. First, it would bring great media attention to Ford's sale of certain 1977 cars and trucks. Second, Ford thought the balloon could set a new world record for a balloon flight across the United States: The existing record of 41 days had been set by wealthy magazine publisher Malcolm Forbes.

A young balloon pilot from Troy, Michigan, Karl Thomas, had come to the attention of Ford after his daring attempt to cross the Atlantic Ocean in a helium balloon a year earlier. The attempt was not successful, and Madigan recounts in his book the miraculous circumstances through which Thomas survived. Apparently, the whole adventure did not deter Thomas from wanting another balloon adventure.

With Thomas in the air, Ford needed someone on the ground to manage the extensive logistics for such an adventure. To handle that, executives turned to none other than Bill Stroppe. Stroppe by this time had been involved in ventures for 30 years with Ford Motor Company projects on land and water; why not handle something in the air as well? His experience with the Carrera

Each member of the automotive press was given one of these folders packed full of press release materials and photos documenting various aspects of the chase. This folder survived and is now part of the vehicle's documentation collection. (Photo Courtesy Drew Peroni)

The Balloon Chaser Ambulance wasn't the first ambulance built by Bill Stroppe. Years earlier, he assembled a white one that was used as a chase vehicle at off-road races. Seen here in action at the 1970 Mint 400 race, a young Willie Stroppe occupies the passenger's seat. Stroppe recalled that the only medical duty they had that day was a racer with some dust in his contact lenses. (Photo Courtesy Trackside Photo)

CHASE VEHICLES — Eight Ford vans, F-series pickups and four-wheel-drive Broncos prepared by Recreational Vans, Inc., of Torrance, Calif., are ground support vehicles for Karl Thomas' cross-country balloon flight. Thomas (left) is shown discussing trip plans with RVI president Bud Blankenship (center) and ground-crew chief Bill Stroppe, veteran off-road racer and vehicle builder.
FORD NEWS BUREAU, 4940 SHEILA STREET, LOS ANGELES, CALIFORNIA 90022   (213) 262-2104

In addition to the copious amounts of words generated in press releases, Ford included a number of staged photos in the press release kits given to the media. Of particular note in these photos is Gopher, the Bronco that Willie Stroppe drove on the balloon chase. It's similar to the Ambulance Bronco but lacked the winch on the front and did not have all of the medical equipment onboard that the Ambulance carried. (Photo Courtesy Drew Peroni)

In addition to building the Broncos and pickups for the chase, Recreational Vehicles Inc. (RVI) created a number of Broncos commemorating the chase and sold them to the general public. The modifications were generally limited to fender flares, tires, wheels, special paint, and badging. These now-collectable vehicles have become known as balloon chasers in the enthusiast community. This example resides at Wild Horses 4x4 in Lodi, California. (Photo Courtesy Dave Loewen)

Panamericana races in the 1950s and off-road races in the 1960s and 1970s prepared him well for the balloon chase, including unexpected schedule changes, unpredictable weather, equipment failures, extreme fatigue, and raw emotions. These challenges were all in a day's work for Stroppe. In addition, Stroppe's son Willie joined him on the adventure in one of his first major projects with his father.

Rolling stock for the venture consisted of eight Ford trucks including two 1977 Broncos, all sprayed orange with crazy 1970s-vibe black stripes by master painter Frank Magoo.

Bill Stroppe added a Warn winch to the project Ambulance Bronco along with bumper braces, dual front shocks, US Indy mags and a roll bar from the Baja Bronco parts bin. The passenger's seat was modified to easily allow stretcher access. Plenty of additional lighting was added for the long nights of balloon chasing.

Riding with Stroppe in one of the Broncos outfitted with ambulance gear was Dick Johanssen of the Los Angeles Police Department. The other Bronco, named *Gopher*, was driven by Willie Stroppe with Larry Weis and journalist Marshall Spiegel aboard.

The balloon's journey began early in the morning of February 1, 1977, at the Santa Anita horse racing track in Arcadia, California. The liftoff was delayed for about an hour due to unfavorable winds. Finally, at 3:00 a.m., Thomas lifted off into the darkness, the balloon glowing like a giant light bulb in the sky.

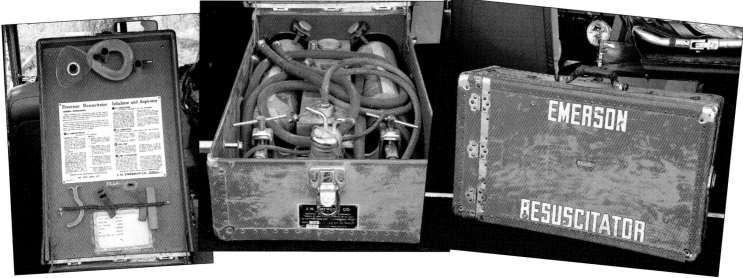

This Emerson respirator apparatus looks positively ancient by today's standards but was considered an essential piece of medical kit for the balloon flight. Thankfully, it was never needed during the adventure. (Photo Courtesy Freeze Frame Images LLC, Al Rogers)

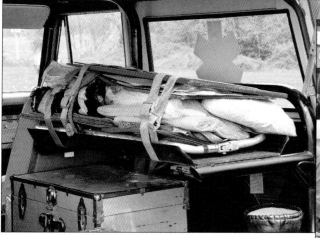

The rear of the Ambulance housed the gurney, backboard, and a wide variety of other medical supplies in various trunks and boxes. Thankfully, it was never needed on the chase and today it adds an interesting dimension of originality when the Ambulance is displayed at shows. (Photo Courtesy Freeze Frame Images LLC)

Willie Stroppe, son of Bill Stroppe, was a young man when he participated in the balloon chase with his father and others in 1977. After the chase, he continued to work with his father in their business and ran it for many years after Bill's death. He's pictured here at the Bronco 50th Anniversary Celebration at the All-Ford Nationals in Carlisle, Pennsylvania, where he was one of the featured guests in 2016. (Photo Courtesy Drew Peroni)

Things went awry from the start as the balloon, at the mercy of prevailing winds, drifted farther south than planned in the Arizona desert. Stroppe kept in sight of the balloon, as were his orders, and found himself crossing the Mexico border, as told in Madigan's book, "by virtue of a lot of arm waving and passing out T-shirts and racing decals." He certainly had plenty of experience with that custom from years of racing in Mexico.

Stroppe continued to trail Thomas as best he could, finally finding the balloon and Thomas in the desert near Puerto Penasco, Mexico. Some quick thinking and paperwork legalities later, the crew was allowed to return to the United States.

On February 5, the team regrouped in Phoenix, hoping for a better shot at heading east. After several days, the weather was still unfavorable and word came from Detroit that Henry Ford II was upset and wanted the adventure scrapped. He had not been told of the event and had not approved it. Willie Stroppe recalls that this was the lowest point in the whole event, as emotions and tensions ran high in the group.

Disregarding Ford's hesitations, Mother Nature intervened with some favorable sailing winds in Montana if the team could get there. Bill Stroppe packed up the entire team and the balloon and headed north.

Imagine this phalanx of lights coming toward you at night! Two adjustable spotlights with red lenses, two overhead long range lights, and a vintage 1970s rotating strobe light gave an official air to the vehicle when in use. Hiding behind all that lighting are additional backboards and a very 1970s sunroof that was added to the hardtop.

It was every man for himself during the race northward. About 20 miles outside Moab, Utah, the alternator quit on Willie's *Gopher* Bronco. The rest of the team continued north while Willie and his passengers waited for a tow truck. With laughter, Willie recalls that Larry Weis had fallen asleep in the back of the Bronco and didn't wake up until *Gopher* was on the tow truck's hook and moving down the road with its nose in the air!

Wintertime temperatures in Montana are far different than February in Phoenix, so the crew scrambled to find winter clothing to prepare for the launch. Willie remembered everyone buying snowsuits from a local snowmobile store. To add insult to injury, the driver's window linkage on Willie's Bronco broke in Montana. The open window made for a very cold ride until they could fix it.

Thomas performed his most challenging section of the flight on a Montana morning: below-zero temperatures, high altitude, and darkness. He managed to successfully pull it off and cleared the tall mountains while fighting frostbite and sickness.

From there, Madigan notes that the pace of the chase picked up considerably with favorable winds. Bill Stroppe managed to pick up three speeding tickets on one road from the same highway patrolman. Daily distances increased from less than 100 miles per day to 300 to 400 with the balloon in the air for more than 12 hours per day.

In South Dakota, some other challenges were presented when the balloon landed in the dark in a deep canyon on the Sioux Reservation in Wounded Knee. The team again couldn't find Thomas until he fired off his only remaining flare, lighting up the night sky to reveal his location. Willie recalled that there were some tense moments on the reservation when some armed locals in a pickup truck weren't pleased with the balloon team being on their land.

Challenges with Ford corporate again reared their head in Lincoln, Nebraska, where the crew learned that Ford again wanted to cancel the whole affair. Bill Stroppe said he would pay for everything out of his own pocket to keep the flight going and issued the ultimatum that if anyone wanted to quit they could. No one left and the trip continued. Willie Stroppe recalls some of his fondest memories from traveling through the Midwestern states. Although the pace was frantic, they reveled in the attention they received in the small towns they visited. Willie recalls with particular emotion one small town where a holiday was declared (including closing the local school) so the residents could watch the balloon's launch.

In Alabama, memories of a small town where the local law enforcement drew their guns on the crew were foremost in Willie's thoughts. The locals reacted strongly when they first encountered the balloon crew, thinking they were moonshine smugglers. After some conversations with the team, they changed their tune, helping them with accommodations for the evening and a police escort out of town in the morning.

On February 18, 1977, Thomas touched down on Bird Island, 15 miles from Jacksonville, Florida. His entire trip had taken 18 days. Ironically, Bill Stroppe missed all the hoopla as he got his Bronco stuck in the sand about 500 yards from where Thomas touched down. He collected eight traffic tickets over the course of his trip in his Bronco and many, many stories.

After all the effort, the trip didn't make it into the *Guinness Book of World Records* due to technicalities in how the flight was recorded. But Ford was happy, as the trip proved, in the end, to be a media juggernaut. Unfortunately, no evidence exists that the sail affected vehicle sales.

After the excitement of the flight was over, the Ambulance remained in Bill Stroppe's possession and returned to California. According to a 2004 *Bronco Driver* article by noted historian Andrew Norton, it was used by Stroppe on occasion as a support vehicle for his various off-road racing efforts during the 1980s. After its race support days were over, it was placed in long-term storage. It is the last vestige of the glory days of Broncos left at Stroppe's shop.

In 1998, several years after his father's passing, Willie Stroppe sold the Ambulance to longtime Bronco parts vendor, James Duff, who moved it to his business in Sequim, Washington. Included with the sale of the Bronco were all the extra medical items on the inside of the truck and a crewman's suit from the chase.

Duff owned the Ambulance until 2011 when well-known Bronco enthusiasts Don and Drew Peroni purchased it. Witnesses to the transaction were none other than Willie Stroppe and Parnelli Jones.

While completing paperwork, the Peronis discovered, much to their surprise, that the Ambulance had never been

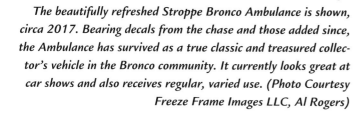

Crew jumpsuits are valuable mementos from the chase. Some photos from early in the adventure show them worn by crew members but they were likely thrown in the suitcase once the real work began. The T-shirt (top right) is a rare shirt commemorating the chase. (Photo Courtesy Freeze Frame Images LLC, Al Rogers)

Period photos show Bill and Willie Stroppe installing the winch and lights onto the Ambulance before the balloon chase began. Bill Stroppe used the Warn 8274 winch on multiple occasions for extractions along the route. The brush guard afforded some protection for the grille, and the auxiliary lights bored holes through the darkness of many rural areas of the chase. (Photo Courtesy Freeze Frame Images LLC, Al Rogers)

The beautifully refreshed Stroppe Bronco Ambulance is shown, circa 2017. Bearing decals from the chase and those added since, the Ambulance has survived as a true classic and treasured collector's vehicle in the Bronco community. It currently looks great at car shows and also receives regular, varied use. (Photo Courtesy Freeze Frame Images LLC, Al Rogers)

titled in its 34 years of existence. That was quickly rectified and the Bronco soon had a pair of Pennsylvania plates.

The Peronis performed some much-needed maintenance on the Ambulance and soon were showing the 35,000-mile rig at various Ford and Bronco-related events around the country. Not just a show truck, Drew Peroni recently completed a 2,000-mile trip through Baja California with the Ambulance. It has become one of the most treasured historical Broncos among enthusiasts due to its exposure in recent years.

The Stroppe Ambulance has been used for a variety of activities in recent years. In 2018, Drew Peroni drove it on trails in Moab prior to heading south for a 2,500-mile trip through Baja. Here it's shown perched on top of a rock on the appropriately named Top of the World trail. (Photo Courtesy Drew Peroni)

NORTHLANDER SAVAGE EDITION

In 1976, after production of the Stroppe Baja Bronco ended, Ford Motor Company approached a young Don Waldoch of Forest Lake, Minnesota, and offered him a Bronco to modify. Waldoch had started building van conversions in the 1970s and caught the eye of Ford.

Along with Broncos, Waldoch modified Ford pickups, and for 1976, the Northlander Savage Edition Bronco was born. Waldoch doesn't know the exact production numbers, but he estimates between 50 and 60 trucks were produced. They all started as well-equipped Broncos with power steering, power brakes, an automatic transmission, and the 4,900-pound GVW package. The Waldoch conversion package, which retailed for $1,300, added fiberglass fender cutouts, a roll bar, off-road lights, body side tape stripes, a sunroof, brush guard, and oversized tires and wheels. Options included winches, tow hooks, headers, dual exhaust, various aftermarket radios, and various tire and wheel options.

Due to the low production numbers and the fact that they were sold and used primarily in Minnesota, where rust is prevalent, very few of the Bronco Savage trucks have survived.

Waldoch Crafts offered a complete suite of converted vehicles in 1976, which included the Northlander Bronco Savage Edition trucks. Don Waldoch estimates that the company modified 50 to 60 Broncos. (Photo Courtesy Don Waldoch)

One of the few remaining Northlander Savage Edition Broncos was rescued a few years ago by a Minnesota collector. As you would expect from a Minnesota truck, it had plenty of rust. It was later sold to another collector who plans to restore it. (Photo Courtesy John Monahan)

These vintage photos show yellow Broncos lined up at Waldoch's facility in Forest Lake, Minnesota, in both their as-received stock and converted Northlander Savage Edition versions. (Photo Courtesy Don Waldoch)

BRONCO MACHO

Another regional edition that appeared for the 1976 Bronco was the Bronco Macho. Modified by the Four-Wheel-Drive-Center in Omaha, Nebraska, owners Larry Hopkins and Roger Darrington added some popular period accessories to the Broncos to make them more off-road worthy. The Broncos received fiberglass rear fender cutouts, Tacoma 15x8 steel wagon-spoke wheels, 10x15 Firestone All-Terrain T/C tires, the Stroppe standard roll bar, Stroppe Cactus Smasher brush guard with two KC fog lights, and a Plastic-Cast center console. A special rear tire cover with the Bronco Macho logo topped off the modifications.

With a retail price of $750 in addition to the Bronco's regular retail price, the Bronco Macho package was an affordable way to purchase a truck with many of the period's desired modifications already installed.

According to a 1976 article in *Off Road*, 50 trucks were initially built for sales at Midwestern Ford dealers. It is not known if any additional trucks beyond the first 50 were built. Like the Waldoch Savage trucks, few Bronco Macho trucks have survived, no doubt due to the Midwest's tough winters and heavy use of salt on the roads.

This 1976 Bronco Macho was a one-owner truck from Nebraska that was discovered by Bronco enthusiast Matthew Kelly in 2018. The original owner was a doctor who used the Bronco to make patient house calls. The truck is in remarkably good condition, considering the harshness of Nebraska's winters. The Stroppe Cactus Smasher push bar and auxiliary lights are still intact. (Photo Courtesy Matthew Kelly)

An unknown number of Bronco Macho trucks remain in existence today. Visible in this example are the Stroppe "Standard" roll bar, fiberglass fender flares, and oversize wheels. The Bronco Macho was a special package put together by an off-road center in Omaha, Nebraska, and sold through Ford dealers. (Photo Courtesy Matthew Kelly)

LIGHTS, CAMERA, ACTION!

Southern California TV automotive journalist Dave Kunz purchased this 1977 medium copper Ranger from the estate of George Wright. Kunz is a Stroppe Bronco fan who decided to base his modifications on the answer to this question: "How would someone modify their Bronco using modern products to enhance its performance with cues gleaned from products that Bill Stroppe sold in the 1970s?"

Kunz removed the heavy Warn 8724 winch and bumper and replaced it with a stock chrome bumper topped by two period-correct Cibie lights. He replaced the stock wheels and hubcaps with a set of 15x7 Western aluminum slot mags rolling on a pair of BFGoodrich All-Terrain tires. The Bronco is a Ranger model without traditional Ranger stripes. Previous owner George Wright didn't reinstall the stripes when the hood was repainted under his ownership.

Kunz continued the Stroppe theme on the interior of his Bronco. In place of the stock steering wheel, he installed a Grant wheel with a slightly smaller and thicker rim than stock that is reminiscent of 1970s aftermarket wheels. A vintage Autometer tach is bolted to the steering column. Kunz's wife made a custom label for the auxiliary lights that makes the extra Bronco hazard switch in the dash blend right in. For tunes, he installed a 1980s vintage Realistic AM/FM cassette stereo in the dash and added controls so he could play music from his satellite receiver or iPod.

In 2018, the truck was featured in a Hagerty insurance commercial that received plenty of air time. In the commercial, the child in the passenger's seat asks her grandfather what the window crank does. The Bronco was also featured in an episode of the popular *Jay Leno's Garage* series in 2018.

Southern California TV journalist Dave Kunz purchased this beautiful 1977 Bronco from the estate of noted Bronco collector George Wright. Kunz believes he is the third owner. The medium copper Ranger, one of the last of the 1977s built, is loaded with nearly every option available. The Bronco, a Ranger model, did not have its stripes reinstalled after a repaint during Wright's ownership. (Photo Courtesy Dave Kunz)

This 1977 Bronco Ranger has become a movie star of sorts in recent years. In 2018, the truck appeared in a widely circulated Hagerty insurance commercial where a grandfather and his granddaughter go for a ride. The Bronco and the actors are seen in this photo between takes. (Photo Courtesy Dave Kunz)

How many Bronco owners get to have Jay Leno take a spin in their truck for a TV show? Not many! California TV anchor and Bronco owner Dave Kunz is obviously enjoying his time with Jay in his 1977 Ranger. (Photo Courtesy Dave Kunz)

Owner Dave Kunz continued the Stroppe theme on the interior of his Bronco. In place of the stock steering wheel, he installed a Grant wheel and added a vintage-looking Autometer tachometer to the steering column. A subtly modified Bronco hazard switch with custom labeling activates the bumper-mounted Cibie lights. A 1980s vintage Realistic AM/FM cassette stereo with modern electronic inputs resides in the dash. (Photo Courtesy Dave Kunz)

1978–1979: BIGGER IS BETTER

> "Four wheeling in the 1978 Bronco is like riding into the backcountry in a Mercedes Benz."

For auto enthusiasts, 1978 may have been the nadir of automotive performance to date. Horsepower ratings continued to drop as auto manufacturers struggled to meet increasingly restrictive emissions requirements. Enthusiasts now refer to this time in automotive history as the "malaise era."

As a counterpoint to the doom and gloom that pervaded the era, Ford's introduction of the new 1978 Bronco was a bright spot on the automotive horizon. After years of touting the features of a smaller, more maneuverable vehicle than their General Motors and Chrysler competition, Ford bowed to the realities of first-generation Bronco sales versus Blazer/Ramcharger numbers and joined the large sport utility club.

History and Development

To understand the popularity of the new model, we need look at the development of the 1978 Bronco. Chevrolet's Blazer, introduced for the 1969 model year, was based on a shortened chassis and body of the Chevrolet pickup truck. Buyers quickly fell in love with the larger Blazer body and by 1972, it was outselling the Bronco by more than 2 to 1. Of course, this data was not lost on the Ford sales department.

Prototype Development

In 1972, development of the new Bronco began with a series of four proposals: Shorthorn (Blazer size), Midhorn (Expedition size), Longhorn (Suburban size), and Widehorn. In a recent interview, former Ford engineer George Peterson shared that the Widehorn was widened about 6 inches over a standard F100 body, requiring cab

Shawn Kleppe of Ossian, Iowa, found this 1979 Bronco Ranger XLT with the Chromatic Stripe package in Alberta, Canada, in 2017, still with its original owner. After jumping through the hurdles to bring it stateside, the clean-up process resulted in the beautiful truck seen here. The only items replaced were gas tank, brake system components, and rear leaf springs. (Photo Courtesy Freeze Frame Image LLC, Al Rogers)

A concept vehicle from 1979, this Bronco featured a light-gold metallic exterior with genuine oak wood trim and a convertible cargo cover made of simulated canvas (actually vinyl). The interior had seats trimmed in simulated sheepwood with beige simulated leather facings accented by tangerine welts and saddle seat bands. It probably never saw anything more rustic than the design studio floor. (Photo Courtesy Ford Motor Company)

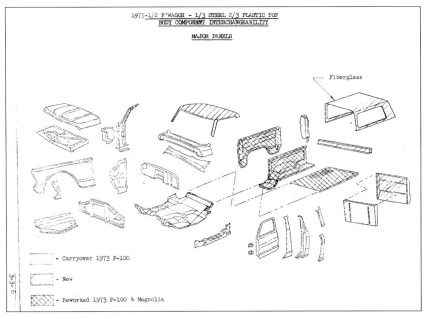

This graphic provides an excellent visual reference to what Ford was able to use from the existing F-Series in the creation of the Shorthorn trucks. A combination of existing parts, reworked panels, and a few all-new panels came together to build the prototypes. (Photo Courtesy Don Wheatley)

running lights due to its width. The Widehorn was reminiscent of the wide Ford Raptor bodies that followed nearly 40 years later.

Ford devoted enough financial resources to the project to construct a version of all four prototypes, although the Shorthorn was the only one with a running engine. The project was down-selected to the Shorthorn version and thereafter the new Bronco project became known as Project Shorthorn.

Peterson was the project design engineer responsible for coordinating the prototype build team at Carron & Company, a local firm responsible for many prototype Ford truck builds at the time. Although the new Bronco would be similar in size to the Blazer, the Light Truck Advanced Engineering team and Light Truck Product Planning knew they wanted to change a few things in the body structure, most notably the top configuration around the doors.

The Blazer had a full-length removable hardtop, which gave it clean lines with the top removed but introduced a greater potential for wind noise and water leaks around the windows as the seals aged. It was decided to keep the F100 doors with integral window frames along with a hardtop section that extended behind the two front seats. To accomplish this, an F100 body was shortened and the cab structure was integrated into shortened quarter panels that should have been a relatively easy integration. Alas, the teams discovered a 1/10-inch mismatch in mating the two panels, which was okay for prototyping but not for production.

Noting the often-chaotic nature of prototype builds, Peterson also noted that they used a modified Blazer hardtop for the Shorthorn prototypes. In addition to the construction challenges, Light Truck Advanced Engineering also faced resistance from Ford brass, who wanted a full-length fiberglass top as on the Blazer. After convincing them of the merits of his design (greater driver/passenger protection, a stiffer body structure, and fewer challenges with wind and water leaks), management relented and adopted Peterson's recommendations.

Body Design

While the prototype construction was underway, work began on the styling of the new Bronco's body. That task was assigned to Dick Nesbitt, an accomplished Ford designer assigned to Ford's Light Truck and Tractor Styling Studio in 1972.

Because Ford specified a requirement that the rear passenger area top be removable, Nesbitt penned four side window proposals with various window shapes and sizes. The final design had four rounded corners because the Production Feasibility Group felt that stress cracks would develop if sharp

These photos are of one of the Shorthorn prototypes mid-construction at Carron & Company in Detroit. Because the rear seat is of the flip-and-fold variety, it's mostly likely the second prototype, Shorthorn 2. (Photo Courtesy Don Wheatley)

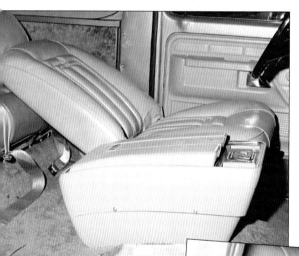

The first of the Shorthorn prototypes, Shorthorn 1, used reclining Maverick LDO (Luxury Décor Option) bucket seats. George Peterson stated that these seats, produced in a tan, supersoft vinyl, were imported from Europe. The rear seat was a bench seat adapted from the Econoline van. (Photo Courtesy Don Wheatley)

corners were used. Apparently, minds changed in the intervening two years because the 1980 design had two rounded corners and two sharp corners, a design that continued through the end of production in 1996.

To further separate the Bronco's appearance from that of the Blazer, Nesbitt proposed a wide Targa band for the B-pillar that wrapped over the roof. Nesbitt had used this same styling feature on the Carrousel van project during the same time period and found that it provided a nice delineation between the steel and fiberglass

Shorthorn 2 used a 60/40 split bench seat with headrests. The passenger's seat pivoted forward on bracketry that resembled that on the Bronco II passenger's seat a dozen years later. Shorthorn 2 also used a flip-and-fold rear seat that found its way into the 1978 Bronco. (Photo Courtesy Don Wheatley)

The Shorthorn and its primary competition, the Chevrolet Blazer, were similarly sized. A Blazer top was used to construct the Shorthorn. (Photo Courtesy Don Wheatley)

1975½ F'WAGON
PROGRAM DESCRIPTION

PRODUCT CONTENT SUMMARY

The 1975½ F'Wagon is a new multipurpose vehicle, to replace the current Bronco. The all-new styling theme is identical to F-100 from the "B" pillar forward and the rear half styling theme derived by the use of shortened Magnolia quarters (box sides) mated with a new rear fiberglass top and a new dropglass tailgate. A full time four wheel drive 4x4 and an optional 4x2 are offered. Compared to the 1973 Bronco, the vehicle features an improved removable top; better occupant ingress/egress; more comfortable seating; larger volume & weight of cargo capacity; improved ride and handling; and additional optional equipment such as bigger engines up to the 460 engine, integral air conditioning, power brakes, and a folding three passenger rear seat.

The F'Wagon overall length is 177.7 inches which is 25.6 inches longer than the '73 Bronco and 6.8 inches shorter than the '73 Chevrolet Blazer. The overall width of 79.8 inches is 0.8 inches wider than the '73 Blazer and 10.7 inches wider than the larger '73 Blazer. This increase in useable interior space than the '73 Bronco. The F'Wagon has more useable interior space is provided by a rear foot well which provides a 14.1 inch rear seat hip to heel, versus 9.8 inch for the Blazer. With the increased hip to heel the couple distance is reduced to 34 inches versus the Blazer's 44 inches. This reduced couple distance provides 37.4 inches behind the rear seat permitting longitudinal tire stowage. The Blazer has 23.5 inches behind the rear seat requiring transverse tire stowage. With the optional flip forward seat the F'Wagon is quickly converted to a 55 inch rear load floor.

The body of the F'Wagon from the "B" pillar lock face forward is carryover F-100 with the exception of the roof panel, floor panel and seats. The front floor is new and the rear load floor is a reworked box floor. The quarter outer panels are reworked Magnolia box panels while the quarter inner panels are reworked F-100 LWB box inners. The unique 1/3 steel 2/3 fiberglass roof construction has a new front steel roof, new "B" pillar header at rear of steel roof, new "B" pillar assembly, and a new fiberglass rear top.

The frame is a ladder-type similar to F-100 with new side rails to accommodate the new wheelbase. Carryover F-100 4x4 and 4x2 crossmembers are used with the deletion of the #3 crossmember due to the shorter length. Body and front end sheet metal are mounted to the frame at 10 locations.

A 240-1V six cylinder, 360-2V eight cylinder and 460-4V eight cylinder engines are offered. Engine positions are identical to the F-Series full time four wheel drive and 4x2 packages. Emission systems are packaged with the objective of using corporate components although unique routing is required due to the shorter wheelbase. The 4x4 version has one single and three double cardan joints in its new driveshafts. The 4x2 version has a new driveshaft with single cardan joints.

The Shorthorn project was also referred to as the 1975.5 F'Wagon project in internal Ford documentation. The project description documents revealed the new Bronco replacement would be available in 4x2 and 4x4 configurations with engine offerings of 240- (6-cylinder), 360-, and 460-ci V-8s. Also highlighted were its dimensions compared to the Blazer, its primary competition. (Photo Courtesy Don Wheatley)

1971 ACCOMPLISHMENTS

· Common Chassis Pickup/Van
    * Nantucket
        Fold Down Seats Converted into Load Floor for Nantucket
    * Centaur
        Pinto Derived Mini-Pickup
            * EA Column and Wheel for 40° Column Angle

1972 ACCOMPLISHMENTS

· Federalized Econoline
    * F-Series Wagon "Shorthorn" ✓
    * Twin-1-Beam Type 4x4 Independent Front Suspension ✓
        * Folding Rear Seat for Shorthorn ✓
        * Tandem Rear Suspension for Motor Home
        * Anti-Skid System Prove-Out and Selection
            1976 Level Exhaust Emission System for 460 CID Engine
            * Next Generation Motor Home Chassis

The year 1972 proved to be a fruitful one for Ford's Advanced Light Truck Engineering Group with completion of both the Shorthorn prototypes and the Twin-Traction Beam 4WD front suspension. The Shorthorn became the 1978 Bronco, but the Twin-Traction Beam had to wait for the next generation of Bronco. (Photo Courtesy Don Wheatley)

The 4x4 front suspension is carryover F-100 coil monobeam providing 4x4 F-100 vehicle height. The 4x2 suspension is a carryover F-100 4x2 with new brackets and springs to accommodate the 1.2 inch higher F'Wagon ride height than F-100 4x2 and 2.3 inches lower vehicle overall height than F'Wagon 4x4.

A full time four wheel drive transfer case is used on all 4x4's. This case is equipped with a torque biased inter-axle differential which simplifies vehicle operation, and eliminates the need for a manual lockout device. With the limited slip differential a small floor mounted lever provides for shifting into high range, neutral or low range.

A standard 15 x 5½" through an optional 15"x7" wheel with a base G78x15 to a maximum 10.00 x 15" tire are offered. Carryover F-100 front disc and rear drum brakes to accommodate all wheel sizes are standard equipment.

The main fuel tank is a new 19.3 gallon steel tank, mounted to the frame aft-of-axle. This fuel tank can be used for the Magnolia. An optional new 26 gallon rear steel tank made from the adjusted base tank tooling and a new 11 gallon mid-ship tank similar to the F-Series are offered. Evaporative emission components are carryover F-series.

portions of the truck. The Targa band also strengthened the body structure because it added a rib to an otherwise flat expanse of sheet metal.

Nesbitt and Peterson both noted that the larger Bronco was originally specified for introduction for the 1974 model year, but the effects of the 1973–1974 oil embargo and resulting economic downturn delayed its release for several years. As a result, the Bronco never used the 1973–1975 F-Series grille it been designed with. For 1978, Ford updated the front end with a more handsome grille than had been used on the 1973–1977 trucks.

F-SERIES WAGON
BASE AND POSSIBLE OPTIONAL APPLICATIONS

2/3 PLASTIC TOP INSTALLED

PLASTIC TOP DELETED- VINYL DROPCLOTH OPTION

SLIDE-IN CAMPER OPTION- WITH WALK-THRU FEATURE

1/3 PLASTIC TOP/ CREW CAB OPTION WITH FIFTH WHEEL APPLICATION

New fifth wheel design required   3-3-16

F-SERIES WAGON
(2/3 PLASTIC TOP INSTALLED)

3-3-17

F-SERIES WAGON
(PLASTIC TOP DELETED- VINYL DROPCLOTH OPTION)

F-SERIES WAGON
(1/3 PLASTIC TOP/CREW CAB OPTION WITH FIFTH WHEEL APPLICATION)

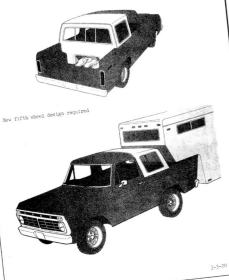

New fifth wheel design required

3-3-20

F-SERIES WAGON
(SLIDE-IN CAMPER OPTION WITH WALK-THRU FEATURE)

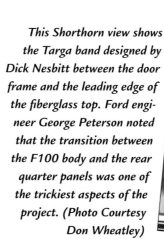

This series of design proposals show the versatility of the Shorthorn concept. The aftermarket responded with a fiberglass cover to essentially convert the 1978–1979 Bronco into a small pickup, but the rest of the proposals were stillborn. Design documents reveal that engineers determined that larger brakes and wheels from the F250 would have been required for the towing requirements of a fifth-wheel trailer. (Photo Courtesy Don Wheatley)

This Shorthorn view shows the Targa band designed by Dick Nesbitt between the door frame and the leading edge of the fiberglass top. Ford engineer George Peterson noted that the transition between the F100 body and the rear quarter panels was one of the trickiest aspects of the project. (Photo Courtesy Don Wheatley)

Shorthorn 1 (left) had a rear liftgate borrowed from a Chevy Blazer. George Peterson stated that his fabricators borrowed and reused parts as required! No word on where the sliding window came from. Shorthorn 2 (right) used a sliding rear window but was manually actuated instead of power-operated as were the production 1978 Bronco. (Photo Courtesy Don Wheatley)

Here, the resemblance to the 1973 F100 is very apparent. The wheel covers are from a Ford car. The ride height on the Shorthorn was slightly lower than the production 1978 Bronco. (Photo Courtesy Don Wheatley)

This is Ford designer Dick Nesbitt's complete design sketch of the Bronco, which he completed in November 1972. Strong visual cues include the Targa band across the top, the wide B-pillar, and the removable fiberglass top. The 1978–1979 production trucks did not have the two sharp corners in the rear window glass because engineers were concerned about stress cracks in the fiberglass. Nesbitt notes with satisfaction that they did adopt his original design for the windows starting with the 1980 models and carried them through 1996. (Photo Courtesy Dick Nesbitt)

These four concepts by Dick Nesbitt are a testament to popular design themes in the early 1970s. Nesbitt notes that vinyl roofs and other add-ons were popular, so his designs included opera windows, various shapes for the rear windows, vertical slits in the body, and sunroofs. Incorporating what are arguably the cleanest aspects of these ideas, Nesbitt fashioned his proposal for the 1978 Bronco. (Photo Courtesy Dick Nesbitt)

Features

The most obvious differences between the 1978 Bronco and its predecessor were of course its size and visual appearance. Front hip room was 15 percent greater, and usable space behind the rear seat more than tripled from 16.6 cubic feet to 49.3 cubic feet.

From the B-pillar forward, it was essentially an F-Series pickup; sharing the sheet metal, powertrain, and drivetrain of its half-ton cousin. Interior details such as the instrument cluster and steering column were also identical.

The initial press introduction to the 1978 Bronco was held in Tucson, Arizona, where journalists were handed keys to new trucks and told to drive them to Los Angeles. Initial reaction from the motoring press was universally positive, border-

The introduction of the new 1978 Bronco was covered with much fanfare in the off-road vehicle publications. The new vehicle received numerous awards including "Four Wheeler of the Year" from Four Wheeler magazine.

ing on effusive. In naming the Bronco as its "Four Wheeler of the Year" for 1978, *Four Wheeler* stated, "Four wheeling in the 1978 Bronco is like riding into the backcountry in a Mercedes Benz."

Tom Madigan, writing in *Off Road*, summarized the new truck thusly, "Ford has gone all out with the introduction of the '78 Bronco to produce a real family-size off-road machine. And we think they have succeeded. If it is any indication of what is to come, then we are in for one heck of a year."

Pickup Van and Four Wheel Drive noted, "This is to say the new Bronco is a performer, versatile, and a welcome addition to the lineup of domestically produced 4WD utility machinery."

Motor Trend titled its article "Has Ford Built the Ultimate Bronco?" and then proceeded to pronounce in the article that it did.

This was the first and most memorable of the 1978 Bronco ads to appear in print publications. With the exception of items 10 and 11 on the list, none of the items mentioned had ever appeared in a Bronco before, although consumers had been wishing for them for years. With the pent-up demand unleashed, the 1978 Bronco was a big hit for Ford. (Photo Courtesy Dick Nesbitt)

1978 Bronco Size Comparison		
	1977 Bronco	1978 Bronco
Wheelbase (inches)	92	104
Overall Length (inches)	152.1	180.3
Overall Width (inches)	69.1	79.3
Front Tread Width (inches)	57.4	64.3
Rear Tread Width (inches)	57.4	64.4
Overall Height (inches)	70.1	74.7
Approach Angle (degrees)	43	38
Departure Angle (degrees)	27	23

Engine

In place of the 302 engine were a pair of new V-8s for the truck line, displacing 351 and 400 ci, respectively. The

351 and 400 were Ford's answer to the need for lighter, emissions-friendly powerplants in the 1970s, replacing the FE-series engines (352, 360, 390, 428), which had been in use in one form or another since the 1950s. The 1978–1979 Broncos were the only generation of Bronco to not offer a 6-cylinder engine option.

351M

The 351 was known as the 351M, to distinguish it from the 351C (Cleveland) and 351W (Windsor). The use of the letter M designation has been the subject of much speculation and debate over the years. It has been alternately claimed to indicate Michigan, Midland, or Modified. In the absence of any definition in official Ford documentation, the debate has continued for years.

The year 1975 brought the introduction of the 351M along with the requirement for unleaded fuel for cars and trucks under 5,500 GVW. In 1977, it made its way into the F-Series trucks, and in 1978, it was installed in the new Bronco. The 351M was a 400 with a shortened piston stroke (back to the original 351C stroke of 3.5 inches). The shorter stroke necessitated taller pistons, but most other parts interchange. Visually, you cannot tell the difference between the two engines.

400

Ford initially started with development of the 400 for use in the 1971 full-size passenger car line. The goal was to have an engine that developed its torque for heavier applications at a lower RPM than the 302 and 351W engines and meet upcoming emissions requirements. Based on the 351 Cleveland block, the 400 was a square engine, featuring a 4.0-inch bore and 4.0-inch stroke, the longest stroke of any Ford pushrod V-8 engine. The 400 was the optional engine in 1978 and 1979, at $165.

The 351M and 400 engines developed 156 hp and 158 hp, respectively, nearly identical in terms of horsepower. The 400's longer stroke resulted in slightly higher torque ratings, 276 ft-lbs versus 262 ft-lbs for the 351M. Both engines had an 8.0:1 compression ratio. Because both engines were designed to be emissions-friendly and weren't performance-oriented, they were only offered with 2-barrel carburetors in the Bronco. The exhaust system consisted of a single exhaust pipe and muffler, with a catalytic converter being added in 1979.

Road tests of the period found few faults in the Bronco, but disappointment with the Bronco's fuel mileage was universal, with most reporting 9 to 10 mpg off-road and about 12 to 13 mpg on the highway. Catalytic converters found their way onto the 1978 California trucks, but the 49-state versions held out until the 1979 model year when emissions regulations changed to require catalytic converters on all vehicles under

The optional 32-gallon fuel tank in the 1978–1979 Bronco featured a skidplate and had more than twice the capacity of the standard tank of the 1977 Bronco. Also visible on this truck is a rear sway bar, part of the Handling package, which also included heavy-duty quad front shocks and heavy-duty rear shocks. Depending on whether the truck was equipped with the Heavy Duty Trailer Towing package, the cost for the Handling package was either $66 or $105. (Photo Courtesy Cliff Brumsfield)

Buried underneath the maze of hoses and wires is a 400-ci V-8 engine, which for 1979 delivered 158 hp at 3,800 rpm. From 1978 on, the Bronco's engine compartment was identical to that of the F-Series pickup. Mounted prominently in the front is an air-conditioning compressor, an option not seen until the introduction of the second generation in 1978. The 351M and 400 engines are visually indistinguishable from each other. (Photo Courtesy Freeze Frame Image LLC, Al Rogers)

8,500 GVW. Road tests of the 1979 models found that mileage on the highway decreased by about 1 mpg due to the addition of the converter and that the engines felt very sluggish and lacked power in off-road situations. Regardless of the fuel economy numbers, Bronco owners could now travel farther on one tank of gas, as the standard tank size increased a whopping 79 percent over the previous years to 25 gallons. An optional 32-gallon tank with a skid plate increased the range even more.

Transmission

Behind the two V-8s, Ford finally offered something that Bronco owners had desired for many years: a 4-speed manual transmission (not available in California). The transmission was an NP435 (or T-18 depending on availability) with a stump-pulling 6.69:1 first gear. The remaining three ratios were similar to the 3-speeds found in the earlier Broncos with a 1:1 fourth gear. Overdrive ratios were still a few years away.

The NP435 and T-18 enjoyed bulletproof reliability and the extremely low "granny" gear was loved by off-road enthusiasts for its compression braking on steep descents and control during technical off-road use. With the 351 engine, Ford used an 11-inch-diameter clutch; a 12-inch unit was specified behind the 400 engine.

The $197 automatic transmission option was the C6, the big brother of the C4 used in the early Bronco. Known as the Select Shift Cruise-O-Matic, the C6 proved to be bulletproof and was a very popular option with buyers of the 1978 and 1979 Bronco. An external transmission oil cooler was an option.

Transfer Case

Ford continued the use of an iron-case, part-time, gear-driven transfer case in the 1978 Bronco with the New Process 205 as the standard offering. The 205 was a 2-speed case similar to the Dana 20, but the low range was only 1.96:1, compared to the Dana 20's 2.34:1. The change probably didn't bother enthusiasts a great deal, as the 1978–1979 trucks did not see as much slow-speed trail work as their earlier siblings, and the higher gearing could easily be compensated for with the ultra-low first gear of the 4-speed manual if so equipped.

Early road tests of the new models found a new fondness for the shifting ease of the new transfer cases. *Four Wheeler* opined, "It goes into gear with the definite firmness that builds more confidence than a backrub from Farrah Fawcett. In short, it is precise and convincing, leaving no question as to its position." Locking hubs were standard with the part-time 4WD system.

For the first time, Ford also offered a full-time 4WD option, the New Process 203 transfer case. The 203, which offered similar gearing to the 205, was offered by all of the Big 3 manufacturers between 1973 and 1979. It was a robust case with both iron and aluminum sections of the case but used a chain in lieu of the gears found in the 205. To allow the transfer case to function in 4WD all the time, a differential was added to the transfer case to allow unequal power distribution between the front and rear axles, similar to the way an open differential

The locking hubs (made by Warn for Ford) are a giveaway that this Bronco was equipped with the part-time New Process 205 transfer case. The wheels are the optional 15x8 styled steel wheels that were originally equipped with 10x15 tires. Also visible are the optional dual front shocks, which helped tame the coil-spring front suspension. (Photo Courtesy Freeze Frame Image LLC, Al Rogers)

works in an axle. The differential could be locked out for equal power distribution like a conventional transfer case if desired.

The shift pattern was Lo-Loc, Lo, Neutral, Hi, and Hi-Loc. Although the full-time 4WD concept was novel, and had achieved a measure of success with Jeep's Quadra-Trac system, its introduction at a time when gas prices were again on the rise signaled its demise after the 1979 model year. The full-time 4WD system was available with the automatic transmission only.

Axles

The axles in the 1978 and 1979 Broncos were similar to those offered in the 1977 models with the obvious change being an increased track width of 7 inches (64.4 verus 57.4 inches). The rear axle continued the use of the heavy-duty rear housing introduced in the 1977 model. The 28-spline axles used in the 1977-and-older trucks were replaced with stronger 31-spline units, raising the axle's capacity to 3,750 pounds. Ratios were 3.00, 3.50 (standard), and 4.11:1. The Traction-Lok, clutch-type limited-slip, was a $175 option for the 3.50 ratio and required with the 4.11:1 ratio. Brakes remained the same size as those used in 1977.

Up front, the Dana 44 also boasted a bit more strength than its narrower predecessor with the use of larger U-joints connecting the stub axles on each side to their respective shafts inside the housing. Ford revised the axle end of the track bar mount for 1978 by making it a cast piece that was welded into the axle housing rather than the previously used formed metal plate. As a result of these changes, the capacity of the front axle was increased to 3,550 pounds, an increase of 550 pounds over the 1977 axle. A limited-slip was again optional for the front differential after several years of absence from the option sheet.

The single-piston disc brakes were a carryover from the 1977 Bronco, although the steering knuckles were revised with the steering arms lowered a few inches and the arm angles changed for revised Ackerman on the new truck. The 1978 Bronco used a vacuum brake booster with a fulcrum linkage to give the right pedal ratio and braking force. The 1979 Bronco linkage was changed so the pedal pushed directly on the booster to activate the brakes. Both used the same overall pedal ratio; the 1979 trucks managed to do it with fewer moving parts.

Steering

Ford also revised the steering on the new Bronco. The integral power steering box was stronger than the previous year's

version and the pitman arm faced forward rather than backward, giving clearance for the optional dual front shocks if so equipped. Ford returned to using the cross-steer linkage that had been used prior to 1976. The drag link attachment point on the tie-rod was moved closer to the passenger-side steering arm to minimize steering forces imparted to the tie-rod.

Manual steering was standard in 1978, and power steering became standard in 1979.

Suspension

One of the biggest changes for the new Bronco was in the suspension system. While employing the same coil-spring/radius-arm front suspension and Hotchkis rear leaf-spring setup from the previous generation, Ford engineers pleased everyone with the optional dual front shock setup, appropriately called quad shocks, for the front suspension. The aftermarket had provided weld-on and bolt-on setups for the first-generation trucks for years, but this marked the first time that such a system was offered from the factory, not just Ford, but any manufacturer.

In addition to the quad-shock setup, Ford increased the stock shock piston diameter from 1 to 1-3/8 inches for increased damping control. The front suspension also benefited from a standard anti-sway bar. If the quad-shock option was not selected, single front shocks on opposing sides of the coil springs were standard. In the rear, the leaf springs were lengthened, which softened the ride but would have increased the body roll without the anti-roll bars Ford offered as options: a 1-inch bar or heavy-duty 1-3/8-inch bar.

For 1978, Ford discarded the Haltenberger inverted-Y linkage used on the 1976–1977 Broncos and returned to the T-linkage used from 1966 to 1975. The intersection of the tie-rod and the

drag link was moved closer to the passenger-side steering knuckle. The Dana 44-9F had a capacity of 550 pounds greater than the version used in first-generation Broncos. (Photo Courtesy Cliff Brumsfield)

Power steering was optional in the 1978 Bronco and standard for 1979. The manual box in 1978 is rare. This particular box is a strong unit and, with some modifications, has become a popular unit to swap into 1966–1977 Broncos. (Photo Courtesy Cliff Brumsfield)

The 1978–1979 Broncos continued the previously used suspension system using forged radius arms and a track bar to locate the axle laterally. The radius-arm brackets were longer, lowering the rear of the radius arms, which gave the front end more caster. Also visible is the bulletproof NP205 transfer case used on Broncos with the part-time 4WD system. (Photo Courtesy Cliff Brumsfield)

In addition to the 1978 shock and steering changes, Ford also increased the caster of the front axle, providing better tracking and straightline stability. Early testing showed some instability at speed and several configurations were tried with the final brackets dropping the radius arm mounts by 2 inches.

Towing Packages

The increased powertrain strength meant that Ford finally decided that Broncos were worthy tow vehicles and offered specific towing packages for them. The Light Duty Trailer Towing package (for trailers up to 2,000 pounds) included an Extra Cooling package, wiring harness, heavy-duty flasher, and of course an emblem to announce that it had the towing package. The Heavy Duty Trailer Towing package (for trailers over 2,000 pounds) included all of those items plus heavy-duty suspension (higher-rate springs), a 60-amp alternator (standard was 40), a 68 amp-hour maintenance-free battery, an external transmission cooler, dual horns, an oil pressure gauge, an ammeter, and large bright recreation mirrors.

Interior

Along with the obvious styling and size changes in the 1978 model, interior refinement and comfort were among the most obvious improvements over the first-generation trucks.

The 1978–1979 doors were a marked contrast to their more utilitarian predecessors. In the richly appointed Ranger XLT trim, chrome door handles, imitation wood paneling, molded plastic door panels with integral armrests, and a large pocket at the bottom of the door signaled to consumers that a new era of luxury had descended on the Bronco. (Photo Courtesy Freeze Frame Image LLC, Al Rogers)

A day's travel in an early Bronco was a taxing and tiresome affair. The new Bronco offered a much higher degree of passenger comfort.

The front seats were again two low-back bucket seats, but the shape of the seats offered greater lateral support than their predecessors, and the material was more breathable and comfortable with a weave that Ford referred to as chain mail. A molded center console with integrated cupholders was optional. A front bench seat was optional to raise the seating capacity to six. In 1979, optional reclining captain's seats with

It's obvious that the original owner checked many option boxes when ordering this Bronco, including cruise control, inside locking hood release, tilt column, air-conditioning, ammeter and oil gauges, and privacy glass on the rear side windows. (Photo Courtesy Freeze Frame Image LLC, Al Rogers)

High-back captain's seats were optional for the first time in 1979 Broncos, a $369 option. The seats had folding armrests on both sides and also reclined. Three-point belts, never available on first-generation trucks, were standard on 1978–1979 Broncos. These seats are in immaculate original condition, thanks largely to the original owner installing seat covers when they were new. (Photo Courtesy Freeze Frame Image LLC, Al Rogers)

armrests were optional as well, increasing interior comfort to new levels.

The optional rear seat, in addition to being wider, also offered a higher back for greater comfort. An optional flip-and-fold configuration greatly increased the rear cargo area capacity when you needed to haul large items in the rear of the vehicle. And if you wanted to remove the rear seat entirely, you simply pulled two pins.

Ford engineers greatly increased rear seat comfort for 1978 by recessing the footwell area for rear-seat passengers.

Within reach of the rear passengers was an optional padded GT bar (the legal department didn't like the term "roll bar"). Optional sliding windows afforded better ventilation in the rear of the vehicle.

Another popular option was air-conditioning, available for the first time in 1978. If the vehicle was ordered with air-conditioning, Ford installed an insulation package to help keep the air-conditioning function as intended. The option of tinted glass on all windows was recommended to lower the heat load in the passenger compartment.

The 1978–1979 Bronco rear cargo area was downright cavernous compared to that of the 1966–1977 trucks (97 cubic feet with the rear seat removed versus 49 cubic feet in the earlier models). The rear seat was a flip-and-fold model that was also removable. The same rear seat was used from 1978 to 1986. (Photo Courtesy Freeze Frame Image LLC, Al Rogers)

The interior of Tom Carper's Bronco is a study in contrasts. The 4-speed manual transmission and bench seat were not usually paired with the Ranger XLT imitation wood grain on the glove box and door panels and the $55 Sport steering wheel. (Photo Courtesy Tom Carper)

This view from the rear of a 1978 Bronco shows exactly how big these trucks are compared to the first generation. The view from the front seat is identical to the pickups from the same year. Because this example has a bench seat, it can seat six people fairly comfortably, an impossible task in the early trucks.

The standard buckets in this 1979 Ranger are probably the nicest original examples remaining in captivity. Although more comfortable than the seats in first-generation Broncos, testers of the new-for-1978 Bronco were not thrilled with them, citing a lack of lateral support. (Photo Courtesy Cliff Brumsfield)

For 1978, the Bronco instrument cluster became a deep, three-binnacle design identical to those used on F-Series pickups. The ammeter and oil gauges shown here were a $32 option if the vehicle was not equipped with the Heavy Duty Trailer Towing package. (Photo Courtesy Cliff Brumsfield)

For the driver, an optional tilt steering column helped with comfort and entrance/egress concerns. An interesting feature of these columns was that one lever handled both the turn-signal functions and the tilt features. Cruise control was another option that was activated by buttons on the steering wheel or by buttons on the end of the turn signal/tilt lever if your Bronco happened to be equipped with one of the Sport steering wheels.

Convenience Group

The Convenience Group option included intermittent windshield wipers, gathered map pockets, and a 12-inch day/night mirror. A lighted visor vanity mirror was popular with passengers, and the Visibility Group option added lighting in the glove box, ashtray, and the underhood area, in addition to instrument panel courtesy lights and a dome light with an integral map light as long as you had front bucket seats.

AM/FM Radio

For the first time, you could buy a Bronco with a radio other than basic AM. Options included an AM digital clock radio, AM/FM radio with a single speaker, AM/FM stereo radio, and (a sure sign of the times) CB radio. The CB was a remote-mount unit with only the handheld microphone visible. The microphone was detachable and could be stored in the glove box to discourage theft.

Security Group

Additional measures to discourage theft were offered in the Security Group option and included a locking gas cap,

inside hood release lock, spare tire lock, and a locking glove box.

Cargo Area/Spare Tire

The standard location for the spare tire was inside on the passenger's side at the rear of the cabin; a vinyl cover for the tire was an option. Ford carried forward from prior years the option of a rear swing-away tire carrier on the passenger's side of the vehicle, and it was an option that most consumers chose, particularly those who carried anything larger than the standard L78-15B tire.

A nice touch was the new rear window assembly that raised or lowered via a keyed switch on the driver's side of the

A swing-away tire carrier continued to be an option with second-generation Broncos. The latch assembly was simplified and rattled less than the first-generation design. The cost with the XLT package in 1979 was $81.00.

This 1979 Bronco still sports the original BFGoodrich 10-15 All-Terrain spare tire on the white-spoke steel wheel. (Photo Courtesy Freeze Frame Image LLC, Al Rogers)

Visible on the left side of the tailgate is the key receptacle that activates the power rear window. The tire cover was stock ($81) with the Ranger XLT package installed on this truck. Visible at the bottom of the chrome rear bumper is a receiver hitch, part of the Light Duty Trailer Towing package, which added $29 to the invoice total. (Photo Courtesy Tom Carper)

tailgate or via a switch on the dash. It was a huge benefit to no longer need to open the tire carrier and then raise a heavy liftgate to gain access to the rear cargo area.

Mirrors

To keep an eye on things behind them, Broncos had three types of mirrors available: the standard-size mirrors that were essentially a carryover from first-generation trucks, the very popular low-mount Western mirrors, and Recreation Swing Out Mirrors, which offered the largest glass size and were the best for towing. The low-mount Western mirrors, which were popular for several generations of trucks, were the most commonly chosen mirrors for 1978 and 1979 trucks.

This 1978 Bronco Custom is equipped with the rare $200 option of the rear sliding side windows. Because engineers were afraid that Dick Nesbitt's original design of two sharp corners in the windows would lead to cracks in the fiberglass, all the corners were rounded for 1978–1979. Barely visible is the optional GT bar (aka roll bar) that cost $105 on the option sheet. (Photo Courtesy Carl Voegtly)

Trim Levels

For 1978, the Bronco was available in two trim levels: Custom and Ranger XLT. Also available was the optional Free Wheeling Package.

Custom

The 1978 Custom trim level trucks are easily identifiable from all others in this generation because they had round headlights. The rectangular headlights were an option and became standard when the 1979 models were introduced. The bumpers were painted black as was the grille. Standard rolling stock was H78x15B tires on 15x5.5 steel wheels with bright hubcaps. A rubber floor mat covered the passenger compartment. The instrument panel and door trim panels were color-keyed with a choice of red, black, blue, green, or tan.

Ranger XLT

The Ranger XLT package, a $669 option, added chrome bumpers, a chrome grille and headlight surround, rectangular headlights (1978), and bright trim molding for the windshield, rear side windows, wheel lips, and lower tailgate section. In addition, it added a bright taillight molding and a body side molding with an inset black vinyl strip.

On the interior, the package included insulation, cut-pile carpeting, door trim panels with a wood-grain accent, seat covering in vinyl or vinyl and cloth, a wood-tone dash with bright moldings, and a "Ranger XLT" badge on the glove box door to let your passenger know they were riding in the top-of-the-line truck.

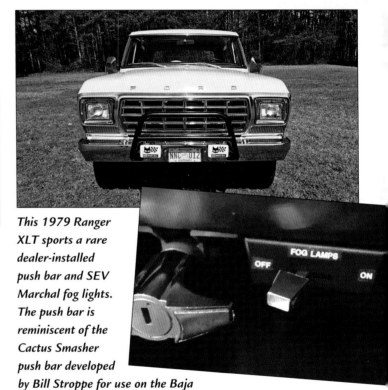

This 1979 Ranger XLT sports a rare dealer-installed push bar and SEV Marchal fog lights. The push bar is reminiscent of the Cactus Smasher push bar developed by Bill Stroppe for use on the Baja Broncos years earlier. (Photo Courtesy Cliff Brumsfield)

Free Wheeling Package

When he originally worked on the 1978 Bronco's styling, designer Dick Nesbitt submitted several proposals for dechromed Bronco trim options with black grille inserts and bumpers, deleted trim moldings, and color accents. Years later, these proposals came to life as a $491 option called the Free Wheeling package, available on either the Custom or Ranger XLT Broncos. An appearance package, it featured tri-color striping (available in orange/tan/cream or blue/white/green, depending on which of 18 base colors were selected).

Black bumpers adorned the front and rear, and the low-mount side mirrors were also blacked out. Inside, your hands were usually wrapped around a good-looking sport

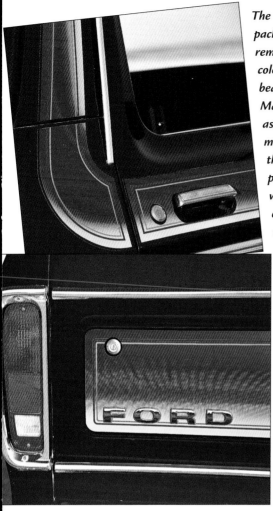

The Chromatic stripe package is a vivid reminder of 1970s colors and still looks beautiful today. Many enthusiasts associate the Chromatic stripes with the Free Wheeling package, but they were separate options. Because the original owner of this truck did not order the Free Wheeling package, he paid $487 for the stripe package to be applied to his black Bronco. (Photo Courtesy Freeze Frame Image LLC, Al Rogers)

steering wheel with a fatter rim (some had standard wheels), and although the Ford brochures claimed the glove box had a black applique on it, it never made it into production.

Rolling stock were 15x6-inch white-spoke steel wheels with raised-white-letter tires or the far more popular 15x8-inch white-spoke steel wheels, often shod with 10-15 Goodyear Tracker A-T tires. Yellow-painted wheels were available, although they were less popular.

For 1979, the Free Wheeling package continued with an option of a so-called Chromatic stripe in lieu of the tri-color striping. The chromatic stripe covered nearly the entire flank of the Bronco in vivid colors, particularly when paired in its usual fashion against a base body color of Raven Black. The Chromatic stripe was also available on trucks without the Free Wheeling package.

Colors and Paint Schemes

The Bronco color palette included 19 options for 1978 and 1979. As a sign of the times, Ford offered an impressive selection of two-tone paint schemes as well. The standard Bronco

paint scheme was a solid exterior body color with a black, sand (1979 only), or white fiberglass top.

To spice things up a bit, the buyer could choose the Special Tu-Tone option, which extended the color chosen for the fiberglass top to the hood and roof area with the rest of the body trimmed in the chosen primary body color.

The Deluxe Tu-Tone option provided an accent color applied within the body line moldings and upper and lower tailgate; the body side molding was included in this option as it served as a perimeter for the accent color.

The Combination Tu-Tone Option combined the Special Tu-Tone and Deluxe Tu-Tone options, making for a beautiful Bronco.

Tires and Wheels

Rolling stock on 1978 and 1979 Broncos was offered in an impressive array of options. L78-15 tires on 5.5-inch-wide steel wheels were standard. For 1978, the wheel covers from the 1977 Special Décor package Bronco were offered as hubcaps for those wheels.

Paying homage to the slot mags from the Stroppe Baja Broncos in the mid-1970s, Ford offered forged aluminum wheels with 5 slots in a 6-inch width. Also offered were the 10-hole forged aluminum wheels, polished to a high luster and polyurethane coated.

The 1970s were the high-water mark for the white steel "wagon wheel" pattern wheels, and Ford offered them in 6- and 8-inch widths. The 8-inch wheels were extremely popular with the off-road crowd.

Collectibility and Production

The 1978 Bronco was a huge sales hit, as evidenced by its sales numbers: 77,917 units, a whopping 436-percent increase over 1977 sales. However, 1978 paled in comparison to 1979, when sales reached six figures for the first and only time in Bronco production at 104,038 units, with 55,764 of those equipped with the Ranger XLT trim package. (Copyright Marti Auto Works, martiauto.com, and used with permission.)

The 1978 and 1979 Broncos long languished in the shadows of their older siblings in terms of desirability with enthusiasts. Due to the higher production numbers and their low cost, they weren't given the same love and care as early as the bobtails were.

As the old adage goes, "a rising tide lifts all boats," as the prices skyrocketed for first-generation Broncos, the 1978–1979 trucks have been able to catch some wind in their resale values as well. A 2018 article in *Hagerty* magazine noted that auction pricing data shows that the trucks of this generation have increased in price by about 130 percent in the last 10 years, and

The 1979 Bronco was the best-selling Bronco of all time with 104,038 units leaving showrooms that year. With handsome examples, such as this two-tone Ranger XLT, it's easy to see why. Comfortable captain's seats were a popular option included on the 55,764 Ranger XLTs sold that year. (Photo Courtesy Ford Motor Company)

Showing the effects of long-term ownership in the Arizona sun, this 1978 Bronco Custom is as comfortable and well-worn as a pair of old cowboy boots. This Bronco is a bit of an anomaly because it's a 1978 Custom model with rectangular headlights; according to Ford specifications, it should have round headlights. Wheels are the optional painted styled steel wheels and it carries the Special Tu-Tone paint job from that year, which was offered in black or white and any of the regular colors. (Photo Courtesy Carl Voegtly)

Standing guard over some carcasses from his older brothers and sisters at the Bronco Ranch in Temperance, Michigan, this 1978 Bronco is a beautiful Ranger XLT model with the Deluxe Tu-Tone paint scheme, a $172 option that included the "Race Track" molding (the thin molding surrounding the primary colored sections of the body). Originally from New Mexico, it moved to Michigan in 2012. Hanging off the front is a vintage Superwinch Ox winch. (Photo Courtesy Tom Carper)

This 1979 Ranger XLT is a virtual time capsule from that year, showing only about 29,000 miles on the odometer. The owner is a 1978–1979 enthusiast and the third owner of this beauty. Nearly everything is original; one of the most obvious changes are the 1977 Appliance Turbo Vec wheels. (Photo Courtesy Cliff Brumsfield)

their popularity is highest with the Gen X crowd behind only the 1966–1977 Broncos.

Although they were produced in the height of the malaise era, their classic good looks and sturdy construction have begun to endear them to collectors. Because so many were used as daily drivers and low-buck four-wheelers over the years, highly optioned models in excellent condition are in short supply and prices are starting to reflect the desirability. Options now exist to compensate for the anemic, smog-era engines.

THE MOSS BROTHERS KEEP IT SIMPLE

In a racing series most frequently identified with expensive Trophy Trucks, the 1979 Bronco of Don and Ken Moss stands out as a monument to simplicity. Since the turn of the century, no off-road racing team has captured more wins or class championships than this humble Northern California race team.

Raised in a rural ranch environment near Bishop, California, the brothers displayed a mechanical aptitude at an early age, eventually earning agricultural engineering degrees at Cal Poly San Luis Obispo.

Long-time desert racing enthusiasts, the brothers decided in the late 1990s to try their hand at racing a truck. With family history of racing Broncos, they focused their sights on a 1978–1979 Bronco, as they felt the longer wheelbase and beefy construction were definite pluses compared to earlier bobtails.

They purchased a 1979 Bronco, planning to race the Baja 2000 as their first race. The Bronco was finished in time for the race, even with the extra work required due to a rollover during testing for the inaugural event.

To begin the buildup, the top was discarded, interior stripped of all non-essential items, and a roll cage constructed from 2-inch DOM (drawn-over-mandrel) tubing gusseted per Southern California Off Road Enthusiasts (SCORE) International rules and tied directly to the frame at numerous points.

The Mosses knew that the original smog-era engines wouldn't be good candidates for a race truck. Instead, Don modestly claims they "just had an engine from an old station wagon in the junkyard." That junkyard engine was a well-built 351 Windsor with plenty of tricks inside. Incredibly, it ran for 12 seasons before it was pulled and another engine installed in 2011. In 2015, it was rebuilt and again installed in the truck.

Behind the engine is stout C6 3-speed transmission controlled by an Art Carr shifter. An NP205 transfer case provides power to the front and rear axles. Don notes that the team uses 4WD about 50 percent of the time on the typical race course.

Transferring the power to the ground is the job of a fabricated Ruffstuff 9-inch rear-end housing with disc brakes and full-floating axles and a heavily trussed high-pinion Dana 44 front end. The Bronco's suspension consists of a pair of coil-over shocks in the front and Deaver leafs in the rear, with 13 and 17 inches of travel, respectively. The Bronco depends on 3-inch King bypass shocks for damping front and rear.

The tires and wheels also help with the ride: 35x12.50 BFGoodrich Baja T/As, mounted on 15x8 American Racing Type 23 wheels, an ideal width that keeps the rims' edges out of the rocks.

Crow Enterprises Harnesses and Beard suspension seats securely contain the driver and passenger. A Parker Pumper system is used to cycle fresh air into the occupants' helmets at all times, a necessity on dusty off-road racing courses.

The team's driving skills, vehicle prep, and continual updating of parts has given them an enviable record of success in the desert circuit. They recorded their 50th class win in the 50th Baja 1000 in 2017, which also happened to be their 13th Baja 1000 win.

Their "KISS" formula of building a stout, reliable, and very simple vehicle has yielded unprecedented results. "If it doesn't break, you don't have to fix it."

Farther down course, their truck covered with mud, the Mosses air out their Bronco on a small rise with a Trophy Truck in hot pursuit. The phalanx of lights bear testament to the long night ahead. High in the air, both axles show ample evidence of bracing to help with the inevitable landings from the jumps. (Photo Courtesy Trackside Photo)

With Arizona mountain peaks in the background and a Laughlin casino visible near the front bumper, the Moss Brothers racing team launches its Class 3 Bronco at the annual SCORE Laughlin Desert Challenge Race. Originally a multi-lap race with laps averaging about 50 to 60 miles in length, the format eventually changed to laps about 12 miles in length and became a fan favorite because they could see the racers more frequently. (Photo Courtesy Trackside Photo)

1980–1986: SMALLER AND LIGHTER

"The Bronco truly is a well-designed, dual-purpose vehicle, matching the best features of a luxury street car with the rugged, go-anywhere capability of a standard 4x4."

Against the backdrop of skyrocketing fuel prices as a result of the second oil embargo crisis in 1979, Ford introduced the 1980 model of the Bronco, the third generation, in the fall of 1979. It was smaller, lighter, more aerodynamic, and offered smaller and more fuel-efficient engines than its predecessor. It was almost as if Ford knew the times were changing and had quickly adapted the Bronco to better meet the needs of the consumer in the financially troubling times. Of course, this wasn't the case because vehicle development takes many years, but it seemed as if the engineers had hit the target with the new Bronco.

History and Development

The development work on the 1980 Bronco, specifically the innovative front suspension, started in the early 1970s. At the time, Ford was looking for a way to incorporate a rugged independent front suspension system into the Bronco to provide a better ride than the monobeam Dana 44 front end then used on the Bronco and the F-Series pickups.

According to Don Wheatley, who was the Bronco engineering supervisor at the time, the first thought on how to accomplish this was to incorporate the Dana-developed V-Drive system into the front end. Developed in the early 1970s, this system used a transfer case mounted behind the transmission that split power to each front wheel via twin driveshafts (hence the "V-drive" name); each one drove a gear drive at each front wheel.

Ford used this system on at least one station wagon prototype and proved that it allowed for a low ride and worked well in a passenger car application. Although it was later used in Ford and

This 1981 Free Wheeling Bronco with chromatic stripe is a rare beast indeed. The Chromatic stripe was a one-year-only option in the third-generation trucks and not many have survived. This Bronco also sports a rare pair of SEV Marchal lights under the front bumper, many likely disappeared due to their mounting location alone. (Photo Courtesy Christopher Lott)

You can tell what was on consumers' minds in 1982: fuel efficiency. Boasts of big-torque 6-cylinder engines, long ranges between fill-ups, overdrive transmissions, and overly optimistic Environmental Protection Agency (EPA) fuel mileage estimates were all part of the advertising strategy for a country still dealing with high fuel prices and a lackluster economy. (Photo Courtesy Ford Motor Company)

The introductory ad for the new 1980 Bronco emphasized the new Twin-Traction Beam front end along with the Bronco's toughness and roomy, comfortable interior. As a sign of the times, the estimated fuel mileage was listed for the first time. (Photo Courtesy Ford Motor Company)

For 1980, Ford redesigned the shape of the rear side windows to include two sharp corners, an acknowledgement that designer Dick Nesbitt's original concept of two sharp corners and two rounded corners was optimal and did not result in cracking of the fiberglass top.

Chevy van 4WD conversions, Wheatley's team determined that it was too complex and too expensive for a pickup or Bronco application. The original designs did not allow for any low-range gear multiplication, which is necessary on a pickup or Bronco configuration; the packaging in the truck chassis was also a challenge.

Soon thereafter, Wheatley notes that he had a eureka moment and realized that a simple U-joint in the middle of the solid axle shaft would mimic Ford's already-existing Twin I-Beam front suspension. Wheatley stated that one of his colleagues immediately tried to dissuade him from trying it because he felt that it wouldn't ride right with the unequal front axles not weighing the same. To test it, Wheatley's team took a regular 4x2 pickup and had the engineering ride team take baseline ride measurements. Then they had Carron and Company (Detroit prototype fabrication company) weld 80 pounds of steel to one of the axles to simulate the weight of a front differential.

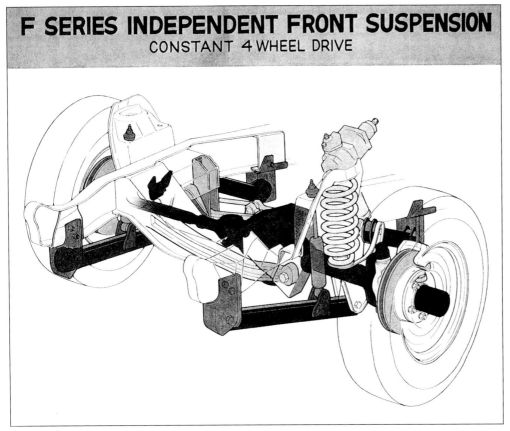

F SERIES INDEPENDENT FRONT SUSPENSION
CONSTANT 4 WHEEL DRIVE

This Twin-Traction Beam concept drawing from 1971 shows how the suspension and links were envisioned at that time. A set of trailing arms that mounted on top of the axle and a set of links behind the axle beams, mounted below the beams, was Don Wheatley's first idea that he patented in 1976. (Photo Courtesy Don Wheatley)

Without telling the ride engineering team exactly what they had done, they had them test it again, and the results came back that it rode better than the baseline setup. At that point, Wheatley felt that they were on solid ground. No good deed goes unpunished, however, and the engineering brass chewed out Wheatley for ruining a good test vehicle. The advantage of Wheatley's system was that it allowed a common frame to be used for 4x2 and 4x4 vehicles and the suspension configuration was similar to the already-existing Twin I-Beam 4x2 front suspension.

Wheatley and coinventor John Richardson applied for a patent on "Independent front suspension for front wheel drive" in 1973 and in 1976, they were awarded US Patent 3,948,337A for the system that became the Twin-Traction Beam independent front suspension system. Wheatley notes that they referred to it as an "independent front suspension system" and the

Project Shorthorn debuted the prototype version of the Twin-Traction Beam 4WD front axle. Visible here are the linkages used to locate the axle beams in the first prototypes of this system. Later production versions of the Twin-Traction Beam relied on traditional radius arms for fore and aft beam location. (Photo Courtesy Don Wheatley)

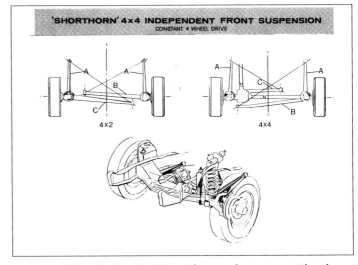

By 1973, the Twin-Traction Beam front-end concept on Shorthorn had been refined a bit. The system now relied on radius arms for fore and aft location similar to the 4x2 Twin I-Beam suspension. However, the differential was still located in the passenger-side beam (it was in the driver's beam on the production version) and the steering was still located behind the beams. (Photo Courtesy Don Wheatley)

"Twin-Traction Beam" moniker was likely conjured up by the marketing department at a later time.

Wheatley went on to win the Henry Ford Technological Award for his invention in 1981. In granting the award, it was noted that his invention allowed lower overall vehicle height, better ride, improved handling, weight reduction, and a cost reduction compared to previously used Ford solid-axle front ends and competitors' moonbeam axles.

Because the axle required a frame change to fit correctly, it was decided to incorporate it into the 1980 trucks rather than the 1978–1979 models. Between 1972 and 1979, axle development was handled by a chassis engineering team led by Ernie Schoenberger. The design went through five stages of evolution until the production units were finalized. A camber adjustment feature was designed in 1977. In 1978, the first engineering prototype was built and tested, and extensive testing and a manufacturing review started. The first axle was built from production tooling in April 1979, and the first vehicle built from production tooling burst forth in June 1979.

Production for the front suspension system was handled by the Dana Corporation. According to Ford engineer George Peterson, the design of the Twin-Traction Beam front axle was the first use of high-power computer-aided design in a truck suspension system at Ford.

Features and Press

To the casual eye, the 1980 Bronco appeared to be nearly identical to the 1978–1979 models that preceded it. And although it did resemble its predecessor in many ways, there were enough differences to distinguish it from its older brethren.

The most significant difference was in weight reduction. The 1978–1979 trucks were portly beasts, and the 1980 trucks trimmed that weight by 300 to 500 pounds, depending on options. Overall length was down 2.7 inches, and it lost 1.1 inches in width. Although the body size was smaller, the cargo capacity of the interior was increased by a full 5 cubic feet. On the exterior, every panel of the body was more squared off and for the first time was sculpted in a wind tunnel.

At the time, Ford advertised that it had spent $700 million in the development of the 1980 Ford pickups and the Bronco. Pavement-centric *Car and Driver* was blunt in its assessment that Ford didn't get its money's worth out of the downsizing program, with editor Rich Ceppos remarking, "We need the new Bronco like a moose needs a new hat rack."

The 4WD press was more sympathetic with *Four Wheeler* naming the Bronco its 1980 Four Wheeler of the Year, stating "The introduction of the first American built four wheel drive trucks with independent front suspension was alone enough to

qualify the entire Ford 4x4 line, but downsizing, new exterior and interior styling and improved passenger comfort unquestionably earned Bronco its second Four Wheeler of the Year award."

Petersen's 4 Wheel and Off Road declared, "The Bronco truly is a well-designed, dual-purpose vehicle, matching the best features of a luxury street car with the rugged, go-anywhere capability of a standard 4x4."

Engine

For the third generation of the Bronco, Ford again mixed up the powertrain options for the truck with a mix of old and new options.

351M

With an obvious nod toward improving fuel economy, the 351M V-8 now sat atop the options list, supplanting the torquey 400 V-8 of the previous two years. Unfortunately, due to ever-tightening emissions regulations, the 351M's rating dropped to a paltry 138 hp, a drop of 18 hp from its 1979 rating. Torque also dropped from 276 to 263 ft-lbs.

302

The mid-level option was the 302 V-8, the mainstay of the first-generation's powertrain. It returned after a two-year absence, and it became the standard engine for California trucks. It was rated at 137 hp and torque was measured at 239 ft-lbs. With almost identical horsepower ratings, the only real advantage to the 351M option was a slight increase in torque.

300 6-Cylinder

For the first time since 1974, Ford offered a 6-cylinder engine in a Bronco. The 49-state standard engine was the 300-ci 6-cylinder, a beloved mainstay introduced in the pickup line in 1965. The Six offered 119 hp and 243 ft-lbs of torque. The 300 was, of course, expected to produce the highest fuel economy ratings of all three engine options and was paired with manual transmissions only until the 1983 model year when it became available with the C6 Select Shift automatic transmission.

The EEC-IV electronic engine control system was added to the engine in 1984, and as with its control of electronic fuel injection systems, it provided ignition spark control and air/fuel mixture adjustments to the carburetor (known as a feedback carburetor) through readings from the oxygen sensor(s) in the exhaust system.

Regardless of the engine choice, all testers of the 1980 Bronco agreed that the engine performance, particularly on the highway, was less than awe-inspiring. This was primarily due to ever-increasing emissions regulations being imposed on the manufacturers and their struggles to tune carbureted engines to meet them. Off-highway, with the advantage of transfer case gear reductions, the complaints turned to praise.

351 Windsor

In 1982, the 351M was phased out and replaced by the 351 Windsor. The engines had similar horsepower and torque ratings, but the 351 Windsor had much greater appeal for after-market modifications and performance accessories.

351 H.O.

In 1984, an upgraded 351 Windsor, known as the 351 H.O., became available as an option in the Bronco. Enthusiasts were happy to know that the H.O. version was rated at 210 hp and 304 ft-lbs of torque, a significant increase over the base 351's ratings of 150 hp and 282 ft-lbs of torque. The increases came through the addition of a Holley 4180 4-barrel carburetor and 4-barrel intake. A pseudo–dual exhaust (only dual pipes behind the muffler) may have helped as well.

The engine continued to be an option through the 1986 model year. Like the 300-ci 6-cylinder, the 351 also received the EEC-IV engine controls for the first time in 1984. Although the electronic processor was a rugged and reliable computer, the carburetor it controlled soon earned the ire and disgust of many technicians who had to work on it. The age of the carburetor was rapidly drawing to a close.

In 1986, "H.O." meant a 4-barrel carburetor and 210 hp. The 351 H.O. had been introduced two years earlier and added about 60 hp over the previous 351 Windsor. Although it doesn't seem significant now, at the time it was a huge step forward in power. (Photo Courtesy David Grinch)

Fuel Injection

Hot on the heels of the 351 H.O., Ford's 302 led the charge into a new era of engine induction with the introduction of electronic fuel injection for the 1985 model year. Unlike some of its competition, Ford leapfrogged over the more commonly used throttle-body setups and used a port injection system with a dry intake manifold and an injector for each of the eight cylinders. Along with a vast improvement in driveability, cold starts, reduced emissions, and slightly improved fuel economy, fuel injection also increased the horsepower rating to 185 hp, a healthy increase of 35 hp over the previous year's carbureted engine. In addition, torque increased by 25 ft-lbs to 275. With the fuel-injected 302, now known as the 5.0, and the 351 H.O., the Bronco finally had the engines that testers had wanted at the model's introduction in 1980.

Fuel was fed to all the engine options from a standard 25-gallon fuel tank from 1980 to 1984. During those years, a Bronco owner could increase range by specifying the 32-gallon tank ($101 option) with a skid plate under it for protection. In a move to simplify the option sheet and save on production costs, the 32-gallon tank was made standard for all Broncos in 1985 and continued to be the standard tank size through the end of production in 1996.

Toolbox

Another underhood option worth mentioning during these years was the plastic toolbox. *Four Wheeler* balked at the price of the toolbox option, $78, but noted that it was an extremely handy and useful item. In 1986, as a cost-cutting measure, Ford changed the retractable hood light to a stationary light.

A handy option in the 1980–1986 Broncos was this underhood light. It was on a retractable reel and had enough cable to be used at various points on the truck, not just in the engine compartment.

Transmission

Behind the three engines, Ford used a variety of transmissions for the 1980–1986 model years. In 1980, choices were limited to the C6 3-speed automatic transmission and the T-18 4-speed manual transmission, both familiar to Ford owners from previous years. The T-18 had a low 6.32:1 first gear, which allowed for excellent low-speed performance off-road and helped quell some of the complaints of low engine output through the use of extremely low gearing.

4-Speed with Overdrive

In 1981, in keeping with the overall theme of greater fuel economy, Ford added the option of a 4-speed manual transmission with an overdrive fourth gear. With a 0.72:1 overdrive ratio, it added reduced RPM on the highway. Unfortunately, due to the low engine outputs at the time of its introduction, it suffered the inverse fate of the T-18: its overdrive ratio was often too high for regular driving, effectively rendering it a 3-speed transmission.

An 11-inch-diameter clutch was used behind the manual transmissions in the third-generation Broncos. For 1984, the linkage was changed from a purely mechanical linkage to a hydraulically actuated linkage, which removed the need for periodic adjustment and provided an extra level of smoothness to its action and engagement. A clutch interlock system was added in 1984 for an extra measure of safety; the engine could no longer be started without the clutch completely disengaged.

4-Speed AOD

The transmission options remained the same until 1985 when, concurrent with the 5.0 electronic fuel-injected (EFI) engine's introduction, Ford also introduced the 4-speed automatic overdrive (AOD) transmission behind the 5.0 EFI engine. With a 0.70:1 overdrive ratio, Bronco owners who preferred an automatic transmission could now enjoy the benefits of reduced highway RPM similar to what their cohorts with 4-speed manual overdrive transmissions had enjoyed since the 1981 model year.

Transfer Case

Unlike the multitude of transmission options offered through the third generation, only one transfer case was offered. Jettisoning the full-time 4WD option offered on the previous generation's models, Ford turned to the New Process 208 transfer case for 1980.

The 208's case was aluminum instead of the cast-iron models used before, shaving 60 pounds in the process. Gear drives were exchanged for a chain-drive setup. Low-range was accomplished via a planetary gearset mounted at the front of the transfer case. Lubrication was provided by a constant-displacement pump, which allowed the Bronco to be towed up to 55 mph for unlimited miles without disconnecting the driveshafts or lifting the front wheels off the ground, a true convenience feature appreciated by many.

Continuing the theme of fuel efficiency, Ford claimed that the part-time case gained 1 mpg over its full-time brethren used previously. The chain-drive cases also were easier to shift than the gear-drives, which made the vehicles more drivable for the average owner. Ford wisely chose a shift pattern for the transfer case that had the lever all the way forward toward the firewall, away from the driver's legs, while in 2-Hi. Low range was a respectable 2.61:1, which when combined with the low gear of the T-18 and 3.50 axle gears, gave an industry-leading 57:1 overall crawl ratio.

Axles and Suspension

As noted earlier, the third-generation Broncos pioneered the use of the Dana 44 Twin-Traction independent front suspension system. The axle's differential case was bolted to the back side of the driver-side beam and was an integral structural member of the beam. From 1980–1982, the passenger-side axle shaft that exited the differential case was bolted to the unit via a collar retained with three bolts. Starting in 1983, it was retained by a snap ring inside the differential case. The axle housings were mounted to the chassis and suspended in much the same manner as their predecessors: radius arms from the axle housings to the frame for fore and aft location and suspended by coil springs with a shock absorber mounted behind the coil spring.

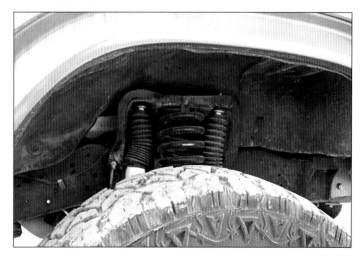

For the third-generation trucks, Ford continued with the option of dual front shocks for each front wheel. Instead of three separate towers used in the 1978–1979 trucks, Ford developed a formed, one-piece coil and shock bucket.

As with 1978–1979 models, a second shock at each front wheel was available and highly recommended as an option for controlling the unsprung mass of the front axles, even though the new front-axle system reduced the amount of unsprung mass by about 100 pounds. Testers noted that trucks with single front shocks "porpoised" on rough terrain.

Axle ratios varied from year to year with the higher offerings either 3.00 or 3.08:1, and lower ratios were 3.50 or 3.54:1/3.55:1, depending on the year and powertrain configuration (49 State, California, or High Altitude). The 4.11:1 ratio returned for the 1985 model year with the introduction of the automatic overdrive transmission behind the 5.0 engine.

As an option for the 1981–1985 model years, Ford listed a limited-slip front differential, a rarity in SUVs. Front axles for all years were rated at 3,550 pounds, except for those vehicles equipped with the Snow Plow Preparation package, which included 3,800-pound axles.

Front Axle Locking Hubs

A new option widely heralded for the 1980 Broncos was automatic locking hubs on the front axle, available with the C6 Select Shift automatic transmission. Gone was the hassle of having to climb out of the vehicle and lock the hubs at each front wheel before engaging 4WD. The hubs locked when the transfer case was shifted into 4WD; to unlock the hubs, you drove the vehicle in reverse for 10 to 15 feet after shifting the transfer case back to 2WD. The automatic locking hubs became available as an option for all transmissions for the 1981 model year.

Rear Axle

The rear axle continued to be the strong and durable 9-inch axle assembly, with a tall 3.00:1 standard axle ratio (V-8s) and an optional 3.50:1 ratio (standard with the 6-cylinder). For fuel efficiency reasons, 4.11:1 gears were discontinued for the early 1980s but made a return to the option list for 1985 when the automatic overdrive transmission was introduced.

The Traction-Lok limited-slip differential was a $197 option in 1980 and continued as an option through 1986, increasing very little in price through the years. The 9-inch was the only rear axle available until 1983, when the 8.8-inch rear end became available as well. Both rear ends were used for the following several years with the 9-inch making its final appearance in the 1986 model year.

The 8.8-inch rear end was similar in strength to the 9-inch rear end but featured a more traditional differential housing integral to the axle housing, as compared to the removable differential assembly of the 9-inch. Both featured 31-spline axles. The 8.8-inch axle shafts were retained via C-clips on the ends of the shafts inside the differential housing; the 9-inch shafts

were retained via a retainer plate outboard of the bearing at the end of the housing.

Towing

The 1980–1986 Broncos could also be equipped for towing. As the engines became more powerful, rated towing capacities increased. For example, in 1984, the Bronco was capable of towing a Class III trailer of up to 6,400 pounds when properly equipped. In 1985, towing capacities increased to 6,800 pounds with the 351 H.O. engine and, surprisingly, up to 8,000 pounds with the smaller 5.0-liter EFI engine due to its 4.11:1 axle ratio.

The tow package consisted of a seven-wire trailer harness, a 60-amp alternator (40-amp standard), a 63-amp-hour maintenance-free battery (36-amp-hour standard), Extra Engine Cooling, an auxiliary transmission cooler mounted in front of the radiator (for automatic transmissions), heavy-duty flashers, and the Handling package that included front and rear stabilizer bars, quad front shocks, and heavy-duty shock absorbers. Ford recommended automatic transmissions and as low (high numerically) an axle ratio as possible as well as a V-8 engine for towing.

An additional helping of beef for the Bronco could be specified when you ordered the Snow Plow Preparation package for your truck. The package added 3,800-pound front axles and springs, a 70-amp alternator, and Extra Cooling package, and the engine block heater was usually selected as well.

The brilliant Chromatic stripe provides a stunning backdrop to the Trailer Special badge on this 1981 Free Wheeling Bronco. For 1981, the Trailer Towing package included a heavy-duty battery and alternator, Extra Engine Cooling, auxiliary transmission cooler, and the Handling package that included quad front shocks and front and rear stabilizer bars. A towing wiring harness, a heavy-duty flasher, and swing-out mirrors completed the package. (Photo Courtesy Christopher Lott)

Interior

As with the exterior of the 1980–1986 Broncos, the interiors of the third-generation trucks were evolutionary rather than revolutionary compared to their immediate predecessors. Despite the fact that the exterior dimensions of the trucks were smaller, the interiors were larger with cargo capacity increasing by more than 5 cubic feet.

The door hardware was redesigned to increase resistance to theft, the door handles were moved lower on the door panels and were more ergonomically shaped for release compared to the 1978–1979 latches. The door panels now had a roomy

The instrument cluster in the 1980–1986 trucks changed from the 1978–1979 three-binnacle design to a more open cluster that included a trip odometer and optional tachometer for the first time. The shift quadrant was also moved from the steering column to the cluster.

The 1980–1986 doors were an evolutionary improvement over previous generations. The door pull had a more natural throw to it and the map pocket at the bottom was more durable. This truck is equipped with the optional power door locks and power windows, both actuated by small switches in chrome binnacles in the door panels.

map pocket molded in, and the speakers were moved for better sound delivery. Power windows were added to the options list for 1981, and power locks joined the list in 1982.

Drivers were also pleased with the new instrument cluster. Instead of the previous generation's cluster with three recessed binnacles, the new cluster offered large, readable gauges, including, for the first time, a tachometer when equipped with the optional Sports Instrumentation option. In addition to the tachometer, a trip odometer made an appearance in the Bronco instrument cluster for the first time.

Warning and indicator lights were arranged across the face of the cluster. The cluster surround was finished in black or a wood-grain finish, depending on the trim level of the truck. An optional digital clock appeared for the first time. The tilt-wheel option continued with the addition of a locking ignition switch on the column for 1980, moving up from the dash location in 1979. Intermittent windshield wipers were again a popular option.

The option of cruise control controlled by buttons in the steering wheel continued, as were numerous sound system options. Radio options changed with the arrival of new technology. An 8-track radio was available through 1982. In 1985, the standard radio became an AM/FM radio instead of AM only and the AM/FM cassette radio increased its capabilities. Ford continued its option of an integrated CB radio for 1980. It disappeared in 1981 due to its high price ($361) and corresponding low sales, along with the fact that the CB's popularity in passenger vehicles was fading.

The third generation of trucks had three options for front seats: low-back buckets, a full-width bench seat with split seatback, and the plush, high-back captain's seats with folding armrests and a reclining feature. The bench obviously gave the greatest seating capacity for the trucks but made access to the flip-and-fold rear seat more difficult.

Another rare accessory was the Ford CB. CBs enjoyed a relatively narrow window of popularity in the late 1970s and early 1980s; Ford offered an integral CB as an option for several years. Its price limited the number of vehicles equipped with it. Most of the functions were contained in the handset as shown here, which meant that vehicles didn't have the typical large receiver boxes hanging below the dashboard. (Photo Courtesy Christopher Lott)

Four Wheeler noted in its July 1982 road test that the "low back vinyl seats are difficult to adjust for good driving position, they don't recline, and they don't give enough lower back support."

In contrast, the captain's chairs were far and away the most popular seating option and received universal praise from all testers. As *Four Wheeler* noted in the same test, "You never seem to get tired when using them."

Another popular option with bucket seats was a plastic center console offering a large amount of storage and two molded cup holders in the lid. Yes, the Bronco was one of the forerunners of the cup holder revolution in modern vehicles.

Behind the front seats, Ford again offered the optional "GT bar" through the 1984 model year. Ford's lawyers ensured that no factory documentation ever referred to it as a "roll bar," as it was called by the general public.

The flip-and-fold rear seat was identical to the 1978–1979 seats and, coupled with the recessed footwell in the floor, was a comfortable place to sit. Rear sliding quarter windows with tinted glass were a popular option.

The standard configuration for the spare tire was an inside mount with a vinyl cover, but the outside-mount, swing-away cover was an extremely popular option. In 1981, the rear window received an optional rear defroster.

Package Bundling

In the early years of this generation of Broncos, buyers could select options mainly by checking boxes for the individual items on the options list. A few options were bundled (Handling package, Snow Plow package, Trailer Towing package, etc.) but autonomy and choice generally prevailed.

Starting with the 1985-model-year trucks, Ford started bundling options into Preferred Equipment packages, also referred to as Rapid-Spec packages. Ford hyped them as easier for the buyer because they simplified the ordering procedure and saved the buyer money. From Ford's perspective, it allowed them to simplify the Bronco build process because not as many variations had to be produced. And much like other bundling packages (think cable TV packages), buyers sometimes complained that they had to accept options they didn't want to get the ones they *did* want.

Trim Packages

Displaying continuity with the 1970s offerings, the 1980 Bronco was available in two trim packages: Custom and the luxurious Ranger XLT with the sporty Free Wheeling package and the "replacement" XLS add-ons to either trim level. Also available was the Eddie Bauer Edition.

Custom

The Custom was, according to Ford, "the value-packed standard trim level." On the exterior, it featured black front and rear bumpers, a black grille with chrome surround, bright hubcaps, bright door-mounted mirrors, and bright tailgate letters. On the inside, it featured low-back, vinyl bucket seats (sliding driver's, fixed passenger's seat that pivoted), an optional bench seat, vinyl seat trim and sun visors, a dome light, a locking steering column, an inside hood release, rubber floor mats, and more.

This 1984 Bronco looks right at home in the beautiful Colorado mountains near the owner's home. It's a Custom model, powered by a torquey 300-ci 6-cylinder engine backed by a 4-speed manual transmission with a creeper first gear. It sports a striking non-factory paint job and a Warn winch rests in an aftermarket bumper on the front of the truck. (Photo Courtesy Gary Gibson)

Ranger XLT

The Ranger XLT package added chrome bumpers, bright rear-side window moldings, and bright lower-body side molding with black vinyl inserts on the exterior. Inside, Ford added luxury with wall-to-wall cut-pile carpeting (including the cargo area), rear quarter panels with integral armrests and storage bins, bright accents on the door panels with the pocket areas carpeted, color-keyed seat belts, an insulated headliner, courtesy lighting activated by the door switches, a simulated leather–wrapped steering wheel, wood-tone accents on the steering wheel horn pad and instrument cluster, and additional insulation in the cabin. Many Ranger XLTs also had the optional captain's seats.

This is a Ranger XLT package door panel from a third-generation Bronco. The power windows, wood-grain insert, and carpeted map pocket announce this is a well-equipped truck. For this generation, the door latches were revised, the locking knobs were more theft-resistant, and the plastic door panels wrapped around the top of the doors. (Photo Courtesy Christopher Lott)

The roll cage, shocks, bumper, and lights give away the true purpose of this otherwise innocent-looking 1984 Bronco. The owner is a longtime Baja racer who uses it (equipped with hand controls) for prerunning race courses in Baja. (Photo Courtesy Dave Moore)

This 1986 Bronco XLT is owned by the grandson of the original owner and has just 87,000 miles on the odometer. The interior is still in excellent condition, which is a rarity, particularly for Arizona trucks. The truck sits slightly taller than stock with a 4-inch lift kit that includes longer radius arms for greater suspension travel.

This is a typical Ranger XLT interior for a 1980–1986 truck. The upholstery pattern on the optional bench seat gives away that it's from one of the earlier years (this example is a 1981). A tilt wheel, power windows, leather-wrapped steering wheel, wood-grain dash, tachometer, and thick carpet are all indicative of a well-equipped truck. The rear window defroster is controlled by the small box hanging below the dash and appears to be an afterthought. (Photo Courtesy Christopher Lott)

Free Wheeling Packages

Positioned as an add-on to the entry-level Custom and the luxury-themed Ranger XLT, the Free Wheeling package once again was Ford's offering for the sporty, youth-oriented market. For 1980, Ford offered the Free Wheeling A package and the Free Wheeling B package, depending on how much fun you wanted to have and how sporty you were.

Free Wheeling A gave you pinstripes or a tricolor tape stripe along the body side, hood, tailgate, and around the door windows. Sport wheel covers (i.e., fancy hubcaps) covered the plain steel wheels, and if you were upgrading a Custom model, you received chrome bumpers front and rear.

Although Free Wheeling A was all about the exterior appearance, Free Wheeling B focused on interior upgrades such as Sports Instrumentation (tachometer, trip odometer, oil pressure gauge, and ammeter), simulated leather–wrapped steering wheel (standard on Ranger XLT), fog lamps with covers on the lower edge of the front bumper, bumper guards, Handling package (front stabilizing bar, quad front heavy-duty shocks, heavy-duty rear shocks), GT bar, and the white wagon-wheel–styled wheels in place of the steel wheels with Sport wheel covers, with 10x15 tires. In short, the Free Wheeling B package was akin to a sport and handling package for the Bronco with the items it added to the truck.

For 1982, Ford renamed the packages: Custom became Standard and Ranger XLT became XLT Lariat. (Seemingly unsure of what to call the top-of-the-line trim package, the XLT Lariat moniker lasted only two years before becoming simply the XLT in 1983. The XLT reigned supreme for two years before being supplanted at the top in 1985 by what became the most well-known trim package in modern Bronco history, the Eddie Bauer.)

The Free Wheeling packages disappeared and were replaced for two years by the XLS package. Included with the changes in the trim packages for 1982 came the only real styling change in the seven-year model run for the third-generation Broncos.

Ford changed the Ford badging on the front of the truck by removing the FORD letters from the leading edge of the hood and replaced them with a prominent Ford oval in the center of the grille, an aesthetically appealing upgrade that was timed perfectly with Ford's increasing use of the Ford oval in its advertising. The grille was changed to have 16 openings instead of the previous 24. The Bronco badges on the front fenders received an updated font and the Ford oval badge replaced the FORD letters on the left-hand side of the tailgate.

XLS

Regarding the XLS, the 1983 Bronco brochure stated, "This youth-oriented Bronco is a real head-turner with eye-catching blackout treatment and special XLS tape striping. Black low-mount Western swing-away mirrors and argent styled-steel wheels add finishing touches to the unique exterior. Interior comfort is well provided for with XLT level seats and full carpeting. XLS adds finishing touches all its own with brushed aluminum appliques on the instrument panel and steering wheel. Bronco XLS, the sporty way to go, either on or off road."

In addition to the black mirrors, the XLS also sported black bumpers and a black grille, along with black gloss treatment on the windshield molding, headlight trim, door handles, locks, and window moldings. The blacked-out treatment and brushed-aluminum interior highlights were a foreshadowing of vehicle treatments 25 to 30 years in the future. Unfortunately, buyers in the mid-1980s weren't interested in such vehicle aesthetics, and the XLS package was rarely seen on 1982 and 1983 Broncos, even when new.

Eddie Bauer

Eddie Bauer was an outdoor retailer that had provided top-quality outdoor gear for enthusiasts since 1920 from its headquarters in Washington state. Bauer held the patent for the quilted down jacket, among other inventions in his long business life.

In what was one of the most unusual and ultimately successful pairings in automotive history, the Eddie Bauer name was added to the Ford Bronco line as the top trim-level package available.

On the outside, the trucks featured a unique two-tone paint treatment not available on other trucks: a Light Desert Tan stripe ran across the lower edge of the body and fenders along with a matching top. The main body color was a contrasting shade: most often Bright Canyon Red, Raven Black, or Dark Charcoal Metallic. Rolling stock was argent styled steel wheels and the spare tire had a special tan tire cover.

On the interior, occupants were coddled in dual front captain's seats with special velour upholstery with forest motifs in the backrests, a matching flip-and-fold rear seat, and privacy glass. When you left the comfortable confines of your Eddie Bauer Bronco, you were reminded that you owned one as you slung an Eddie Bauer garment bag over your shoulder and carried your Eddie Bauer tote bag in your hand.

The Eddie Bauer Edition Bronco became a popular trim package. The two-tone paint combinations, in particular, have stood the test of time well.

Colors

The available colors on the third-generation Bronco once again covered a wide-ranging spectrum with 19 offered for 1980. The fiberglass roofs were offered in 6 colors for even more combinations.

Two-tone paint jobs, Tu-Tone in Ford parlance, were still popular and Ford offered them in three formats. The simplest was an accent tape stripe down the side of the body that matched the fiberglass top color. The Deluxe Tu-Tone had the accent coloring the body side panel. And the fanciest of the three, the Victoria Tu-Tone had the accent coloring on the front of the roof, hood, around the door window, and covering the lower body side. Other than the most basically equipped Custom Broncos, most had one of these two-tone combinations.

By 1986, the last year of this generation, 11 body colors and 4 top colors were on the option sheet. The decreasing number of color choices mirrored the trend among other automotive manufacturers of narrowing the number of choices available on the option sheet, which in turn lowered inventory and production costs.

Tires and Wheels

As the new decade dawned, the Bronco's tire and wheel choices displayed continuity with those offered at the end of the previous decade. Namely, the base offering was steel wheels with optimistically named "bright" hubcaps. Options were the commonly optioned painted white spoke wheels, aka wagon wheels, often shod with Goodyear Tracker A-T 10x15 all-terrain tires in the early 1980s.

Vehicles more for street use had the 10-hole polished forged aluminum wheels. The fancier hubcaps were called Sport Wheel Covers. The option of five-slot brushed aluminum wheels, commonly called slot mags, was still available.

The year 1982 brought P-series radial tires to the Bronco line for the first time, much to buyers' delight, as they appreciated the better ride that radials offered over bias-ply tires. Forged-aluminum wheels disappeared in 1982, as the slot mag style faded in popularity. In their place was a cast-aluminum wheel. Joining the lineup for the first time was a steel argent wagon-style wheel with a bright trim ring that ultimately proved to be popular with this generation of truck, particularly as it was standard on the Eddie Bauer trim-level Broncos in later years.

Bearing an eerie resemblance to John Travolta, this caballero looks ready for something standing next to the Ford Bronco Montana Lobo concept vehicle in 1981. Built on a 1977 Bronco chassis and shown at the 1981 Chicago Auto Show, Lobo was a two-seater with a mixture of traditional (winch behind the foam front bumper) and outlandish (the removable plexiglass doors and airfoil). (Photo Courtesy Ford Motor Company)

A stainless steel 102-inch whip CB antenna was de rigueur in the age of CB when the Montana Lobo was built. Handy storage boxes are mounted at each rear corner of the bed that featured a retractable loading ramp. The large rear window offers an open feeling between the cabin and the rear compartment. Not visible is the digital dash and ventilated seats. (Photo Courtesy Ford Motor Company)

Most serious Bronco prerunners have their spare tires mounted inside, and this one is no exception: a large T-handle attaches it to the rollcage. A form-fitting cage with padding for the passenger's head and "taco" gussets at some of the corners indicate that this is a serious and professional build. (Photo Courtesy Pete Olson)

The wheels options list followed the same path as the paint list, decreasing to just two steel-wheel choices in 1985: the white wagon spoke and the steel argent wagon-style wheel.

Production Numbers and Collectibility

After the stunning production numbers of the 1979 models (104,038 sold), the 1980 Bronco sales numbers took a deep dive, plummeting to 44,353 units. This must have been a bitter disappointment for Ford, particularly because the Bronco was a new model for the year. Factors affecting sales may have been the second oil embargo and a general slowdown in the economy.

Sales hovered around 40,000 units per year through the 1983 model year, reflecting the generally poor US economy during those years. In 1984, sales increased to 49,253 units; their best showing of the decade to date. Steady increases to 54,562 sales in 1985 and 62,127 Broncos in 1986 were encouraging, no doubt buoyed by an increasingly healthy economy, stronger engines, and the Eddie Bauer trim package.

Legacy

The 1980–1986 Broncos, particularly from the first several years of production, have not been popular with enthusiasts. Low-output engines with finicky carburetors and restrictive exhaust systems have given them an undesirable reputation with the general public, a situation in which most vehicles from the malaise era find themselves. As with all Broncos, their value has started to climb slowly in recent years, riding the coattails of their more popular cousins. In particular, the 1985 and 1986 Eddie Bauer Editions (the most likely to have received good care and maintenance) are becoming more sought after.

Up front, Vels Parnelli Jones Racing added another shock to each front wheel (for a total of three). They gusseted the radius arms and added Charlie Haga's Haga Balls in the springs as a form of secondary suspension. This was high tech for a build in 1984. (Photo Courtesy Pete Olson)

This 1984 Bronco was originally owned by Eddie Wachs, who spent $55,000 in 1984 to have it built and modified at Vels Parnelli Jones Racing. The engine, drivetrain, and interior were rebuilt and strengthened for the rigors of off-road use. (Photo Courtesy Pete Olson)

In the early 1980s, the next evolution of Ted Nugent's love affair with the Bronco developed and was documented again in a 1982 issue of Four Wheeler. This camouflaged monster was built for the Motor City Madman by Bill Stroppe's shop in conjunction with Ford Motor Company and Four Wheeler.

ON THE 8TH DAY, the gods created a man they told to have great wisdom; to teach our children good things with his ways and his rock-n-roll music; and to construct a four-wheel-drive transportation machine to help deliver the message to wherever he wanted to go. They called him..."Uncle Ted" Nugent.

By Duane Elliott
PHOTOS BY THE AUTHOR

Some of you may know him as the "Motor City Madman," "Uncle Ted," "Nuge," or just by the fury of his rock-n-roll music that always leaves you doing the "Wango Tango" when the songs are over.

But that's only half of the story. *Off-Road* heard of another side of Ted. One that was more down to earth than most people could ever realize; a side that tells of Nugent's efforts to help get kids off drugs and out into the woods to appreciate

life, and, a side that reveals Nugent's long-time desire to get down and get dirty in low-lock four-wheel drive with the rest of the guys. That is, if they could keep up with him!

Fortunately for us though, we

GOING GONZO... AGAIN!

...chase the "Weekend ...d his one-of-a-kind, ...'90 Bronco through ...nd swamps of his ...(because we would ...there!). Instead, Bill ...editor of *Off-Road*, ...drived our way into ...f the Zebra-striped

Bronco, strapped ourselves in, and got a first-hand view of how things worked—including the double live, 800-watt, JBL "Stormtroopin'" stereo!

THE SECOND TIME AROUND

This machine is actually a second-generation version of Nugent's "big-n-bad" '82 green and brown camouflaged Bronco that Bill Sanders, Bill Stroppe and Ford had helped build with Nuge back when it was new. This time around though, Ted wanted something really unique; he wanted to put a new body on the '82 chassis and rebuild the old chassis from the ground up. Not only

that, he wanted the B... up in a Zebra-striped... color scheme to match... of "zebra-camo Te... Wackmaster" bow hun... ment. (For more infor... cerning Nugent's huntin... door adventures, se... column in *Off-Road* be... the pages preceding this...

So once again he re... expertise of the Ford M... and they got the Carron... company that builds shou... side of Detroit for var... manufactures) to revitaliz... Ford into one of the wil... we've seen in a while.

Ted Nugent's 1980 Bronco, like the Motor City Madman himself, has evolved through the years. Originally built by Bill Stroppe in the early 1980s, it has sported several different camouflage paint schemes, suspension systems, and body panels through the years. It now wears body panels from a 1992–1996 Bronco. (TedNugent.com and Brown Photography)

LITTLE MULE

The 1980–1986 Broncos haven't had as much screen time as some of the other generations of trucks (particularly the first-generation models), but 1984's hit movie *Romancing the Stone* found a Bronco sharing the screen with its two high-profile costars, Michael Douglas and Kathleen Turner, for a few glorious minutes. The Bronco helped the two stars elude the evil Colonel Zolo and his henchmen while roaring through the jungles of Colombia. As with all good movie chase scenes, it culminated in a big jump, in this case over a river, which left the bad guys in the water.

Known as the *Little Mule*, the automotive star was actually three Broncos, as is often the case when vehicles are jumped and thrashed during the filming of a movie or television show.

According to the January 1985 issue of *Four Wheeler*, famed car customizer and painter Dean Jeffries was given the job of modifying three 1983 Broncos for the movie. Bronco 1 ended up being the camera truck, covered with mounts to film nearly every aspect of the vehicle. Broncos 2 and 3 were the stunt trucks; 3 was the primary rig and 2 was the backup.

The engines were gone through by Art Chrisman Special-

ties in Fountain Valley, California, to give the needed oomph for better performance. Upgrades included typical beefing such as a more aggressive cam, 4-barrel carburetor, and manifold and headers. In other words, it was a vintage 1980s build to wake up a smog-choked stock engine. B&M built the heavy-duty automatic transmission.

Each front corner had three Bilstein shocks and the rears had two each. Polyurethane engine mounts and suspension bushings were installed. Jeffries' biggest problem, according the article, was breaking stock bolts in the vehicle due to impacts, so every nut and bolt was replaced with Premier Supertanium fasteners, standard race car fare.

Cragar made special 15x10 steel wheels that allowed the 33-inch Goodyear Wrangler tires to be run at a low air pressure to help absorb the shock from the landings.

A coat of black paint, Hooker chrome side pipes, and a chrome brush and grille guard holding a Warn winch finished off the exterior modifications.

Supposedly set in Colombia, the actual shooting took place in Veracruz, Mexico. In addition to building the vehicles, Jeffries

LITTLE MULE CONTINUED

was also a stuntman, so he did the driving as well. Wearing Bell belts, a special vest, and sitting on a rubber, air-bag type of seat, Jeffries neared the river ramp at about 100 mph, which had a small kicker on it to lift the front of the

Bronco into the air to prevent an endo on the other side.

Success! It took only one take to capture the Bronco's jump and resulting 53-foot bounce on the other side. Both the Bronco and Jeffries were unscathed.

Jeffries continued his career until his passing in 2013, and according to the *Four Wheeler* article, two of the Broncos went on the Ford show circuit after the movie was finished. Their current whereabouts are unknown.

THE ■ LITTLE MULE

Romancing the Stone's workhorse Bronco

By Ken Koonce

"ROMANCING THE STONE"
Script written by Diane Thomas

145 EXT   **JUAN'S COMPOUND—DAY**   **145**

Zolo's Jeeps pull up and stop. Zolo and his men leap out and take positions on the upper patio in front of Juan's compound.
BLAM! A vehicle blasts through a shed's rickety doors, passing Zolo and his men. A super-charged Bronco done up in Western style, "The Little Mule" emblazoned on its doors, does an incredible wheely off the ledge of the patio onto the street below, which the death squad has just driven up. Zolo and his men scramble in confusion.

145A THE BRONCO   **145A**

The Little Mule blasts down the street.
JUAN
What do you think of my "Little Mule" now she's warming up?
JACK
(ad lib)
We're gonna run over those guys. Are you crazy?

154 INT. BRONCO   **154**

A river lies dead ahead
JUAN
See that river?
The Bronco quickly nears the river bank.
JACK
Juan, where the hell ya going?
JUAN
To "Lupe's Escape." I used it many times in the past.
He produces a small electronic box similar to a garage door opener, points it straight ahead.

155 RIVER BANK   **155**

road at the edge of the river a narrow steel lip lifts and drops into place, acting as a ramp, as giant grind it into place.

RONCO   **157**

ct to what seems to them a terrible oncoming crash. Juan casually points off screen.

VER BANK   **158**

visible at the last moment; the Bronco roars out to its edge and soars across the remaining gap.

ONCO   **159**

ds on the other side of the river.

One of 1984's hit movies, Romancing the Stone, featuring Michael Douglas and Kathleen Turner, also starred a Ford Bronco known as Little Mule. *The Bronco roared through the jungle, helping its human costars elude the bad guys, culminating in a big jump over a river.*

1987–1991: CLEAN AND AERODYNAMIC

For Ford, the 1980s was the decade of aerodynamics. Starting with the 1983 Thunderbird and continuing with the groundbreaking 1986 Taurus, front ends were rounded, headlights covered, and flanks smoothed in an effort to not only lower drag coefficients and raise fuel mileage, but also to create a more aesthetically pleasing package than the blocky, squared-off body shapes that had dominated Ford products since the 1960s. The Bronco was fairly square-cut for the first three generations as well, although the 1980–1986 trucks did receive some aero work as part of their development.

For the 1987 model year, Ford turned its attention to restyling the Mustang, the F-Series truck, and the Bronco. Like the Mustang, the Bronco received revised front-end styling, which was markedly smoother than its predecessor and visually more attractive. The sheet metal was more curvaceous, and the headlights were now flush-mounted to the grille and fenders, which helped create an aerodynamic look. The front bumper was a smooth-contour shape that wrapped around the front of the truck. The body received some minor sculpting along its sides, new taillight housings, and fender openings that helped complete the aero overhaul.

The headlights, in addition to directing airflow, were also easier to service than the previously used sealed-beam headlights. The new headlights consisted of a plastic housing with a replaceable bulb that was easily removed and replaced without the use of any tools and required no readjustment after the bulb was replaced. The grille now had three rows of cutouts, replacing the four-row version from 1986. Ironically, in spite of all this smoothing aero work, this generation is known today as the brick nose by enthusiasts.

The Alpine Green Metallic Eddie Bauer Bronco was a handsome unit as it splashed through this mountain stream in 1987, introducing the sleek, aerodynamically styled fourth-generation Bronco. Eddie Bauer Broncos such as this example have become more collectible in recent years, and values for clean examples are on the rise. (Photo Courtesy Dick Nesbitt)

The fourth-generation Bronco continued the use of large swing-away mirrors to view objects to the side and rear. All examples from the factory were chrome and offered excellent visibility. The swing-away feature was much appreciated by owners in tight quarters where tree limbs or other obstacles sometimes folded the mirrors back against the door with a resounding **thunk.**

Dick Nesbitt's Targa band design feature was still evident on Bronco roofs three generations after its introduction. In addition to being a styling feature, it also served a functional purpose by adding stiffness to a large, relatively flat surface.

Engine

For 1987, the Bronco continued with the same three engine offerings: 4.9 (300-ci) 6-cylinder, 5.0 (302-ci) V-8, and 5.8 (351-ci) V-8, as had been offered for 1986. However, the big news for 1987 was the introduction of electronic fuel injection for the 300 Six.

300

Like its V-8 brother, the 302, the 300's fuel injection was a multiport system with an injector at each cylinder, controlled by Ford's EEC-IV computer. Coinciding with the addition of fuel injection, the compression ratio of the engine was raised from 8.0 to 8.8:1 with a fast-burn cylinder head.

In addition to the greater reliability, easier cold starts, and better fuel economy offered by the fuel injection system, the 300 also really woke up when injection was added. Horsepower jumped from 120 hp in 1986 to 145 in 1987 and torque increased from 223 to 265 ft-lbs. Hydro-elastic motor mounts were added during the year, which reduced noise, vibration, and harshness (NVH). The 300 Six increased slightly in its horsepower rating (5 hp) for 1990, as long as an axle ratio other than 3.08:1 was selected. Otherwise, it remained unchanged for the fourth-generation's run.

302

The 302 (5.0 liter), which had received electronic fuel injection a few years earlier, continued without changes. Magazine testers at the time noted that the 5.0 was plenty peppy in most situations, although they admitted that if you were going to get a V-8, there wasn't much of a reason not to order the 5.8. As multiport fuel injection was still relatively new on the scene, they also noted that the engine compartment was a "snakes nest" of hoses and wires compared to those of carbureted or throttle-body-injected engines.

351

In 1988, the last carbureted holdout in the Bronco family, the 351, finally received electronic fuel injection to control its fuel delivery. As with all of Ford's other fuel-injected engines, it received multiport injection controlled by an EEC-IV com-

Underneath that maze of hoses, tubes, and wires is an electronically fuel-injected 5.0 V-8. Period magazine tests frequently commented negatively on the complexity of the engine compartment compared to the competition that used throttle-body injection systems, but the port injection system used by Ford proved to be superior in terms of overall efficiency. (Photo Courtesy Rosaleen O'Byrne)

puter. The Bronco's fuel injection systems were batch-fire (i.e., each bank of cylinders received an injection of fuel at once).

Unlike the 300 6-cylinder's dramatic power increases when it received injection, the 351's output ratings remained nearly the same: the horsepower remained the same at 210 and torque increased only slightly to 315 ft-lbs. With electronic fuel injection, the 5.8 also received a serpentine-belt front accessory drive, a welcome change from the old multiple V-belt system. Other than a change from a two-piece to single-piece rear main seal in 1990, the 5.8 remained the same throughout the life of the fourth generation.

Transmission

In 1987, transmissions continued to be the 4-speed manual transmission with the creeper or granny low first gear, the 4-speed manual with an overdrive fourth gear, the C6 Select Shift 3-speed automatic transmission (with the 351 engine), and the 4-speed AOD, available with the 5.0 EFI engine.

Many Bronco owners' prayers were answered in 1988 when Ford introduced a new series of truck manual transmissions. The new transmissions were both 5-speed manuals, known as the M5OD and M5OD-HD, respectively.

M5OD

The Manual 5-speed with Overdrive (M5OD) was manufactured by Mazda for Ford. The R2 variant was used in a number of Ford vehicles including Econoline vans, F150s, and Broncos. It featured an integral bellhousing and synchronized first gear along with a synchronized reverse gear, for which Mazda received a US patent.

The clutch was a 10-inch-diameter unit actuated by a hydraulic slave cylinder. The slave cylinder was mounted inside the bellhousing, which many owners found to be expensive to replace. Ratios were 3.90, 2:25, 1.49, 1.00, and 0.80:1 overdrive, with a reverse ratio of 3.39:1. The M5OD proved to be a worthwhile replacement for the 4-speed overdrive transmission with the additional gear between first and fourth gear adding versatility for street driving.

Due to the torque rating of the transmission, it was offered behind the 300 Six and 5.0 V-8 engines only. Although the M5OD has received some bad press regarding its strength over the years, many owners have found it to be a durable unit providing many years of reliable service.

M5OD-HD

The M5OD-HD, Ford's moniker for the ZF S5-42, was manufactured by the ZF Group, a German car parts company. The ZF was the replacement for the BorgWarner T-18 used in previous Broncos and featured a 5.72:1 low creeper gear

and a 0.76:1 overdrive fifth gear (the best of both worlds for many drivers). The good news surrounding the arrival of the M5OD-HD transmission was short-lived, however, as it was used in the Bronco for less than a complete model year and then behind the 300 6-cylinder engine only.

According to the 1988 Ford Truck Data Book, it was phased out before the end of the 1988 model year and replaced with its predecessor, the BorgWarner T-18 4-speed. Why it was so quickly removed from the options list in the Bronco remains a mystery, as it continued to be offered in several Ford trucks. The Warner T-18 4-speed stayed on the options list for 1989 and 1990 Broncos before disappearing from the factory offerings list for good.

E4OD

In the world of automatic transmissions, the AOD continued to be offered with the 5.0 engine. The 5.8 had the beefy C6 Select Shift 3-speed automatic through part of the 1990 model year when the Electronic 4-Speed Overdrive (E4OD) automatic transmission was introduced to replace it. The E4OD was available behind the 300 6-cylinder and the 5.8 engines.

Compared to the C6, Ford promised improved fuel economy, performance, and shift feel with the electronically controlled valve body compared to its vacuum-shifted contemporaries. For towing, the overdrive could be locked out via a button on the dash.

The E4OD continued in use in Broncos through 1996.

Transfer Case

Behind all of the transmissions offered for fifth-generation Broncos resided the BorgWarner 1356 transfer case, which, like the NP 208 that preceded it, was an aluminum-cased chain-drive unit with a planetary gearset mounted in front for the low-range gear reduction. In this case 2.69:1, slightly lower than the 2.61:1 ratio of its predecessor.

For 1987, a new option was the Touch-Drive electric shift transfer case option. Available that year only with the most advanced engine and transmission combination, the 5.0 EFI V-8 and AOD 4-speed automatic transmission, Touch-Drive deleted the floor shifter for the transfer case and replaced it with a small switch panel on the dash where the user pressed a button (marked "4x4") to engage high-range 4WD and another button (marked "Low Range") for low range. Four-wheel drive could be engaged or disengaged at any speed and was advertised as an "on the fly" system.

Although not many full-size Bronco owners found themselves scraping their transfer cases on rocks, the transfer case skid plate was an option for many years until becoming standard equipment for the 1988 model year. Reflecting the

Retained by five bolts, Ford's automatic-locking front hubs resembled regular locking hubs but lacked a knob and blatantly proclaimed that they were automatic! This example is on a 1988 Bronco.

increased sophistication (softening?) of buyers, automatic locking hubs became standard across the line for Broncos mid-year in the 1989 model year, regardless of whether they were equipped with Touch-Drive or not, and manual hubs became the option.

Axles and Brakes

Fourth-generation Broncos continued the use of the Twin-Traction Beam independent front axle and 8.8-inch rear axle of the previous generation. For 1987, the Twin-Traction Beam front end gained the ability for caster adjustability for the first time (previously it had been adjustable for camber only). Lubed-for-life ball joints were installed and twin-tube gas shocks were available to help better dampen the motions of the Twin-Traction Beam front axle.

A limited-slip differential for the rear axle was optional for all 1987–1991 trucks. The front limited-slip option, which had disappeared for the 1986 model year, again made it onto the option sheet for 1988. In 1989, the standard front axle rating increased from 3,550 to 3,800 pounds. Previously, the 3,800-pound rating had been used exclusively with the Snow Plow package.

As with the previous generation, magazine tests of the time raved about the front suspension's low-speed compliance and maneuverability while being less enthusiastic about the system's high-speed and on-road handling, noting steering vagueness, wandering, and some bump steer.

Anti-Locking Brake System

For 1987, the Bronco gained an important safety feature with the introduction of a rear anti-locking brake system (ABS), the first offered on a full-size SUV. Active in 2WD only, the ABS system used a combination of sensors, the vehicle's computer, and hydraulic pressure-control valves to modulate the hydraulic pressure in the rear brake lines. Pre-

mature rear brake lockup had long been a safety concern with short-wheelbase SUVs, so the ABS, despite its limitations, was a welcome addition. The computer continuously monitored the system and a light on the dash illuminated to notify the driver of a system malfunction.

The basic brake hardware was essentially unchanged from the previous generation. In fact, most of the components could be traced to the introduction of disc brakes on the 1976 model. For 1987, Ford switched from a cast-iron master cylinder to an aluminum-bodied unit with a translucent plastic reservoir with a screw-on cap so the brake fluid level could be checked at a glance, and the fluid topped off more easily.

Not one of its better ideas, Ford used a different type of locking hub and hub/rotor assembly (manual locking hubs only) on 1987 and early 1988 Broncos. Essentially a larger version of the pieces used on the Ranger and the Bronco II, the system used a flange-style locking hub that slipped onto a one-piece (aka top hat) hub and rotor assembly. The hubs were aluminum, so if bad wheel bearings or a dragging caliper caused excessive heating of the hub assembly, the plastic knob and/or the hub distorted, causing the hub to lock or jam. Ford issued a Technical Service Bulletin addressing the problem, but because replacement parts are rare and expensive, most owners have elected to convert their trucks to the pre-1987/post-1988 style of hubs and rotors.

Interior

The interior of the 1987 Bronco was updated to impart a smoother, cleaner design to go along with its new aerodynamic exterior. Gone were the squared-off edges and straight

Climate controls in the 1987–1991 Bronco were a mix of old and new. The layout was intuitive and easy to use. This was the last generation to use sliding levers instead of rotary knobs. This Bronco still sports its original AM/FM and cassette radio with digital tuning and separate controls for base and treble, balance, and fade. (Photo Courtesy Rosaleen O'Byrne)

The instrument cluster introduced on the 1987 trucks was more aerodynamic than its predecessor with more curves and fewer sharp corners. The A-frame steering wheel was used on a variety of Ford products at the time. (Photo Courtesy Rosaleen O'Byrne)

lines of the 1980–1986s. In their place was a new instrument panel with a curved shape that positioned the speedometer centrally in front of the driver for an unobstructed view. Standard gauges included fuel, oil pressure, water temperature, and ammeter. In addition to the standard backlit panel, the pointers on the gauges were now lit for better nighttime readability. The optional tachometer resided to the right of the speedometer when it was specified. Redundant warning lights for the engine temperature and oil pressure gauges were also part of the instrument cluster. Flanking the instrument panel were two air vents. If the Bronco happened to be equipped with Touch-Drive, that panel resided below the passenger-side air vent.

The center pod was revised with the radio and climate controls switching locations from 1986. The climate controls were now easier to reach, and the radio, although mounted lower than in previous years, was still not far out of reach. All radios for 1987 were now tuned electronically (the tuning dial became a thing of the past), and all of them featured digital clocks. Ergonomically speaking, because the radio didn't need to have a dial turned for tuning, its placement wasn't as critical as in years past. The AM radio could be deleted for a credit. The passenger had a new, small cargo shelf in front of him or her on top of the glove box, which was now larger than the one used in third-generation trucks and also removable.

The front passengers found themselves seated in either standard, low-back bucket seats, an optional front bench seat, or dual front reclining captain's seats (standard on Eddie Bauer, optional on XLT). If the captain's seats were selected, the popular center console between the seats with built-in cupholders was a popular option. Once again, three passengers easily fit

on the flip-and-fold rear bench seat that was also removable.

For the first time in 1987, tinted glass (albeit a light tint) was standard on the Bronco. If you went for the Privacy Glass option, rear passengers thanked you as the quarter windows in the hardtop were tinted a darker shade with a slight reflective hue to the glass.

Drivers with the Custom package gripped a black vinyl steering wheel with a new A-shaped center section. XLT and Eddie Bauer owners gripped a leather-wrapped steering wheel or an optional tilt steering wheel with the cruise control buttons on the center ribs of the wheel.

Trim Packages

The 1987–1991 Bronco came in three trim packages: Custom, XLT, and Eddie Bauer. The Silver Anniversary Edition and the Nite Edition also became available.

Custom

As you would expect, the Custom, which replaced the 1986 Standard Bronco, was the low-line version, featuring vinyl upholstery, vinyl floor mat, and color-keyed door panels. The Custom, as well as all other trim levels, now had black accents on the interior door handles, window regulators, door lock buttons, dome light bezel, and door scuff plates. In previous years, the lowest trim-line Broncos made do with a Bronco emblem on the front fenders. For 1987, even Custom vehicles had a trim badge below the emblem on the fender.

Driven by a third-generation Bronco enthusiast, this 1990 Bronco Custom calls Tucson, Arizona, home. Primarily used as a commuter these days, it's powered by a 5.0 engine and a 5-speed manual transmission. It features a few custom touches on both the interior and exterior, courtesy of the owner's grandfather. (Photo Courtesy Eric Zuercher)

And in case there was any question after 21 years of production, Ford added a 4x4 emblem under the driver's headlight.

XLT

"Bronco XLT is a good-lookin' truck, if you're in town or in the back forty. And it gives you all the equipment to make you feel at home in both places," announced the 1987 Ford brochure in describing the XLT package. The XLT package added an extra measure of luxury to the Bronco that was popular with many buyers. The Custom's black grille was replaced with a chrome version with bright surround around the headlights. The Custom had a chrome bumper but the XLT package added a black rubber rub strip that broke up the broad expanse of chrome and provided some measure of protection against light scuffs, etc. Additional brightwork included quarter window moldings, wheel lip, and lower body side protection moldings. Out back, the tailgate featured a brushed-aluminum applique.

Along with the sharp-looking exterior, XLT owners could bask in a comfortable, quiet interior that included color-keyed carpeting, a cloth headliner, and cloth sun visors. The door panels had cloth inserts and the stock seats had poly-knit cloth bucket seats standard or cloth captain's chairs as an option. In 1989, Ford revised the bucket-seat mounting bracketry to allow the front seats to tip and slide for better ingress and egress to the rear seat, a foreshadowing of appeasing customer desires that resulted in four-door SUVs. In the back, a rear cargo light made identifying items after dark a bit easier.

Eddie Bauer

For the Eddie Bauer Edition, Ford's marketing hype said it best, "If Bronco owners are special people, the Eddie Bauer driver is even more so. Eddie Bauer's list of standard and optional features is impressive. So impressive that one fact stands out: Whether it's the Grand Canyon in July, Mount Washington in December, or the Club on Saturday night, you're never out of place with the Eddie Bauer Bronco."

Eddie Bauer interiors are a lush and plush place to spend time. Comfortably padded velour captain's chairs with armrests, a lockable center console, faux wood accents surrounding the instrument cluster, thick carpeting, and power windows and locks ensure a pleasurable front-seat trip. (Photo Courtesy Rosaleen O'Bryne)

This 1990 Bronco XLT is a Dark Grey Metallic with a black fiberglass top for what Ford called the Two-Tone effect. Rolling stock consists of 31x10.50x15 tires on the 15x8 modular aluminum wheels that joined the options list in 1991. The sticker price was $22,516. (Photo Courtesy David Grinch)

Just in case there was any doubt, the person sitting in the passenger's seat of a fourth-generation Bronco knew he or she was sitting in an Eddie Bauer Bronco with this emblem attached to the dashboard. (Photo Courtesy Rosaleen O'Byrne)

The colored tree motif is in keeping with the outdoor theme of Eddie Bauer trucks. The velour-like upholstery did not prove to have long-term durability and few examples of this upholstery have survived in excellent condition. (Photo Courtesy Rosaleen O'Byrne)

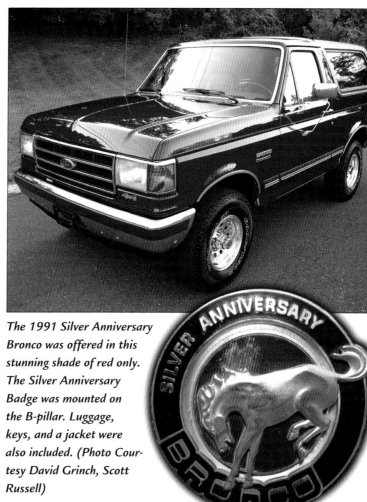

The 1991 Silver Anniversary Bronco was offered in this stunning shade of red only. The Silver Anniversary Badge was mounted on the B-pillar. Luggage, keys, and a jacket were also included. (Photo Courtesy David Grinch, Scott Russell)

Eddie Bauer models had dual reclining cloth captain's chairs with inboard armrests as standard equipment and covered in Eddie Bauer–specific upholstery patterns. The cabin received additional insulation beyond what the XLT package had for even more luxury. In 1991, front and rear carpeted floor mats with matching Eddie Bauer logos were introduced to coddle owners' feet. On the exterior, the Eddie Bauer package included the outside swing-away spare tire carrier with a Bauer-specific chestnut cover.

Silver Anniversary Edition

The 1991 model year also saw the introduction of two new trim packages for Bronco owners, each catering to unique demographics in the new decade. One catered to the more mature owner who loved tradition and favored a taste of luxury. The other targeted a younger owner who wanted a truck with modern graphics and colors that were in vogue.

It was the 25th anniversary of the Bronco, and Ford responded by offering a limited-production model called the Silver Anniversary Edition. The body and top were finished in Currant Red along with the rub strip on the front bumper. Adorning the body were Silver Anniversary front fender emblems, emblems on the B-pillar, and a Silver Anniversary logo on the outside spare tire carrier.

Inside, it featured charcoal leather seating surfaces with dark red trim, the first time leather was offered in a Bronco. The 22-ounce carpet was even thicker than that found in the Eddie Bauer Bronco, and special Silver Anniversary floor mats with silver lettering covered the carpet. Trim panels, dash, and door panels were of course color-matched.

The 5.0 engine was standard with the 5.8 as an option. Some sources state that production was split evenly between the two engines. In any case, befitting its status as the understated, most luxurious edition of the Bronco, the E4OD automatic transmission and Touch-Drive 4WD system were standard equipment. Rolling stock consisted of 31x10.50x15 Goodyear Wrangler Radials on the new-for-1991 forged aluminum modular wheels.

As with the Eddie Bauer Bronco, owners received special swag when they purchased a Silver Anniversary Bronco: a bag, a jacket, and Silver Anniversary keys announced to the world that they had purchased the ultimate Bronco.

Ford reportedly produced 3,000 Silver Anniversary trucks.

Nite Edition

On the opposite end of the spectrum was the Nite Edition Bronco. Based on the XLT Bronco, the Nite appealed to trendy, youthful buyers and truly was a truck for the early 1990s. The body and top were painted Raven Black and all the body trim was blacked out. A Nite decal in a period-correct font resided at the top rear corner of each quarter panel.

The 1991 Nite Broncos are rare; this Raven Black truck is an exquisite example of the model. With the exception of the chrome nerf bars, this truck is stock. The monochromatic black paint scheme with vivid contrasting color tape and decal scream early 1990s. (Photo Courtesy Jason Dougherty)

Dark Charcoal is the interior color of this 1991 Nite Bronco. The 1987–1991 door panels were more sculpted and aero-looking compared to the previous generation's panels. The door pull was similar and the power window controls were mounted lower, which sometimes came in contact with passengers' knees. (Photo Courtesy Jason Dougherty)

This 1990s-style (color and font) decal on the rear quarter panels was also a key visual identifier of the Nite package. This truck has Aegean Blue decals. (Photo Courtesy Jason Dougherty)

All 1991 Nite Edition Broncos had this Nite badge on the top of the dashboard in front of the front passenger's seat. Only 383 Nite Edition Broncos were built for the 1991 model year, making them extremely rare today. (Copyright Marti Auto Works, martiauto.com, and used with permission; Photo Courtesy Jason Dougherty)

Paint and Colors

For fourth-generation Broncos, colors and two-tone combinations displayed the greatest consistency year-to-year to date.

In 1987, Ford introduced a new color combination: the Two-Tone effect. This coloring scheme consisted of a solid body color with the fiberglass roof painted one of four colors. The top colors for the Two-Tone effect, as well as the other two-tone schemes were White (also called Colonial White), Light Chestnut (also called Tan), Deep Shadow Blue, and Black (also called Raven Black).

The exterior color palette consisted 11 colors for 1987, including an Eddie Bauer–specific Alpine Green Metallic hue.

A body side tape stripe ran the length of the body along the beltline. The stripes came in two colors: Aegean Blue and Azalea Pink. Aegean Blue–striped trucks had Crystal Blue and Dark Charcoal interiors. Those who opted for the pink stripe found themselves sitting in a Scarlet Red interior.

The dashboard on the passenger's side featured a Nite badge, and the floors were covered with color-keyed Nite floor mats front and rear. Rolling stock was similar to the 25th Anniversary Edition with the new, sharp-looking modular aluminum wheels shod with slightly smaller P235/75R-15 radials.

For 1988–1991, the choices were increased to 12 colors with the addition of Dark Chestnut Metallic.

In 1987, three interior colors (Regatta Blue, Canyon Red, and Chestnut) were offered. In 1988, a medium gray interior color option was added to the XLT trim level. For 1989, the medium gray was changed to dark charcoal, and those four interior colors continued through the 1991 model year.

In addition to the aforementioned Two-Tone effect paint scheme, Ford continued its offerings from previous years of the Deluxe Two-Tone and Victoria Two-Tone paint schemes. The Deluxe Two-Tone consisted of the accent color on the center body side area and tailgate between the mid-body side tape stripe and the lower body side protection molding. The rest of the body was covered in the body color. The Victoria Two-Tone included the accent color on the hood, upper fenders, around the door windows, and on the lower body side below the lower body side protection molding.

A popular option beginning with the 1990 model year was the 15x7 modular aluminum wheels. A classic design with fake rivets surrounding the inner perimeter of the wheel, the design is still popular. The five-bolt auto-locking hub is also shown on this Bronco. (Photo Courtesy Jason Dougherty)

Tires and Wheels

The base tire size for all Broncos of this generation was P235/75R-15 all-season radial tires with black sidewalls. The same size with outlined white letters was optional, as was an all-terrain tread pattern. For the ultimate in tire sizing, 31x10.50x15 all-terrain tires could be selected with all trim levels (Custom beginning in 1988).

By the late 1980s, the classic white-spoke steel wheels were starting to lose favor with buyers, both OEM and aftermarket, and Ford dropped them from the lineup for 1987. They continued with standard stamped-steel wheels that could be covered with Sport wheel covers (i.e., fancy hubcaps) as an option. Taking a lead from an option first introduced on Eddie Bauer Broncos, the top-of-the-line option became deluxe argent styled-steel wheels with chrome trim rings, a tasteful replacement for the white-spoke steel wheels.

In 1991, in conjunction with the introduction of the Nite and 25th Anniversary trucks, Ford for the first time introduced an aluminum modular wheel as an option on the Custom and XLT trucks. They were standard on the Eddie Bauer, Nite, and 25th Anniversary packages. With simulated rivets around the perimeter of the rim's center, the modular wheels proved to be a popular option and a timeless design that still looks good today.

Production and Collectibility

Despite its new good looks and additional powertrain upgrades, the 1987 trucks didn't sell as well as the 1986 models, with sales dropping to 43,074 units. That number proved to be the nadir of the decade, although 1988–1990 trucks sold at higher levels. Despite the introduction of the 25th Anniversary and Nite packages in 1991, sales plunged more than 50 percent from 1990 totals to 25,001 units.

Don Waldoch ventured into Broncos again in the 1980s with a run of John Elway Ford Broncos in 1989. Waldoch built between 6 and 10 of them and noted that they were not strong sellers, despite Elway's popularity at the time. Total sales matched (or nearly matched) the number 7 on Elway's jersey. (Photo Courtesy Don Waldoch)

Why such a precipitous decline? The United States was again in an economic downturn during this time, which hurt all auto sales. Beyond the economic situation, however, the answer can be seen in changing consumer tastes. The Bronco II had handily outsold its full-size brother for years, and the Bronco II's successor, the Explorer, was introduced for the 1991 model year. Offering better fuel mileage, and more important, four doors, the new Explorer proved to be an incredible hit for Ford, outselling the Bronco by 10 to 1 for 1991.

In terms of collectability, the 1987–1991 Broncos are climbing the desirability scale. They have performed yeoman duty for many years as daily drivers for families and young drivers, particularly young males. The 25th Anniversary models, in good condition, now command higher prices and desirability among enthusiasts. The relatively low number of Nite models produced has also made them desirable. Eddie Bauer and clean XLT versions are also gaining in popularity.

This beautiful 1988 Eddie Bauer Bronco now resides with its third owner. Sporting only 88,000 miles on the odometer, the previous owners used it as a vehicle at their second home in Lake Tahoe, Nevada. According to the owner, the 5.0 still purrs so smoothly you can hardly tell it's running. Retail price was just over $21,000 when new. (Photo Courtesy Rosaleen O'Byrne)

Sporting the latest in fashion, circa 1989, Denver Broncos' quarterback John Elway poses with a Waldoch Elway Bronco. The Elway Bronco featured a wide array of cosmetic upgrades while it remained stock under the hood. (Photo Courtesy Don Waldoch)

K Bar S was best known for its early Bronco parts business, but in later years, it sold parts for the later generations as well. This was its 1989 Bronco, which could go four-wheeling as well as tow a trailer with its race Bronco on it. This Bronco featured a supercharger and was also used as a guide vehicle for the K Bar S Nevada ghost town tours led by John Karp. (Photo Courtesy Ed Gudenkauf)

1992-1996:
THE FINAL LAP

"Ford engineers have kept the Bronco at the forefront of SUV technology, changing things that need to be changed and leaving the rest as it was."

In 1992, a recession was affecting sales, but there was another factor that was changing Americans' affection for large, two-door, V-8–powered 4WD SUVs: smaller sport utilities that offered better fuel economy and, more important, four doors. Ford's own Explorer outsold its bigger brother by more than 13 to 1 for the 1992 model year. Despite these sales disparities, the Bronco remained on the market for four more model years and continued to be the United States's best-selling full-size sports utility, as it had been since 1979.

By 1992, the Bronco had reached its zenith in terms of body shape, design, and general powertrain development. For its fifth and final iteration, changes were limited to small tweaks and changes in refinement and styling with some additional safety features along the way.

Ford called the 1992 Bronco "the smartest Bronco ever," a general statement that referred to several aspects of the truck, including its exterior styling. The new grille featured 12 openings, lending a cleaner look over the 1991 model's 16. The fenders and hood were revised slightly for a cleaner-looking front end. The flanks, doors, and top were the same, but new, aerodynamic side mirrors (manual were standard, electric were optional) added sleekness to the body.

Reviews

Phil Howell, writing in the July 1994 issue of *4Wheel Drive & Sport Utility Magazine*, summed up this generation of Bronco well when he said, "The Bronco has been around for a long time, and the bugs have been worked out of it . . . Ford engineers have kept the Bronco at the forefront of SUV technology, changing things that need to be changed and leaving the rest as it was."

With its Dark Toreador Red Metallic and Light Saddle Metallic Two-Tone paint glowing in a Ford press photo, this 1996 Eddie Bauer Edition of the Ford Bronco was a handsome rig. It had come a long way in 30 years since its introduction as a bare-bones roadster. (Photo Courtesy Dick Nesbitt)

A rare option seen only on the 1996 Broncos is this flashing-red turn-signal feature in the sideview mirrors. This installation was the first instance of the flashing arrows in a US vehicle and became a popular feature on many vehicles in later years. (Photo Courtesy David Grinch)

Engine

For 1992, the three engine choices that had been offered for the previous decade returned: 4.9 (300-ci) 6-cylinder, 5.0 (302-ci) V-8, and 5.8 (351-ci) V-8. Paired with an M5OD (Mazda R2) 5-speed manual overdrive transmission or the E4OD 4-speed automatic transmission, 1992 proved to be the 300's last showing in the Bronco and was in the Custom and XLT packages only.

From 1993 on, the standard engine across all trim levels became the 5.0 V-8. In 1994, the 5.0 received a bump in horsepower, rising from 185 to 205 hp. Curiously, published torque ratings declined, from 300 to 275 ft-lbs. For 1996, the ratings declined slightly to 199 hp and 270 ft-lbs of torque.

5.8 Upgrades

The optional 5.8 (351-ci) V-8 was rated at 210 hp through 1995, not much more than the 5.0. However, its torque rating of 325 ft-lbs made it a popular upgrade with many owners, and the 5.8 trucks command a premium in today's market due to their desirability. For 1994, 5.8 engines gained another desirable feature, a roller cam. Roller camshaft engines are desirable because of less wear and reduced friction compared to their flat-tappet cousins.

In addition, the 5.8 received an upgrade in 1995 (1996 for the 49-state versions) to a mass-air air-metering system for the fuel-injection system. It was a more precise method than the previously used speed-density setup.

In conjunction with the mass-air intake system, Ford also instituted an abbreviated onboard diagnostics engine management system (OBD-II) on the Bronco for 1996 (in 1995 for California vehicles). Mandated by the federal government for all 1996 vehicles, OBD-II allowed more complete monitoring of engine systems and sensors than the previously used OBD-I system and provided for common trouble codes across all platforms.

Like its smaller 5.0 brother, the 5.8's horsepower rating declined slightly for 1996 to 205 hp, but its torque output increased to 328 ft-lbs.

An engine block heater was optional on all engines across all years as well.

Transmission

Behind the engines resided the 5-speed manual Mazda R2 transmission, which had proven to be fairly popular in previous-generation trucks after it was introduced in 1988. It offered a nice balance of a reasonably low first gear for crawling along with an overdrive gear for lower stress highway cruising. The R2 continued to be the standard transmission through 1996. Not available behind the 5.8 V-8, the 5-speed used a 10-inch-diameter clutch when mated to the 4.9 Six and an 11-inch unit behind the 5.0L.

Despite the versatility of the 5-speed manual, most consumers opted for the automatic overdrive transmission, either AOD (1992–1993) or E4OD (all years), as more owners found themselves wanting greater luxury, comfort, and general ease in the driving experience. The automatic overdrive transmission had proven itself to be reliable by the time this generation of Bronco was released, and tow ratings were also much higher with the automatic transmission. Broncos with the 5.0 and 5.8 with automatics were rated to tow trailers weighing 6,600 and 7,100 pounds, respectively, compared to a 3,000-pound maximum rating with the 5-speed manual behind the 5.0 V-8.

The Trailer Towing package for the fifth-generation Broncos included a trailer wiring harness, heavy-duty turn-signal

For fifth-generation Broncos, the overdrive button was moved from the dash to the end of the column shifter. The button allowed the overdrive gear to be locked out in situations such as climbing steep hills or towing when the transmission's tendency to hunt for gears was annoying and put undue stress on the transmission.

flasher, rear stabilizer bar, quad front and heavy-duty rear shock absorbers, heavy-duty battery (84 amp hours, 850 cold cranking amps that was standard on Eddie Bauers), and Super Engine Cooling, which included an auxiliary transmission oil cooler with the automatic transmission and 5.8 V-8 engine.

Transfer Case

As with the previous generation, all transmissions were backed by the BorgWarner 1356 transfer case. Together with the front hubs, three 4WD actuation methods were available: standard were automatic locking hubs with a floor-mounted shift lever. Electric Touch-Drive, introduced on the fourth-generation Bronco, was again available and proved to be a popular option. For those who desired total mechanical control of their 4WD system and were touched with perhaps a hint of nostalgia for days gone by, manual-locking front hubs were an option with a floor-mounted shifter inside the cab.

One of the popular conversions with late-model Twin-Traction Beam Broncos is to convert them to solid-axle front ends. James Duff Enterprises has developed a Solid Axle Swap kit that allows incredible front-end articulation, as evidenced here on its 1996 Bronco company truck. (Photo Courtesy Suzanne Duff)

The Touch-Drive transfer case used in the 1992–1996 trucks was controlled by these two push buttons on the dashboard to the right of the steering wheel. 4WD could be engaged with the push of a button at speeds up to 50 mph. It was recommended that the vehicle be stopped to shift into low range. (Photo Courtesy David Grinch)

Axles and Suspension

The newly restyled Bronco continued the use of the old standbys in the axle department: Twin-Traction Beam Dana 44 independent front suspension and an 8.8-inch rear differential out back with available ratios of 3.08, 3.55, and 4.10:1. The limited-slip front and rear axles were still optional and when equipped, made for formidable traction capabilities in rough terrain.

Quad front shocks were still a popular option for the front suspension and Ford still found reasons to offer five front spring ratings for the front coil springs, corresponding to various engine and transmission combinations as well as options such as the Heavy Duty Service package, which included the quad front shocks and a rear stabilizer bar. The rear suspension was five-leaf springs with a 3,770-pound rating.

In 1993, Ford made a big step forward in the safety department by upgrading the Bronco's brakes from rear-wheel-only ABS (introduced in 1987) to four-wheel ABS. Advances in vehicle electronics made new technologies more powerful with each passing year. The addition of ABS hardware to the front wheels necessitated some design changes in the spindles that had essentially been the same since 1980.

Interior

Along with the new, sleeker exterior styling, Ford also modernized the shape and feel of the Bronco's interior for 1992. Gone was the A-frame steering wheel of the 1987–1991 trucks. In its place was a new steering wheel with a thickly padded rim and a center section that closely resembled that of other Ford products of the era; Ford referred to it as a half-moon design. The cruise-control buttons were more pleasing to the eye and had a better tactile feel than their predecessors as well.

The dash featured restyled gauges with oil pressure, water temperature, a voltmeter (replacing the ammeter), and fuel level to the left of the center-mounted speedometer. The tachometer, available on the XLT and Eddie Bauer, was located to the right of the speedometer. For the first time, a digital odometer was used in the instrument cluster, combining the odometer and trip odometer functions in a single gauge.

The air vents flanking the cluster were moved lower, and the headlight switch, wiper switch, and Touch-Drive buttons (if so equipped) were moved to the top. The overdrive button to control the automatic overdrive transmission was moved

It never got any more sumptuous than this. The leather interiors on the fifth-generation Broncos were a comfortable place to spend time. Thick carpeting, the leather-wrapped steering wheel, outboard seat belts in the rear, cupholders and ashtrays for the rear passengers, and a center console with cupholders for front-seat passengers were a far cry from the first Bronco interiors introduced 30 years earlier. (Photo Courtesy Dick Nesbitt)

For the 1992–1996 Broncos, Ford once again swapped the radio and climate controls from the previous two generations. Climate controls now consisted of three rotary knobs, and the radio had larger buttons than its predecessor. Barely visible is the Power Point (an additional auxiliary 12V port) a nod to the increasing use of electrical accessories in vehicles in the 1990s. (Photo Courtesy Ben Bauman)

The 1992–1996 instrument cluster is arguably the most handsome of all generations and still looks great today. It continued the theme of the third- and fourth-generations' clusters offering a speedometer, a tachometer, and four gauges. The digital odometer/trip odometer was a new addition to the cluster during these years.

from the dash to the end of the shifter on the column.

The climate controls and radio also switched places again, back to their 1980–1986 location with the radio on top; the radio now fed a four-speaker sound system. For the first time since 1978, the climate controls were no longer controlled by sliding rods but by rotary knobs. The three-knob setup controlling fan speed, temperature, and mode continued to be used on many Ford trucks long after the Bronco had been put out to pasture.

In lieu of the cigarette lighter, Ford now offered a Power Point electrical outlet, which was essentially a 12V power port with a cover. It was in recognition that consumers needed outlets for 12V electronics not a lighter for lighting tobacco products.

Leather Seat

Following the lead of the Silver Anniversary Edition available in 1991, leather seating surfaces were available for the first time in 1992 on the optional captain's chairs available in the XLT, Nite, and Eddie Bauer. In addition to the leather, the captain's chairs also gained power lumbar supports for the first time.

In the doors, the power window controls and power door locks were moved to a more ergonomically pleasing location, which eliminated complaints from the previous generation's placement, which seemed to draw inadvertent actuation from driver and passenger knees and legs. The door panels also received more modern styling. A popular new option was the Light and Convenience Group, which placed an updated console between the two front captain's chairs. The console, now more than just a large molded plastic bucket, had a built-in cupholder, coin holder, and cassette holder.

Reflecting Ford's continuing efforts with passenger safety, the rear-seat passengers (the outboard ones anyway) gained an additional measure of protection for 1992 with the addition of three-point safety restraints, replacing the previous lap belts. In addition, the plastic surfaces on the inside of the rear quarter panels were restyled for a more modern appearance, and outboard passengers now had their own ashtray and cup-

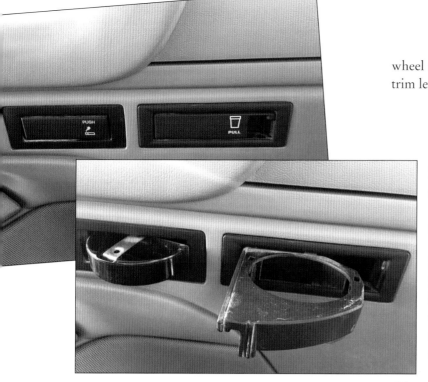

wheel rim (always black, leather-wrapped on XLT and higher trim levels).

Trim Levels

For 1992, Ford offered four trim levels for the Bronco (Custom, XLT, XLT Nite, XLT Sport) as well as the Eddie Bauer Edition.

Custom

The Custom was again the most basic with vinyl bucket seats standard with optional cloth and vinyl bucket seats or a cloth-and-vinyl bench seat. Full instrumentation (except a tachometer) along with interval windshield wipers also found their way onto the standard equipment list. The new aero-style external door mirrors were chrome but were manually actuated.

In 1994, the Custom became the XL package, and although the name changed, the standard features essentially remained the same for the rest of the years of the Bronco's existence. The Custom and XL package Broncos of this generation became long-serving staples of many municipalities and government agencies including the US Forest Service, which outfitted its rigs in the familiar Forest Service Green color.

XLT

The XLT package added significant standard features above that of the Custom including cloth captain's chairs (which included power lumbar), air-conditioning, rear

Rear-seat passengers in fifth-generation Broncos had allowances for two vices while en route. Swing-out ashtrays and cupholders were handy and did not intrude into the passenger's space when not in use.

holder. Both were plastic pieces that rotated out from the interior panel for use and sat flush to the panel when not in use.

In 1994, Ford upped the safety game even further by adding a standard driver-side airbag to the steering wheel, standard across all trim levels. The new wheel featured a larger center section to house the airbag, as compared to the 1992–1993 wheels with cruise-control buttons (when equipped) residing in the perimeter of the wheel inboard of the well-padded

The 1994–1996 Broncos sported this airbag-equipped steering wheel that also included cruise control and horn buttons. Wiper controls were moved from the dash to the turn-signal stalk in 1992. (Photo Courtesy Ben Bauman)

Seeing a sharp increase in value in recent years, this beautiful 1996 Bronco XLT with optional forged Alcoa wheels and BF-Goodrich All-Terrain tires represents the culmination of 30 years of Bronco production and the unfortunate consequence of forever being known as an "O. J. Bronco." (Photo Courtesy Mecum Auctions)

The XLT trim package featured cloth upholstery on the seats. The cloth upholstery did not prove to be particularly durable in Broncos and excellent examples like these are difficult to find today. (Photo Courtesy Ben Bauman)

window defroster, Privacy Glass, power door locks and windows, Light and Convenience Group, cruise control and tilt wheel, tachometer, AM/FM stereo with cassette player and digital clock, and argent styled-steel wheels. A color-keyed, two-piece full-length headliner helped insulate the top from exterior noises and added to the overall feeling of luxury.

XLT Nite

For 1992, the XLT Nite package returned for its second year on the Bronco trim package option sheet. Ford called it "a bold choice for 1992," a "mode for those of you who want something with a distinctly different appeal." Once again, befitting its name, the Nite truck came in Raven Black in blacked-out trim with exterior Nite decals, a black fiberglass roof, and special body side tape stripes with Aegean Blue with Crystal Blue and Dark Charcoal interior or Azalea Pink with a Scarlet interior.

In addition to the model-specific interior colors, passengers knew they were in a Nite Edition Bronco because the dash displayed a Nite badge and their feet sat on color-keyed front and rear Nite floor mats.

Nite Broncos had the 5.0 V-8 as the standard engine, forged-aluminum deep-dish wheels, and five P235/75R15 all-season tires with outlined white letters. The Nite trucks also had the Handling package (heavy-duty front springs, heavy-duty rear shock absorbers, 6450 GVWR, and rear stabilizer bar) and a black tire cover on the exterior tire carrier with the word "Nite" on it.

It doesn't get much better than this: a stealthy, well-built white 1996 XLT Bronco prerunner is on a camping trip somewhere on a gorgeous beach in Baja. (Photo Courtesy Kris Hernandez)

The 1992 Nite Bronco was a beautiful rig with blacked-out trim and era-perfect bright vinyl decals. The package was discontinued after 1992. (Photo Courtesy David Grinch)

XLT Sport

After the Nite package disappeared following the 1992 model year, Broncos did not offer a monochromatic paint scheme until the 1995 model year when the Bronco XLT Sport package was introduced. The XLT Sport was an exterior appearance package that featured a color-keyed grille, headlight surround, bumpers, and cab steps. The exterior door mirrors were black electric aero-mirrors.

The interior was that of the XLT model including cloth captain's chairs with power-adjustable lumbar supports and a tachometer. Ford proclaimed, "If you're ready to go 4-wheeling, it's ready and willing to go when you are." The XLT Sport was offered in Bright Red Clearcoat and Oxford White Clearcoat colors.

This popular package was available in 1995 and 1996.

Eddie Bauer

The top trim package was once again the Eddie Bauer. Like the XLT and Nite packages, the Eddie Bauer came standard with cloth captain's chairs with power lumbar support; leather seating surfaces were an option (also available on the rear seat). The four-speaker sound system and Light and Convenience Group were standard as were chrome electric aero-mirrors. The Light and Convenience Group, carried forward from the previous generation, consisted of interior amenities such as a headlights-on audible alert, underhood light, and dual-beam dome/map light.

In 1994, Ford added items to the passenger compartment including an electrochromic rearview mirror that automatically dimmed to reduce headlight glare, illuminated visor mirrors, overhead console, cargo net across the back of the truck, and retractable cover to hide the area between the back seat and the tailgate. The overhead console gave the driver additional information, such as outside temperature, a compass, map lights, garage door opener storage, and a storage pocket.

The auto-dimming rearview mirror, overhead console, and cargo net were optional on the XLT and standard on the Eddie Bauer. The year 1994 also marked the first time that an AM/FM radio with a CD player was offered as an option across the XLT and Eddie Bauer lines.

The Eddie Bauer package gained the cab steps in 1995 that were also introduced on the XLT Sport that year along with the so-called "turbo slots" in the front bumper. The latter gained their name from their use on the Ford Powerstroke turbocharged diesel pickup that was introduced around the same time. The slots effectively offered more exposed cooling surfaces on the front of the truck, a real asset for turbocharged vehicles. The XLT package gained the slots for the 1996 model year.

Deep-dish aluminum wheels were standard rolling stock, motivated by the standard 5.0 V-8 backed by the E4OD automatic transmission. In 1994, pursuant to federal regulations, the air-conditioning system on all Broncos was changed from R12 refrigerant to R134 in an effort to eliminate chlorofluorocarbons (CFCs) from the atmosphere.

Tires and Wheels

Standard for all fifth-generation Broncos were P235/75Rx15 black-sidewall all-season tires. A step up was the same-size tire in an all-terrain configuration with a slightly more aggressive tread pattern and tougher construction with white-outline lettering. The largest size available was P265/75Rx15 with white-outline lettering, the nearest metric equivalent to 31x10.50x15LT tires used in 1991.

Full-wheel hubcaps were finally gone during these years. The base wheels were still standard steel wheels in 1992, but in 1993 and beyond, the standard wheel became argent styled-steel wheels in a directional style with chrome plastic caps over the lug nuts and hubs. Optional was essentially the same wheel with a sharp-looking chrome finish. For Nite and Eddie Bauer versions, the standard wheel (optional on Custom and XLT)

This 1996 Eddie Bauer is an exquisite example with 223,000 miles on the odometer. It originally hails from Coeur d'Alene, Idaho, and is now with its fifth owner. Eighteen months of restoration work has netted a beautiful Bronco that the owner uses as a driver and cruiser.

was again the top-of-the-line forged aluminum deep-dish wheels.

In 1992 and 1993, these wheels resembled two-piece modular wheels with fake rivets around the perimeter of the center section. In 1994, Ford introduced a more modern version of this wheel: a one-piece forged-aluminum wheel manufactured by Alcoa for Ford. These wheels immediately became a consumer favorite for their looks *and* for their ease of cleaning compared to their predecessors, which had a multitude of cracks and crevasses to clean around the faux rivets. These wheels are still prized by Bronco enthusiasts for their classic good looks and strength and are often retrofitted to earlier generations of the Bronco and other classic trucks.

Forged Alcoa wheels were an option on the 1994–1996 Broncos. Because they didn't have rivets, they were easier to clean than those found on earlier Broncos. Their classic looks and strength have made them popular retrofits for other vehicles as well. (Photo Courtesy David Grinch)

Paint and Colors

For 1992, Ford offered 13 exterior colors across the various trim levels on the Bronco, up from 12 offered the year before. Although the Custom and XLT packages could be selected with all 13 options, the Eddie Bauer Edition was limited to 6 of those colors and the Nite was again limited to Raven Black, following Henry Ford's Model T axiom of "you can have it in any color you'd like as long as it's black." Interiors were again offered in 4 colors.

For 1993, Ford offered just 5 exterior colors but expanded the list again to 10 in 1994. With the Eddie Bauer secondary color now called Tucson Bronze, Eddie Bauer gained Desert Copper Clearcoat as a model-specific color for the first time. In 1995, Colonial White Clearcoat joined the list as an additional Eddie Bauer-specific color for that year only.

The 1992 redesign also brought changes to the paint schemes on the exterior of the Bronco. Since 1980, Ford had offered two two-tone paint schemes on the Bronco: Deluxe Two-Tone and Victoria Two-Tone. The Deluxe Two-Tone consisted of an accent color on the center body side area and the tailgate, between the mid-body side tape stripe and the lower body side protection molding. The rest of the body was the primary color.

For the 1992 model year, the body side Two-Tone replaced the Victoria Two-Tone. Whereas the Victoria included a wide swath of the body color on the side of the vehicle, the body side only had a small section of the body color above the mid-body side tape stripe. The accent color covered the majority of the body side, including the rocker panels. The body side Two-Tone was offered for the 1992 model year only, making it a rare sight on the road.

From 1993 to 1996, the only two-tone paint scheme offered (other the Eddie Bauer paint offerings) was the Deluxe Two-Tone pattern, and it was only offered on the XLT package.

Production and Collectability

The production total of 25,516 in 1992 was only a slight improvement over the abysmal 1991 numbers, which were the

A 1996 Bronco XLT Border Patrol Bronco is in a location far removed from the country where it earned its keep two decades earlier. The owner, a former Border Patrol agent, found his truck reduced to a dilapidated hunting truck in the southern United States. As part of the restoration, he recreated the rear window bars. It is one of 129 Broncos rebuilt in a 2001 $750 million program. (Photo Courtesy Ben Bauman)

This 1994 Bronco XLT eases down a rocky trail in the central Arizona desert terrain near Phoenix. Used primarily as a daily driver, it also sees occasional forays into the Arizona backcountry with friends. The previous owner, like many former Bronco owners, wishes he still owned it today. (Photo Courtesy Michael Bucher)

This 1994 XLT has nearly 150,000 miles on it and is the owner's daily driver. After the purchase in 2014, a significant amount of time has been spent restoring it cosmetically and mechanically. The owner's goal is to keep it as factory as possible. (Photo Courtesy Travis Muller)

these trucks in the western United States has been their repurposing as desert prerunners.

Desert Prerunners

As a vehicle model ages and examples become less ubiquitous in daily traffic, its use and owner demographics change as well.

The vehicles, after several owners and the passage of time, start to wear out with the inevitable higher mileage and reduced maintenance, whether due to financial constraints or general neglect. At this point, the car or truck usually experiences one of two scenarios: it eventually ends up in a junkyard or it's rescued by a collector or enthusiast willing to spend the time and resources to keep it on the road.

In the case of the last generation of the Ford Bronco, many examples have been rescued and repurposed into desert prerunners. What's a prerunner, you ask? As a member of a small automotive enthusiast subculture, it's a vehicle built to mimic a type of truck with a specific function in the motorsports world.

For many years, racers were allowed to travel a race course several weeks in advance of the race to learn the course and its intricacies so they would have fewer surprises on race day. In time, this became known as prerunning. The first prerunners were stock vehicles that the racers used to traverse the course. They might even be a street-legal version of the vehicle they raced. In recent times, racers have discovered late-model Broncos, specifically 1992–1996 models.

Off-road racing enthusiasts have known for years that the Twin-Traction Beam front end provided rugged dependability and a great deal of wheel travel at a reasonable cost compared to the more traditional torsion-bar and A-arm systems of competitive offerings. The stock Twin-Traction Beam offers about 8 inches of vertical travel in stock form; modified suspensions can offer 14 to 18 inches of travel with a few modifications. Longer and stronger shocks or a coil-over conversion, extended radius arms, and modified axle beams together increase the performance of the front suspension and drive axles.

For the rear suspension, leaf springs are usually upgraded to higher-leaf-count springs (similar to those used on race vehicles) for a more progressive rate, better ride, and more wheel

lowest since 1977. The nation's growing appetite for smaller SUVs similar to the Explorer and the continuing economic troubles contributed to the lower numbers. Totals improved slightly for the final four model years of production, ranging between 32,281 in 1993 and a high of 37,693 for 1995.

Collector interest in the 1992–1996 Broncos has increased markedly in recent years. Although many of the trucks have been retired from daily-driver duty, they have continued to be purchased by enthusiasts for use as relatively low-cost backcountry exploration vehicles. Higher-trim models, in particular the Eddie Bauer, in good condition and with lower miles have seen a significant increase in value. One popular use for

This 1992 Bronco is built as a desert prerunner with seating for four. Boasting a coil-over suspension, cut-and-turned Twin-Traction Beams, custom leaf springs, and a full roll cage, this truck is capable of traveling at high speeds in the desert Southwest and the Baja peninsula. (Photo Courtesy John Cole)

This 1994 Bronco catches air somewhere in Baja. The owner, a motorsports photojournalist, considers his Bronco one of his most important tools in his job. It allows him to travel with confidence far into remote areas to capture stunning race photographs along the course. (Photo Courtesy GetSome Photo)

travel. Shock absorber choices mirror those found on the front end: from a simple monotube shock absorber to the most exotic bypass shocks. The most serious trucks ditch the leaf springs altogether in favor of a system of links to locate the axle. Suspension on linked trucks usually consists of a coil-over shock absorber at each rear corner in conjunction with a bypass shock.

Another distinguishing feature of the prerunner Broncos is the bumpers. They're usually of a minimalist design and constructed of steel tubing. In this regard, they follow the design aesthetic of their more serious race brethren, where a bumper isn't needed for much more than some slight impact protection from other vehicles or perhaps an errant bush or two that might jump out.

As in a race truck, occupant protection is a key feature for most prerunner vehicles that are used for their intended purpose in the desert. A good starting point is a stout roll cage, usually constructed of 1.75- or

A well-built Bronco is also apparently a big draw for members of the opposite sex. A glance in the rear fenderwell reveals a forest of 2-inch-diameter remote-reservoir gas-charged racing shock absorbers to help dampen the motion of the leaf springs. This build philosophy was typical before the advent of larger-diameter shocks (2.5 to 3 inches) in recent years. (Photo Courtesy Junior Hinkle)

The rear axle of this 1996 Bronco prerunner displays plenty of beefing for its Baja sojourns. Large-diameter bypass shock absorbers are visible inboard of the frame rails. Long-travel leaf springs, with many more leafs than stock, are clamped to the axle with a heavy-duty spring plate, which also doubles as the lower mount for an axle-limiting strap, limiting the travel of the rear end. Wilwood four-piston disc brakes bring the axle to a stop; a Cone Industries full-floating rear end and 5/8-inch-diameter wheel studs ensure that the tire and wheel never part company. (Photo Courtesy Kris Hernandez)

Resplendent in its element, this 1996 Bronco XLT is affectionately known as Minty, a nod to its color as named by a previous owner and eagerly embraced by the current owner's daughters. It rides on 37-inch all-terrain tires mounted on 17-inch aluminum rims. Fiberglass additions to the body include front and rear fenders to accommodate the widened axles and the hood. (Photo Courtesy Sam Snyder)

2-inch-diameter tubing. Many Bronco owners find, with hard use, that the body's sheet metal in the cowl area cracks and tears, so bracing is added to the front of the cage, extending it into the engine compartment and encompassing the engine. The engine cage might also serve as mounting points for coil-over and bypass shock absorbers.

Because prerunners often travel in remote areas at night and at higher speeds than a regular Bronco, owners often add off-road lights. They sometimes add multiple individual lights or an LED light bar to the front bumper and to a roof rack if so equipped.

Many Bronco prerunner owners swap in aftermarket seats to replace the original versions. Suspension seats have proven to be extremely durable and comfortable. Some Bronco owners swap out the rear bench seat and replace it with a single suspension seat in the rear of the truck, turning their vehicles into three-seaters. In addition, the single rear seat allows for more cargo space, a welcome benefit on such a size-constrained vehicle.

Tires and wheels are also of prime concern for a Bronco prerunner. Impact absorption and ride comfort in rough terrain are key priorities for a vehicle that hits stuff. Broncos generally run 33- to 37-inch tires on aluminum wheels. Forged wheels are preferred for their increased strength, but many have no issues with cast wheels. Bead locks are often added to

the wheels to help keep the tire bead seated on the wheel during low-PSI operation.

For the late-model Bronco owner, the 8.8-inch rear axle is always a source of concern in terms of durability. Serious Bronco prerunners might have it replaced with a stronger 9-inch axle assembly from an earlier truck or custom unit. For the ultimate in strength, the owner may opt for a full-floating rear end, which removes the necessity of retaining the wheel from the axles from the axle shafts themselves and transfers that function to much stronger spindles and bearings attached to the axle housing

The growth of the Bronco prerunner movement has meant new life for many older trucks. It has grown to include an enthusiast base that's building more trucks every year. The lessons learned from these builds are good information for all late-model Bronco enthusiasts looking to improve their trucks for increased durability, safety, and usefulness, whether they're pounding pavement or cruising a lonely dirt road in Baja.

The popularity of the Ford Raptor has led to the development of Raptor-esque fiberglass for the fifth-generation Broncos. Here, Dick Gray airs out his Raptor Bronco somewhere in the wilds of Baja. (Photo Courtesy GetSome Photo)

THE O. J. CHASE

The murders of Nicole Brown Simpson and Ron Goldman on June 12, 1994, resulted in what some called the Trial of the Century. Central to the story was a car chase, probably the most famous car chase in US history, and the car being chased happened to be a Ford Bronco.

The famed football star–turned actor, O. J. Simpson, was the primary suspect in the murders of his ex-wife and her friend from the moment the bodies were discovered. However, it wasn't until the morning of Friday, June 17, 1994, that the Los Angeles Police Department announced that Simpson needed to surrender. Murder charges were filed and Simpson was scheduled to surrender by 11 a.m. that morning.

Simpson didn't surrender, and he was soon declared a fugitive after police were not able to find him at several locations. An arrest warrant was also issued for Al Cowlings, a friend and former teammate of Simpson's who had left the San Fernando Valley home with Simpson when he decided not to turn himself in.

Simpson's whereabouts were unknown, and at 5 p.m. that evening, Simpson's attorney held a press conference and read a note from Simpson that implied he was going to take his own life. At 5:51 p.m., Simpson placed a cellphone call that was traced to Interstate 5 in Orange County, California, near Lake Forest. Five minutes later, the California Highway Patrol (CHP) located and began pursuit of a white 1993 Ford Bronco with Simpson inside, owned and driven by Al Cowlings.

News helicopters swooped in, and within minutes, every network was broadcasting the white 1993 Bronco XLT cruising slowly along Southern California freeways with a phalanx of CHP cruisers following behind. Cowlings had called the CHP and asked them to back off, as Simpson allegedly had a gun to his head during the chase.

The chase lasted about two hours, and as news spread, people along the route came out on freeway overpasses and along the roadsides to witness one of the most surreal moments in American history. An estimated 95 million television viewers tuned in to watch Simpson, never visible in the Bronco, travel to the driveway of his Brentwood home where Cowlings parked his Bronco and they both surrendered to police.

So what happened to the Bronco? In 1995, Simpson's former agent Mike Gilbert and two partners reached an agreement with Cowlings to buy the Bronco for $75,000. Remarkably, it sat in a parking garage for the next 17 years.

In 2012, the Bronco went to the Luxor Hotel in Las Vegas as part of a memorabilia display. After four years, it returned to Gilbert's garage then resurfaced again in 2017 in an episode of *Pawn Stars*, where Gilbert offered the Bronco to host Rick Harrison for $1.25 million. Harrison ultimately decided to pass on the purchase, noting that defining the value for an item with such an unusual backstory is hard to determine.

As of this writing, the infamous Bronco is on display at the

Motorists wave at O. J. Simpson during the slow police pursuit along Southern California freeways. Simpson didn't see all the motorists though, as he was crouched in the backseat, talking on his cell phone to police and at times allegedly holding a gun to his head. The infamous white Bronco belonged to his friend Al Cowlings, who drove the truck on its 90-minute journey through Los Angeles. (Photo Courtesy Getty Images)

Today, the "O. J. Bronco" resides in the Alcatraz East Crime Museum in Pigeon Forge, Tennessee. Following its famous trip on the California freeways, it languished in a parking garage for many years, was on display in Las Vegas, and made an appearance on the Pawn Stars *TV show.*

Alcatraz East Crime Museum in Pigeon Forge, Tennessee, where the general public can view it. Approximately 20 miles have been added to the odometer since the chase.

The Bronco's association with O. J. Simpson has never been replicated in American history. There are other vehicle and personality comparisons: Porsche Speedsters and James Dean, Lincoln Continentals and John F. Kennedy, and green Mustang fastbacks and Steve McQueen, but none as strong as an early 1990s white Bronco and the former football player and actor. It was the moment when seemingly the whole nation learned what a Ford Bronco looked like, for all the wrong reasons.

More than 20 years later, people still make jokes about the "O. J. Bronco," and every Bronco owner has probably been the recipient of a wisecrack or two. Among enthusiasts, the 1992–1996 trucks are often referred to as an OJB (O. J. Bronco) as a way to identify this particular bodystyle.

1984–1990: BRONCO II: THE DEUCE

> "Bronco II has it all over the early Bronco in looks, convenience, and utility space."

The 1979 oil crisis had a huge effect on automotive manufacturers. As they observed the effects of high fuel prices and looked at their vehicle portfolios, it was painfully obvious that sport utilities were large, heavy, and used prodigious amounts of fuel. Small pickups from foreign manufacturers were starting to carve a serious dent in domestic sales and small domestic pickups were on the horizon to replace their badge-engineered brethren. And so, the events of 1979 birthed the Chevrolet S-10 Blazer, Ford Bronco II, Jeep Cherokee, and a few years later the Toyota 4Runner, Nissan Pathfinder, Isuzu Trooper, and Mitsubishi Montero.

The Bronco II was introduced in March 1983 as a 1984 model. Its family heritage was evident from its first viewing and *Four Wheeler* breathlessly proclaimed in its first article, "Ford has borrowed several good ideas from other 4x4s, combined them with some original ideas of its own and produced a vehicle that will turn heads and start tongues wagging wherever it goes." Comparisons to first-generation Broncos were inevitable and frequent. *Four Wheeler* continued in the same article, "Bronco II has it all over the early Bronco in looks, convenience, and utility space."

The Bronco II's wheelbase was 2 inches longer than its brother's at 94 inches. The early Bronco was slightly taller at 73 inches versus 69. The Bronco II was longer (158.4 versus 153.8 inches) and narrower (65 versus 69.1 inches). Compared to its contemporary Bronco, its wheelbase was 10 inches shorter, overall length was 19 inches shorter, 9 inches narrower, and 5 inches shorter in height. In addition to its smaller size, it weighed 800 to 1,000 pounds less than its full-size brother.

Due to its looks and suspension system, testers praised the Bronco II's truck-like characteristics, from its ride height to its handling, both on- and off-road. In comparison tests with other new down-sized 4WDs, the Bronco II was usually noted to have the firmest suspension ride and perceived ruggedness and durability.

Sporting a Deluxe Tu-Tone paint job, the 1984 Bronco II XLT was a stylish mode of transportation for this family of happy skiers. (Photo Courtesy Ford Motor Company)

Longtime Bronco vendor James Duff Enterprises branched out in the 1980s to include the new Bronco II in its suite of products. Duff bought a brand-new Bronco II in 1984 and immediately started using it as a product development platform. The little Deuce is still in its stable more than 30 years later and running strong! (Photo Courtesy Suzanne Duff)

1984–1988

Like the 1978–1996 full-size Bronco, the Bronco II shared its DNA with a pickup: the Ford Ranger. Known internally as the "Yuma" program, both vehicles were built at the Ford assembly plant in Louisville, Kentucky. The Bronco II shared the same front sheet metal (fenders, doors, and hood) with the Ranger, along with the front cab section. The vehicles were essentially identical from the B-pillar forward.

The Bronco II arguably had two generations: 1984–1988 and 1989–1990. From 1984 to 1988, the Bronco II grille had 21 openings with the small Ford oval in the lower corner on the driver's side. The first generation could be divided into two sub-generations; 1984–1985 trucks had a number of differences that separated them from 1986–1988 versions.

1989–1990

For 1989, the Ranger front end was restyled and the Bronco II followed suit. The grille and front end were given a more aerodynamic and arguably more handsome-looking nose with a grille having 16 openings. Matching the large Bronco and F-Series trucks, the Ford oval was mounted front and center. The vent windows in the doors were replaced with one-piece glass. The new front bumper was of a wraparound type.

The 1989 and 1990 Bronco IIs were slightly larger than the

preceding years: 161.9 versus 158.3 inches in length and 70.4 versus 68.2 inches in height (4WD models).

The 1990 model year marked the end of production for the Bronco II as it was discontinued to make way for its successor: the Ford Explorer. It was an abbreviated model year with production ending in January 1990.

Styling and Features

Aft of the B-pillar were two of the Bronco II's most distinctive visual features. Rather than

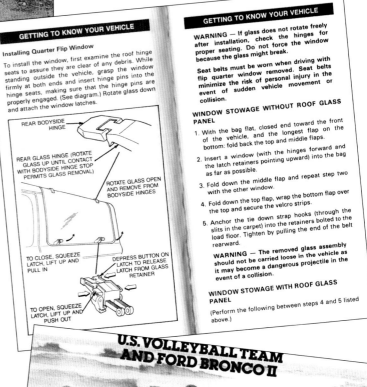

The 1985 Bronco II owner's manual devoted several pages to an option that never made it into production. Ford planned to make the rear side windows removable for an open-air feeling in the back. The ad shows smiling, happy people hanging out in the windowless openings but alas, consumers were never able to share in that joy in production vehicles.

a removable rear top similar to the full-size Bronco, the Bronco II sported rear side windows that curved up into the top of the roof for better visibility from the rear seat, a feature shared with the Dodge Ramcharger. Ford's early press releases and some Bronco II advertisements noted that removable side windows would be an option soon after production began, and the owner's manuals for some of the early years gave instructions on how to remove the windows if equipped with latches and hinges. But alas, some illustrations and instructions in the owner's manual didn't make it happen and the idea apparently never made it into production. Fears of water leaks and perhaps safety concerns doomed the idea.

At the rear, the traditional fold-down steel tailgate was replaced with a fiberglass one-piece liftgate. The lighter weight of the liftgate was made easier to open thanks to the use of gas-charged struts. As an optional feature in 1984–1985, the glass window in the liftgate was able to be opened separately from the liftgate. It also opened with the assistance of gas struts. The trucks with the opening rear glass did not offer the options of the rear window defroster or the rear window wiper.

The most popular exterior option was the swing-away rear tire carrier. The standard spare-tire configuration was inside the passenger compartment, but with interior space at a premium, the swing-away rear tire carrier was usually selected. An optional ski and roof rack also helped free up valuable interior space inside the small truck. A flip-open and removable sunroof was an option more popular in the early years. Bright low-mount Western swing-away mirrors were also a popular option, as the standard black door mirrors had poor visibility.

Engine

Unlike its Ranger cousin, which was offered with 2.0- and 2.3-liter engines, the Bronco II came standard with the engine that was also the top-level offering in the Ranger: the 2.8-liter Cologne V-6 (170 ci). Also offered were the 2.8 V-6, 2.9 V-6, and 2.3 turbo diesel.

2.8 V-6

The 2.8 was a V-6 with European roots, produced since 1965 in Cologne, Germany. It was among the first mass-produced V-6 engines and had a cast-iron block with cylinders cast in a 60-degree configuration. The engine was fed by a 2-barrel carburetor and had an 8.7:1 compression ratio. Although 115 hp doesn't sound like a lot, the engine's output received positive reviews in the early 1980s, when V-8 engines were producing only 30 to 50 more horsepower.

The 2.8's horsepower and torque ratings (150 ft-lbs) were similar to those of the 2.8 V-6 offered in the S-10 Blazer.

Although it was carbureted, the 2.8 was controlled by an EEC-IV system. According to Ford, the system offered self-test, spark control, battery charge control, programmed choke control, a knock sensor, and keep-alive memory. Generally speaking, the computer adjusted the air/fuel mixture and ignition timing for cold starts and constantly balanced the air/fuel mixture and ignition timing during operation for maximum power and efficiency. Although the system promised great results, these early attempts at electronic controls on the engine were often crude and didn't perform as advertised, particularly as they aged and accumulated many miles and years of use.

2.9 V-6

In 1986, the 2.8 was replaced by the 2.9 (179-ci) V-6, also from the Cologne V-6 family and was similar to the 2.8. It had the same bore (3.66 inches), but the stroke was increased slightly from 2.7 inches to 2.835 inches. It used a timing chain to drive the camshaft instead of the 2.8's gear drive, so the camshaft turned in the same direction as the crankshaft. The heads had a slightly different exhaust-valve arrangement and a three-port exhaust manifold.

The larger displacement brought more horsepower (140) and the torque increased (170 ft-lbs), thanks to the longer stroke. The compression ratio was also raised (9.3:1). The biggest change with the introduction of the 2.9 was the introduction of multi-port fuel injection. Although the 2.9 offered better drivability than the 2.8, it too was plagued with reliability issues as the engines aged, specifically cracked cylinder heads due to overheating and lack of maintenance.

The problems were addressed in late 1989 when a redesigned cylinder with better rocker bases was introduced. However, none of these heads made it into production engines before the Bronco II was discontinued; some were installed as Ford warranty replacements, according to the rangerstation.com history of the Bronco II.

Feeding the engine in all years was a 23-gallon fuel tank. A Super Engine Cooling package and engine-block heater were offered as options for the V-6 engine.

2.3 Turbo Diesel

A rare addition to the engine option list was a 2.3 turbo diesel, which became available for the 1986 model year and perhaps a portion of the 1987 model year. The engine, manufactured by Mitsubishi, made only 86 hp and 134 ft-lbs of torque, making it a poor performer in both performance and sales.

This is an exceptionally clean version of the 2.9 V-6 with EFI that was introduced in the 1986 models of the Bronco II. The 2.9 proved to be a better engine than the 2.8 that it replaced, although cracked cylinder heads were common as the engines aged. (Photo Courtesy David Grinch)

The Bronco II had a more sporting pretention with the automatic transmission shifter on the floor, something never offered on its full-size cousins. The transfer-case shifter was close at hand for those models that didn't have electronic shifting and was definitely more petite than those found in Broncos. (Photo Courtesy David Grinch)

Transmission

At its introduction in 1983, the Bronco II found itself at a point in mini-truck history where 4-speed manual transmissions were still being used, and for the 1984 model year only, the standard manual transmission was a 4-speed, made by Toyo Kogyo, with ratios of 3.96, 2.08, 1.39, and 1.00:1. A 5-speed manual with overdrive was optional and certainly the better choice with the fifth gear offering a 25-percent overdrive.

In 1985, the 4-speed was dropped and the 5-speed manual became standard. Toyo Kogyo, Mitsubishi, and Mazda made the 5-speeds used in various years. All the manual transmissions used a 9-inch-diameter clutch.

The automatic transmission offered in 1984 Bronco IIs was a 3-speed automatic transmission known as the C5. It was similar to the C4 3-speed automatic offered in 1973–1977 Broncos. The primary differences were in the hydraulic circuits, and the C5 had a centrifugal-locking torque converter, which did not require the use of electronics or hydraulics to actuate.

Early in the 1985 model year, Ford replaced the C5 with a 4-speed automatic overdrive transmission known as the A4LD, a French-built unit. It featured ratios similar to the C5 with a 26-percent overdrive ratio in fourth gear. The A4LD featured a torque converter that locked in fourth gear and the upper range of third gear, resulting in lower engine RPM, less heat, and greater fuel efficiency. Unlike the torque converter in the C5, the A4LD's torque converter locked electronically via signals from the EEC computer.

Until the Bronco II was restyled for the 1989 model year, all transmissions, manual and automatic, were shifted by floor shifters. The transfer case shifter, when so equipped, resided to the left of the floor shifter, regardless of whether it was an automatic or manual shifter.

Transfer Case

The Bronco II was offered as a 4WD during all years. Its standard, manually shifted transfer case was a BorgWarner 1350 2-speed unit featuring a 1:1 high range and 2.48:1 low range. Similar to the transfer cases offered in full-size Broncos, it was a three-piece, aluminum-cased unit with a chain drive and a planetary gearset for the low range.

Beginning in late 1986, the 1350 was offered with an electric shift option, called Touch-Drive. Offering the convenience of "shift on the fly" at any speed, the push-button controls were located in a pod in the roof between the sun visors until the 1989 redesign, when they were moved to the dash to the right of the steering wheel. An electric motor on the side of the transfer case handled the shifting between gears when commanded by the interior buttons. The Touch-Drive option required automatic locking front hubs.

From 1986 to 1989, the BorgWarner 1350 electric shift transfer case was used as part of the Touch-Drive system. In 1990 the BorgWarner 1354 electric shift transfer case was introduced and went on to be used in the Explorer.

Unlike its big brother, the Bronco II was also offered in a 2WD configuration starting in 1986. Their unusual feature

Axles

The Bronco II used downsized versions of the axles found on the larger Bronco and F-Series pickups. The front was a Dana 28 Twin-Traction Beam axle with a 6.625-inch-diameter ring gear (the Dana 44 Twin-Traction Beam used an 8.5-inch-diameter ring gear) and a rating of 2,640 pounds.

In 1990, the front axle changed to a Dana 35 Twin-Traction Beam with a 7.56-inch-diameter ring gear. The Dana 35 was used in Ford's Explorers and Rangers after 1990. The rear axle was a smaller version of the 8.8-inch solid axle used in the Bronco and had a 7.5-inch-diameter ring gear. The track width was 56.9 inches front and rear, compared to 65.1 of the full-size Bronco.

Limited-slip differentials were optional in both front and rear axles, through 1985, when the front limited-slip was discontinued. Available with various engine/transmission combinations through the years and also in California-specific configurations, axle ratios were 3.45, 3.73, and 4.10:1. Manual-locking hubs were standard and auto-locking hubs were an option with the floor-mounted shifter (through 1985) and standard when Touch-Drive was chosen as an option.

There was significant internal debate within Ford on whether to use the Twin-Traction Beam axles in the Bronco II or go with a more conventional MacPherson strut or SLA (short-long arm) suspension. Yuma Program prototypes had been constructed with MacPherson strut front ends. According to some documents, a group of engineers within Ford felt that it was a better system in terms of handling and rollover resistance. Ultimately, the decision was made to go with the Twin-Traction Beam front end. Some sources suggest that it may have been driven by a senior management's penchant for the Twin I-Beam front end (longevity and durability). Ford may have regretted that decision in later years.

Suspension

The front suspension consisted of a coil spring at each corner with a single, gas-pressurized shock absorber to dampen ride motions. The Bronco II never had the quad shock option that was so popular on the full-size Bronco. In the rear, single-stage leaf springs, mounted over the axle, provided the suspension with a single, gas-pressurized shock at each wheel. Front and rear stabilizer bars were standard.

2WD Bronco IIs were probably the only 2WD vehicles that had a transfer case, or at least a shell of one. In what must have been a cost-cutting move, Ford gutted the 2-speed transfer cases of the 4WD models and essentially used them as a spacer in the driveline, shown here with a large 8MA decal on it. (Photo Courtesy Zach Abbott)

The front ends of 2WD Bronco IIs were downsized versions of the F-Series Twin I-Beam front end that was also used on Ranger pickups. The beams were located by radius arms and the suspension used coil springs. (Photo Courtesy Zach Abbott)

was that they too had a transfer case, or something that looked like a transfer case. The unit, a BorgWarner 1359, transmitted power from the transmission directly to the rear driveshaft via a main shaft in the case. There were no guts to the transfer case and the front output shaft hole was covered. This was likely a cost-saving effort.

By using the dummy transfer case, Ford only had to use one transmission configuration, one driveshaft, and all the associated mounting brackets and hardware associated with the powertrain. Some Bronco IIs in 1990 had a more conventional 2WD configuration with an adapter on the back of a 2WD transmission that attached to the driveshaft.

Snow Plow Package

Following in the footsteps of the first-generation's utilitarian roots, Ford offered a Snow Plow package for the Bronco II through the 1988 model year. The package included heavy-duty front coil springs with rubber air bags in them, heavy-duty rear springs, and heavy-duty shock absorbers. An auxiliary transmission cooler and a 60-amp alternator were included. The front air dam was deleted, presumably because it interfered with the linkage of the plow. After the automatic overdrive transmission was added in 1985, it became a standard part of the package as well, along with P205/75R-15 raised white-letter radial tires.

Steering and Brakes

Power steering was standard, and the turning radius was an impressive 32.5 feet. Ford boasted that the steering linkage had rubber-filled ball sockets, which eliminated the need for periodic lubrication.

Power brakes were also standard for all years of the Bronco II with 10.9-inch-diameter discs in front and 9-inch drums in the rear. In 1987, Ford upgraded the brake booster to a dual-diaphragm unit and introduced rear ABS to the Bronco II. On 4x4 Bronco IIs, the anti-lock function engaged only when the vehicle was operated in 2WD mode.

Towing

The Bronco II could be ordered with a Trailer Towing package which allowed towing of trailers weighing up to 5,000 pounds, when equipped with the 4.10:1 axle ratio. The optional Trailer Towing package included Super Engine Cooling, a trailer wiring harness, heavy-duty turn-signal flasher, and an auxiliary transmission cooler if the automatic transmission was selected. The heavy-duty battery was also recommended for towing.

The option no longer appeared in sales literature after 1985, but the main key components, such as the 4.10:1 axle ratio, auxiliary transmission cooler, and Super Engine Cooling package remained on the options list if an owner wanted to configure his or her vehicle for towing.

Interior

The Bronco II interior was a familiar space to anyone who had sat in a Ranger pickup interior in the preceding year. As with the exterior, the interior forward of the B-pillar was essentially identical to that of the Ranger. For the 1984 model year only, the driver's hands wrapped around a four-spoke steering wheel described in a *Motor Trend* review, as "plainly plain and awful with a rim far too thin."

Ford used this steering wheel in the Bronco II until 1985 when it was replaced with the new A-frame wheel that was used by many other Ford products at the time. Like many early 1980s Ford products, you had to push in the turn-signal stalk to activate the horn, an oddity that most people didn't like. The wheel and general dash layout were shared with the Ford Ranger. (Photo Courtesy Suzanne Duff)

Beginning in 1985, the wheel was changed to the A-frame wheel used in other Ford vehicles. If the truck was equipped with the optional cruise control, the actuation buttons were located in the spokes of the wheel. Thankfully, the newer wheel had a thicker rim and a tilt-wheel option.

In front of the driver, two centrally located instrument dials afforded excellent visibility. The one on the left showing fuel level, engine temperature, oil pressure, and an ammeter. The one on the right housed the speedometer and odometer. *Motor Trend* described it as "typical Ford; pleasant if a bit bland," noting that there was no tachometer, a situation that Ford did not rectify until the 1986 model year.

The radio and climate controls were centrally located in the center stack and received good reviews for their placement and function. The Bronco II radio offerings reflected its era: simple radios with mechanical tuning in the early years moving to full-featured electronic controls by the end of the decade. Air-conditioning was an option for all years.

The glove box area had a unique arrangement, with a traditional locking glove box located below the centerline of the dash; above it was an open compartment for storage of readily accessible items. The aftermarket soon offered a mesh net for this area to keep items from bouncing out on rough roads.

Overhead, an optional console between the sun visors housed a digital clock and a pivoting map light. The console option went away when the Touch-Drive 4WD option was introduced in 1986, and the shift controls pod took over the console space.

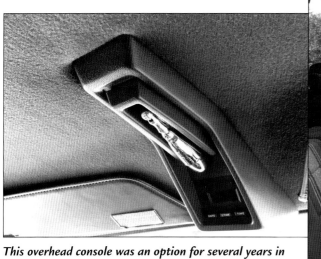

This overhead console was an option for several years in the Bronco II, and it included the folding map light and digital clock. The map light was made of chrome-plated plastic and broke easily. (Photo Courtesy Suzanne Duff)

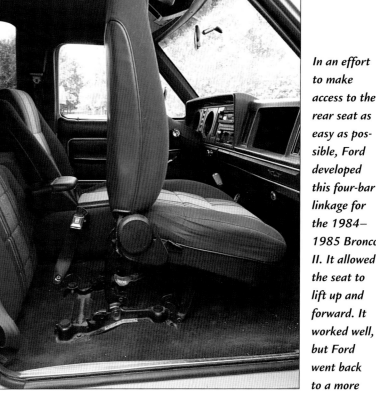

In an effort to make access to the rear seat as easy as possible, Ford developed this four-bar linkage for the 1984–1985 Bronco II. It allowed the seat to lift up and forward. It worked well, but Ford went back to a more conventional sliding linkage for 1986. The high-back buckets with a fairly soft, velour-like material were comfortable if not particularly durable. The flip-and-fold rear seat is also visible behind the front seats. (Photo Courtesy Suzanne Duff)

As part of the 1989 redesign, the dash changed to resemble the 1987–newer Ford full-size Bronco dash. The instrument panel had new foam-in-place construction to help eliminate noise. The instrument cluster gained a more open look with all the gauges mounted in one cluster behind a clear plastic cover. The fan control changed from a sliding lever to a circular knob. The open glove box binnacle was exchanged for a shelf on top of the area where the revised air vents now resided. The seating was updated with new standard high-back bucket seats and revised optional high-back captain's chairs.

The 1989 revamp also included a new molded headliner for increased noise insulation and better fit and finish, plus additional cabin noise reduction and insulation.

"The rather ordinary looking bucket seats are also surprisingly good" is how one road test described the Bronco II front bucket seats. Even the base-level seats had a reclining mechanism with a wide adjustment range. The base upholstery was a knitted vinyl with matching color-keyed vinyl door panels.

On the passenger side, 1984–1985 trucks had a clever four-bar linkage mechanism making the seat easy to lift up and flip forward for ease of access to the rear seat. Access still wasn't stellar, but it maximized the door opening area.

In 1986, the pivoting linkage was replaced with a simpler, sliding-track mechanism. In 1986, the Bronco II offered five-passenger seating for the first time with the introduction of a 60/40 front bench seat, upholstered in cloth, and a folding center armrest. The driver-side bucket seat gained a tip-and-slide function similar to the passenger-side seat in 1988, which helped access even more.

Eschewing the standard vinyl floor mat often found on lower-trim vehicles, the Bronco II offered a full-length, color-keyed, carpeted floor across all trim levels, although carpet delete (with a vinyl mat

The 1989–1990 Bronco II also adopted its revised dashboards, door panels, and seats from the Ranger. These updates for 1989 gave a much more modern appearance and feel to the dash. The revised door panels had a more integrated look and higher quality feel than those of the 1988-older trucks. (Photo Courtesy Gary Gayda)

A look inside the 1989 Bronco II shows the flip-and-fold rear-seat configuration that was available on 1989–1990 Bronco IIs only. The seat flipped down into a recessed footwell area behind the front seats, which freed even more cargo space in the rear. The retractable cargo cover, visible in the rear, helped shield items on the floor from prying eyes. (Photo Courtesy Gary Gayda)

Ford called this interior color Scarlet Red; others had less flattering names for it and it seems as if every other Ford made in the late 1980s had it. This interior is on an 1988 Bronco II, which has the newer A-frame steering wheel. The last year for this interior configuration was 1988. (Photo Courtesy David Grinch)

installed instead) was an option in 1984–1985. Rear quarter trim pieces were also color-keyed and offered ashtrays and padded armrests. Four coat hooks were standard across all models as were four color-keyed passenger-assist handles, one for each seat.

Overhead was a matching, cloth, color-keyed headliner that ran the length of the roof. It's no wonder that reviews of the period highlighted these features in stark contrast to the first-generation's more crude, utility-centric interiors.

The rear seat was another feature where the Bronco II was more versatile than first-generation Broncos as well as its contemporary full-size cousins. As a compliment to the standard carpeted floor, the backs of the rear seat were carpeted to match. Following the lead of subcompact cars, the Bronco II rear seat was a 50/50 split fold-down seat that offered more seating versatility.

In 1984, a rear-seat delete option could be chosen if a purely utilitarian configuration was desired.

In 1984–1985, dual captain's chairs in the rear were optional, with taller headrests than the standard split-bench seat.

With the restyle in 1989, the rear seats changed to a 50/50 split flip/fold configuration, which moved the rear seats up against the back of the front seats when desired, as in full-size Broncos.

Trim Levels

At its introduction in 1983, the Bronco II was available in three trim levels: Standard/XL, XLS/XLS Sport, and XLT. A

few months later, at the official start of the 1984 model year, these packages were joined by a fourth: the Eddie Bauer.

Standard/XL

The Standard trim level included many features beyond Ford's statement of the obvious: large vertical taillights! Halogen headlights and dual, outside, foldaway rearview mirrors were features appreciated by buyers. Chrome bumpers front and rear added a bit of flash; wheels were standard steel wheels with sport wheel covers.

Inside, front reclining bucket seats upholstered in knitted vinyl were standard along with color-keyed, vinyl door panels. The instrument cluster surround was a pewter-tone applique. The rear compartment was completely trimmed out with no bare-metal surfaces.

In 1987, the Standard was renamed to the slightly more regal-sounding XL. Tinted glass was standard on all the windows with a darker tint shade on the liftgate windows and rear quarter windows, a welcome addition considering the large area of glass in each.

Depending on the year in the 1984–1988 era, Ford offered flip-open, pivoting front vent windows as an option (or not available) in the Standard/XL trucks, reserving it as standard for the other trim levels.

In 1989, a floor-mounted heater vent was added for the comfort of the rear passengers.

XLS/XLS Sport

The sporty trim package for the Bronco II was the XLS; "Lean, clean, and slightly mean" in Ford parlance. Arguably the trim level that has aged the least gracefully since the 1980s, the XLS package was instantly recognizable thanks to its rocker molding, fender spats, and bold "XLS" graphics applied to the doors and rear quarter panels.

At the Bronco II introduction, many of the first road test vehicles and trucks featured in advertisements were XLS packages. Despite the frequent appearances of the XLS package in the press, few were sold and seeing one today is a rare sight.

The XLS tape stripe applied to the body was three colors. The lower door edges, rocker panels, front spoiler, and wheel spats were also a separate color than the rest of the body, matching one of the colors in the three-color hue of the XLS decal.

The grille and bumpers were blacked out. In 1984, the surround was also blacked out but for 1985, it received a chrome finish, offering a contrast to the black grille. Deluxe, cast-aluminum wheels were standard as were heavy-duty shock absorbers.

Inside, the XLS interior continued the sporty theme with fully trimmed cloth door-trim panels with the color-keyed molding, cloth insert, and map pocket. The instrument panel and the flocking in the storage bin above the glove box were color-keyed, and each model year received the deluxe steering wheel. In 1985, a tilt wheel, interval windshield wipers, and cruise control were standard with the package. As Ford sales materials proudly proclaimed, "XLS is Bronco II's sporting proposition."

The XLS disappeared after the 1985 model year, and the lineup lacked a sporty model until 1988 when a similar trim level called the XL Sport package entered the options list. Known as Preferred Equipment package 922A, the XL Sport package was offered from 1988 to 1990 and featured the Sport Appearance package, which included a brush/grille guard, fog lamps, wheel spats (revived from the XLS package), a black wraparound front bumper, and black tubular rear bumper with stone deflector. It also included a special two-tone paint treatment, a tachometer, and 15x6 cast-aluminum modular wheels.

Appearing first on the late 1987 trucks and optional with the XL Sport (and also the XLT) was the Sport tape stripe. It ran along the body side only with monotone paint in a horizontal pattern, and rose at an angle at the B-pillar, continuing toward the rear of the truck in a fading pattern. Sporting a heavy metallic finish, it was iridescent in sunlight and proved to be a striking pattern that has aged well, styling-wise.

XLT

Available across all years of the Bronco II, the XLT represented solid luxury and was, as Ford stated, "Beau-

tifully equipped for Value." The grille and headlight frames were bright chrome and a body side accent stripe ran the length of the truck. The bumpers were chrome with black end caps and the small, standard black mirrors were replaced with chrome, low-mount, breakaway Western mirrors.

Inside, the reclining front seats were upholstered in cloth and vinyl and the seat belts were color-keyed and had tension eliminators. In a step up from the Standard Bronco II, the door trim panels were trimmed in cloth and featured a swath of carpet on the lower section (matching the floor carpeting) as well as on the map pockets. An optional floor console featured a trash bin, cassette-tape tray, coin tray, two cup depressions, and a Graphic Warning Display Module, which had a number of lights that came on if you needed to add wiper fluid, fuel, etc.

Windshield wipers with variable speed control (standard on all models beginning in 1988), a leather-wrapped steering wheel, and sound insulation added to the feeling of increased luxury and comfort in the XLT. In the rear compartment, passengers were treated to integral, padded armrests (apparently passengers in Standard-trim Broncos had to make do with folding their arms), their own speakers, and behind the rear seat, a liftgate-operated cargo lamp along with three additional storage compartments in the rear quarter panels, including one that was lockable.

Eddie Bauer

In 1984, the Bronco II was the first vehicle in the Ford lineup to receive an option that became one of the best-known trim packages in automotive history: the Eddie Bauer package. The pairing of Eddie Bauer and Ford seemed unusual, yet natural, at the same time. Ford's marketing used phrases

This 1987 Eddie Bauer model is an excellent example of the top trim package for the Bronco II. This specimen sports a chrome push bar popular in the era along with aluminum modular wheels. (Photo Courtesy Mecum Auctions)

such as "Two names known for toughness and quality get together in the special Eddie Bauer Bronco II, a fine way to enjoy the great outdoors. Rugged Bronco II is field-tested and built-Ford-tough. Eddie Bauer survival gear has been field-tested, too; right to the top of Mount Everest!"

To differentiate it from other Bronco II trim packages, the Eddie Bauer Edition was always easily identifiable by its special Tu-Tone paint treatment with accent stripes. Cast-aluminum wheels and larger P205 all-terrain radials with raised white letters were standard. On some years, the outside swing-away tire carrier was standard on the Eddie Bauer; it was always an option on all the other trim levels.

Inside, standard dual captain's chairs in Eddie Bauer Tan were trimmed with special cloth-and-vinyl seat fabric and featured power lumbar supports and folding inboard armrests. Cruise control and a tilt wheel were standard in addition to all the XLT trim and courtesy lighting. Power window controls were also standard on the Eddie Bauer.

The icing on the cake for Eddie Bauer Bronco IIs was the special Eddie Bauer swag that was included with the vehicle's purchase. Depending on the model year, it included a large Eddie Bauer gear bag, a travel blanket with case, a visor organizer, map case, and a garment bag, all trimmed in tan or green cloth and leather.

Tires and Wheels

Standard wheels for Bronco IIs were 15x6–inch steel wheels covered with sport wheel covers. Usually seen only on the Standard and XL trucks, most buyers opted for these handsome choices.

Available through 1987 was a 15x6–inch four-spoke, white sport styled-steel wheel. The white color offered a 1980s vibe that fit well with the early years of the truck. The standard wheel on the XLT and the XLS for a number of years was the Deluxe wheel trim. It too was a steel wheel that featured an argent-colored center section with eight spokes and a bright trim ring around the perimeter, with bright lug nuts offering a nice contrast against a black hub cover.

The top-of-the-line wheels for all years were five-spoke cast-aluminum that still looks good today. They were standard on Eddie Bauer Bronco IIs and optional on all other trim levels. In 1988, these wheels were joined by another cast-aluminum offering: an aluminum modular wheel with 12 holes in the center section and faux rivets around the outer edge of the center section. Mirroring the popularity of this wheel style in the aftermarket at the time, Ford referred to them as "deep-dish" aluminum wheels. They were slightly wider than other wheels, 15x7 inches, and were standard on the XL Sport trim package and optional on others.

This optional five-spoke cast-aluminum wheel was the top of the line for all years of the Bronco II and is a sharp-looking, classic wheel today. (Photo Courtesy David Grinch)

From 1984 to 1990, the Bronco II was offered with two tire sizes: P195/75R-15 and P205/75R-15. They came in a variety of tread patterns in both raised-white-letter and black-wall configurations. All were of a radial-belted construction with both glass-belt and steel-belt construction.

Paint and Colors

When the Bronco II was introduced in 1983, it was offered in 15 colors. Six months later, when the 1984 model year officially began, that number was lowered to 12, where it remained through the end of production in 1990.

The Eddie Bauer package usually had one exterior color that was exclusive to that package and featured a special Two-Tone paint treatment with a chestnut color across the fender arches and lower flanks of the vehicle.

Mirroring the choices found on the full-size Bronco, the Bronco II was available with two-tone styles through 1986: Regular Two-Tone and Deluxe Two-Tone. The Regular Two-Tone featured an accent color applied to the lower body side and liftgate below the beltline crease. To help differentiate the color split, Ford applied a two-color tape stripe at the intersection of the two colors. The Deluxe Two-Tone featured the accent color applied to the mid-body side and liftgate below the beltline crease and above the rocker area. Two-color tape stripes were applied at the breaks in the colors.

From 1987 to 1990, the only two-tone color scheme offered was the Deluxe Two-Tone, arguably the better looking of the two color schemes and one that has aged well.

Production and Collectability

In terms of sales numbers, Ford hit a home run with the Bronco II, with first-year sales (a longer sales year due to the

Komfort Koach offered an add-on luxury package for Bronco IIs in 1985 that was available through Ford dealerships. Three exterior paint schemes along with a push guard, grille guard, custom wheels, and a rear continental kit were offered. In addition, fog lamps and an accessory known as a Magik-Rak (a multiple-purpose rack) were offered.

This 1989 Bronco II is a rare survivor whose use belies its splendid appearance. The owners are not afraid to exercise their steed on trails around Southern California and neighboring states. The 1989 and 1990 Bronco IIs adopted the revised front-end styling that was also used on Ranger pickups during those years. (Photo Courtesy Gary Gayda)

early introduction) of 155,311 units. For perspective, that's more than three times the number of full-size Broncos sold in the same year. For the rest of the Bronco II run, it sold between two and three times more units each year than its larger cousin, with an all-time high of 158,351 sales for the 1988 model year.

As for collectability, the Bronco II has ranked near the bottom of the Bronco world. Despite favorable comparisons to the first-generation Bronco at its introduction and many similarities, it has never caught on with collectors.

From the rear, the decals on this Bronco II bear witness to the various trails it's tackled over the years. It has the swing-away rear tire carrier, which frees up interior space for trail gear. (Photo Courtesy Gary Gayda)

BRONCO II STABILITY CONCERNS

The story of the Bronco II isn't complete without mention of the safety concerns and history of rollovers that dogged it from nearly the beginning of its existence. According to *Engineering Ethics: An Industrial Perspective* by Gail Baura, stability problems arose in the 1981 design phase and during verification testing in 1982. Engineering documents eventually revealed that the Bronco II stability index was too low compared to its competition. The stability index is calculated using several variables, including vehicle track width and center-of-gravity height. If a vehicle is too tippy, it has a low index rating.

During the Bronco II development phase, some rollovers were noted in the J-turn test and the accident-avoidance test. Concerns raised to management were countered by Ford's concern about time-to-market and, specifically, losing market share to the newly introduced Chevy S-10 Blazer, which is a typical engineering versus marketing conundrum.

Before Bronco II production began, Ford's General Counsel office collected more than 100 documents related to the vehicle's handling problems. Baura noted that 53 of these documents disappeared, a foreshadowing of lawsuits that came in later years. Some changes were proposed to help improve the stability index prior to its introduction, but no serious improvements were implemented.

In 1989, negative media attention increased with headlines in *Automotive News,* *the Wall Street Journal,* and *Washington Post* to go with a number of articles about unfavorable test results coming from *Consumer Reports* magazine. The National Highway Traffic Safety Administration (NHTSA) opened a formal study of the Bronco II in 1989. According to a March 16, 1989, article in the *Los Angeles Times,* 43 Bronco II single-vehicle rollovers caused fatalities, which was 19 of every 100,000 vehicles. After NHTSA determined its rollover rates were similar to other small SUVs, it closed its investigation.

A 1997 *Los Angeles Times* article noted that 260 people had died in Bronco II rollovers and disclosed that Ford had paid about $113 million to settle injury and wrongful-death lawsuits (including a suit by jockey Willie Shoemaker). The largest single payout came in the form of a $62.4 million case, according to a 1995 article in *Automotive News.* Ford settled a class-action lawsuit with owners by providing new safety warning decals, owner's manuals, and videocassettes to educate the owners. In addition, Ford agreed to pay owners $100 toward the replacement cost of worn-out shock absorbers.

In time, the memories of these Bronco II tragedies have faded and were overshadowed by the infamous Ford/Firestone debacle in the next century with Explorer rollovers. The design debate was not resolved until the introduction of a newly redesigned Explorer in 2002.

BRONCOS IN COMPETITION

"Almost from the moment the Bronco was introduced, Ford made sure that it was fielded in off-road races in Western states and the Baja California peninsula."

"Race on Sunday, Sell on Monday." It's an old adage from the glory days of the American car industry that held true for many years. Fans and buyers went to showrooms and purchased cars based on what happened at the racetrack the preceding weekend.

Although the saying is most closely aligned with sports car and passenger car sales, it also held true to a degree with the Bronco. No other off-road utility vehicle has been tied so closely to off-road racing. Even today, more than 40 years after the Bronco ended its dominant reign in Baja, the racing lore from those early years is one of the key memories that enthusiasts cite when talking about their love and admiration for the trucks.

In addition to its feats in the desert, the Bronco has also seen competition, and success, in other areas of motorsport, including autocross, sand drags, mud bogs, monster trucks, drag racing, and off-road racing.

Autocross

Autocross? In a Bronco? A narrow track width, short wheelbase, and a high center of gravity are not on your usual wishlist for an effective autocrossing machine. But Bill Kinsman has given it a go anyway. After all, his mantra is, "It's really all about having fun with cars."

The Southern California resident has owned an early Bronco for many years and wanted to build a version of his favorite vehicle to carve the corners on courses

By 1966, Bill Stroppe had a fleet of racing Broncos and was on his way to developing his reputation in off-road racing. Featuring V-8 engines and hopped-up 6-cylinder engines, these Broncos were an impressive sight when they rolled up to a race on the back of Stroppe's transporter. (Photo Courtesy Motor Trend Group LLC)

Sand Drags

Broncos competed for many years in sand drags and in sand and gravel hill climbs such as the infamous Gravelrama in Cleves, Ohio.

This is probably the only autocrossing early Bronco in the country. The owner has competed in numerous competitions at the Goodguys hot rod shows in the Southwest for several years. His truck is a 1972 Bronco frame and body with a Mustang II front end. Power comes from a Ford Explorer 5.0 junkyard engine backed by a T-5 5-speed transmission. It has almost 50/50 weight balance and weighs around 2,900 pounds. (Photo Courtesy Terry Lysak)

at Goodguys hot rod shows and other venues. His truck certainly gets attention in a field of Camaros, Corvettes, and Mustangs.

Kinsman started with a 1972 Bronco and retained the frame and uncut body. Because 4WD was no longer needed, he jettisoned the front axle and the transfer case, removing hundreds of pounds in the process. In its place he installed a Mustang II tubular front end with Mustang Cobra disc brakes, sway bar, and coil-over shocks. The disc-brake Explorer rear end is suspended by a custom three-link suspension with coil-over shocks.

For motivation, Kinsman swapped in a 1996 Explorer 5.0 EFI V-8 with a mild cam. The transmission is a T-5 5-speed manual. Fuel is stored in a Harmon Racing Cells fuel cell. Rolling stock is obviously much smaller and stickier than a regular Bronco's tires: low-profile Falken tires mounted on American Racing Wheels. The Bronco weighs about 1,000 pounds less than its stock 4WD counterpart, which helps immensely with acceleration and braking on tight courses, although Kinsman admits he's always thinking about more tire and more horsepower.

As a nod to his favorite Bronco racer, Kinsman plans to eventually build a *Big Oly*–style wing for the top of his roll cage and add an *Oly*-style wrap.

Kinsman has been racing the Bronco for three years and finished first or second in class in most of his outings.

Charlie Erickson's trick 1966 Bronco sand dragster was capable of mid-5-second times for a 100-yard run, traveling at speeds of up to 80 mph; not bad for a 170-ci 6-cylinder! Traction was delivered via 11-inch-wide Goodyear Blue Streak grooved sand tires. Erickson hated decals on his rig and painted the interior and exterior a bright white color.

A pioneer in the sand drag world was Bronco salesman Charlie Erickson. He started selling Broncos at Ken Roggy Ford in La Puente, California, when they were introduced and later became the Bronco specialist at Fairway Ford in Placentia, California. For years, his smiling caricature was a fixture in off-road magazine ads.

Erickson built a 1966 Bronco for sand drags soon after the Bronco was introduced. His Bronco was not only special because it was one of the first, prettiest, and fastest ones built but because of his choice of powerplant. Most drag machines have a powerful V-8 to propel the vehicle down the drag lane. Instead of a V-8, Erickson chose a 170-ci 6-cylinder as the stock engine. Internally, he beefed it with stronger pistons, moly rings, and a ported and polished head. A Moon cam actuated the valves. Fuel was supplied by two Stromberg carburetors feeding a Paxton supercharger. Erickson used a stock 3-speed transmission backed by a chain-drive single-speed transfer case that sent power to all four wheels. This powertrain setup was stout enough for times in the mid-5-second range for a 100-yard run, topping out at speeds of up to 80 mph!

Rolling stock was 15-inch-wide Goodyear Blue Streak 11x16 grooved sand tires. Erickson eschewed decals on his rig and painted both the interior and exterior white. He drilled holes in the frame to keep weight down, along with replacing the front fenders with fiberglass units.

In 1967, Erickson won the Pismo Hill Climb and the San Jacinto sand drags. He repeated both of those wins in 1968, and in 1969 he won the Oceanside Drag Championships. In 1970, he sold the truck to Utah resident LeRoy Page, who continued to race it for many years at sand drags and snow hill climbs in Utah. In 2011, the Page family, led by LeRoy's son, Brian, restored the truck to its original configuration and showed it at a number of western car shows. Today, the truck remains an integral member of the Page family.

Erickson's 170-ci 6-cylinder still looks good today. It also moves the Bronco smartly thanks to some trick internals and that big Paxton supercharger forcing air into it.

Restored in 2010–2011, Charlie Erickson's former race Bronco is resplendent in its original white color sans any decals, as Erickson didn't care for them. The wide Goodyear tires helped him move through 100 yards of sand in just over 5 seconds.

Monster Trucks

In the 1980s, that uniquely American phenomenon known as monster trucks took hold, and Broncos were not spared from its influence. Each of the three generations produced at that time had a representative in the genre.

The recipe for a monster truck in those days was pretty simple. Stock frames were sometimes used with the smaller 48-inch tires, but a new or secondary frame of much larger tubing was usually constructed to handle the stress of the 2.5- or 5-ton military axles and tires up to 73 inches in diameter. Heavily arched, stiff leaf springs were used at each corner with a forest of hydraulic shock absorbers attempting to provide damping duties. Most of the trucks had four-wheel steering.

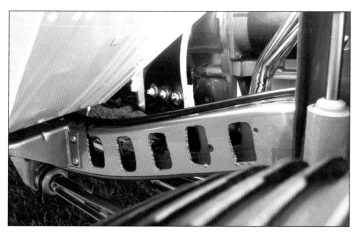

Charlie Erickson was serious about cutting weight from his sand dragster. Visible here is the frame rail with some serious chunks of metal removed. He also cut out pieces of the radius arms.

The first third-generation Bronco built into a monster truck during the 1980s craze was Desert Beast, a 1981 XLT Bronco sporting 48-inch Goodyear Terra tires with a blown 427 Ford turning out 800 hp under the hood. Owner Gael Morgan claimed 15-second times to 100 mph.

HORSE POWER

Bustin' Bronco

THREE BOBTAILS BUILT FOR BATTERING By Eric Borsum

In every job that must be done there is an element of fun. Once you find the fun, the job's a game. Charles Flynn knew his job was going to be fun. The Alabama off-roader began his Bronco buildup with the desire to own the world's tallest bobtail and ended up with a '74 Ford monster known as Hog Machine. Dennis Edmonds and Mark Bontrager followed suit with a '69 Bronco and an '84 Bronco II respectively. Their 4x4s may not be as tall, but they're exceptional pieces of equipment. These three heavy horses are some of the finest in the land, so get ready to enjoy a lot of horse power.

HOG MACHINE

HOG MACHINE

The Southern monster gets bigger

Text and photos by Michael Bargo Jr.

Down in Henagar, Alabama, anything that likes to keep its nose in the mud is called a "hawg." It's not surprising that Charles Flynn's 1974 Bronco-turned-monster is called the "Hog Machine," a 12½-foot-high mechanical mud chewer on 74x44x32-inch rubber that digs its way through the thickest muck to be found in the South or anywhere else.

Two things are particularly impressive about the Hog. The first shock of the vehicle is its height. At 12½ feet tall, one of the tallest of all monsters. The second thing is a head-scratcher: since the Bronco looks virtually identical to a stock 1974 model, one has

Left and Facing Page: Hog Machine was likely the most famous of the Bronco monster machines. It received the most magazine coverage by far. Owner Charles Flynn of Henagar, Alabama, added a separate subframe under the stock Bronco frame to keep the 73-inch Goodyear tires in check. The bobtail behemoth was powered by a 454-ci Chevy engine.

The powertrain consisted of a high-horsepower big-block engine topped with multiple carburetors and more often than not a supercharger. Transfer cases were often salvaged from the same trucks that donated the axles. A wild paint job, a phalanx of lights, some strategically placed chrome accessories, and voila, you had a fire-breathing car-crushing beast. Sadly, many of these monster trucks did not survive. The *Showtime* Bronco monster truck has recently been recreated by its original owner.

Drag Racing

The desert wasn't the only place that Broncos played in the early days. For a brief time in the mid-1960s, famed drag racer Doug Nash enjoyed his Bronco a quarter mile at a time at dragstrips throughout the country. He did well enough with it that many enthusiasts still remember the unique dragster today.

When the Bronco was introduced for the 1966 model year, Nash was 24 years old, and he had already raced 10 Ford and Mercury drag racers according to the November 1966 issue of *Car Craft*. Assistance from the Ford Truck Division is mentioned in period articles, but the company's specific contributions to the project are not known.

Nash tried to keep the weight low for the best possible horsepower-to-weight ratio. To that end, Nash and fabricator Tom Smith constructed the chassis and roll cage from aluminum. The main frame rails were a wispy 1.5x3 inches, and the roll cage was constructed with 2x0.125-inch-thick tubing. The front axle, radius bars, steering linkage, and spindles were steel and suspended by coil-over springs. The front axle was constructed from 2-inch-diameter tubing with a brace on the underside for additional strength.

The rear end, a 9-inch Ford housing pirated from a 1966 Galaxy 427, was narrowed, equipped with 4.57:1 gears, Airheart disc brakes, suspended by Air Lift bags, and located by a Watts linkage and trailing arms. The

Showtime was a 1978 Bronco monster owned by Brian Shell. Like other monsters, it followed the theme of a big-block engine (514-ci Ford) topped by a blower and large-capacity carbs. A forest of shocks and twin steerable 5-ton axles gave it excellent maneuverability. (Photos Courtesy Marty Garza)

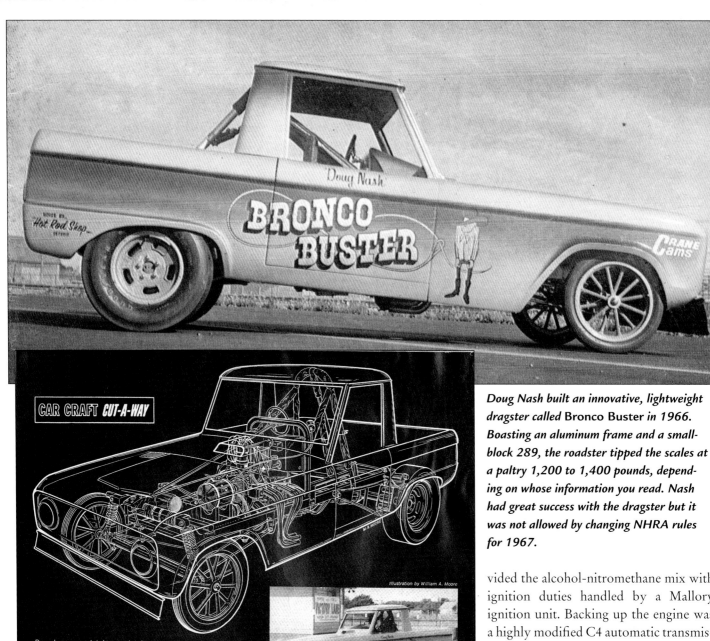

Doug Nash built an innovative, lightweight dragster called *Bronco Buster* in 1966. Boasting an aluminum frame and a small-block 289, the roadster tipped the scales at a paltry 1,200 to 1,400 pounds, depending on whose information you read. Nash had great success with the dragster but it was not allowed by changing NHRA rules for 1967.

CAR CRAFT CUT-A-WAY

Illustration by William A. Moore

Based on a completely new aluminum chassis assembly, Doug Nash's super-lightweight match race car is the wildest. This fiberglass-bodied Bronco pickup sports a healthy fuel-burning, injected 289 cubic inch mill, and has blasted the quarter mile in nine seconds at speeds above 150 mph on initial trial runs. Weighing in at only 1400 pounds, the beautiful "Bronco Buster" delivers an excess of "ponies" to those big Goodyears through a racing Cruise-O-Matic.

resulting 57-inch rear track width was similar to the production Bronco, although the wheelbase was lengthened to 112 inches.

The front wheels were 12-spoke American magnesium models carrying motorcycle-size tires. Out back, Halibrand mags were shod with 9x15 Goodyear drag slicks.

According to several sources, Nash was offered a 427 SOHC engine for the dragster but turned it down for a "little" 289 instead, as he was familiar with the engine and it weighed a lot less than the 'Cammer. The block was O-ringed and an aluminum main support girdle was added for the crankshaft, but otherwise the block was stock. Custom rods, pistons, and cam were used inside. A Hilborn fuel-injection system pro-

vided the alcohol-nitromethane mix with ignition duties handled by a Mallory ignition unit. Backing up the engine was a highly modified C4 automatic transmission from a Mustang, again chosen for its weight advantage over a C6.

The body, which mimicked a Bronco half cab, was a custom fiberglass unit by Walt Phillips. It was a two-piece affair with the front clip and cab flipping forward to allow access to the engine and passenger compartment.

When completed, the Bronco tipped the scales at a feathery 1,200 or 1,400 pounds, depending on the source. His early runs were in the 9-second range at 160 mph. Later, after adding a supercharger, he was able to eke out an 8.33-second run at over 181 mph.

Bronco Buster and other vehicles like it were outlawed for the 1967 season when the NHRA nixed both Funny Car pickups and aluminum-framed dragsters, so the squirrelly colt became obsolete. The car was sold; according to some online posts by Nash's daughter, the body ended up in a Detroit junkyard. So, alas, *Bronco Buster* is no more.

Off-Road Racing

Almost from the moment the Bronco was introduced, Ford made sure that it was fielded in off-road races in Western states and the Baja California peninsula. Ford knew that it had a willing and able partner in Bill Stroppe, who was matched with Ford racing giant Holman & Moody when the Bronco was introduced.

Bill Stroppe

Stroppe had first raced in Mexico in the La Carrera Panamericana races in the 1950s, achieving great results with a team of Lincoln sedans that he built and raced for the luxury division of Ford. He impressed Lincoln brass, not only with race wins but with his level of vehicle and team preparation and ingenuity in vehicle builds and pit-stop execution.

When the Bronco was introduced, Ford summoned Stroppe to Dearborn to pick up the remains of numerous test rigs to build into race Broncos. Willie Stroppe fondly recalls traveling to Detroit with his father and visiting the infield of Ford's Dearborn Proving Grounds to pick up the Broncos.

From those test vehicles, Bill Stroppe built several race Broncos with both 6-cylinder and, later, V-8 engines. Stroppe hired Ray Harvick of Hemet, California, a well-known Ford West Coast stock car racer, as his first driver. In November 1965, 6-cylinder Broncos took first and third places in the hill climb and second place in the obstacle course and drag races in Afton Canyon in California.

This cabin of a racer illustrates the utter starkness of one of the early Stroppe racers. The stock instrument cluster is still in place, but all climate controls, windshield, and the floor mat have been removed. A lone tachometer and one other gauge resides in the dash and the 3-speed column shift has been moved to a Hurst floor unit. A fire extinguisher is barely visible on the passenger's floorboard. (Photo Courtesy Motor Trend Group LLC)

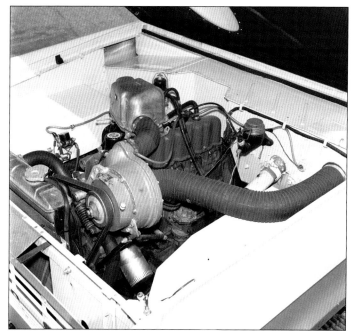

This is an impressive 6-cylinder racing engine in one of Stroppe's racing Broncos. Even the 6-cylinder could move the bobtail with some authority thanks to the supercharger residing on the front of the engine. The air intake has been moved to the passenger compartment; it was a move that became one of the hallmarks of Stroppe's later builds. (Photo Courtesy Motor Trend Group LLC)

One of Stroppe's earliest race trucks was Ray Harvick's Bronco, shown here with its Riverside Grand Prix wins noted on the rear quarter panel. This truck had molded-in rear fender flares, a Hurst floor shifter, and high-flotation tires on steel wheels. Note that the stock rear fuel filler is still in place. (Photo Courtesy Motor Trend Group LLC)

CHAPTER ELEVEN: BRONCOS IN COMPETITION

In the mid-1960s, California Jeep dealer Brian Chuchua began holding races in the Santa Ana river bottom in Riverside, California. Called the Riverside Grand Prix, the courses were brutal, featuring bumpy straightaways, at least four water crossings per lap, steep drop-offs, and short sandy climbs. Vintage movies show drivers bouncing like rag dolls while their vehicles leaped and jumped across the rough terrain at almost unmanageable speeds.

Stroppe entered Broncos in the 1966 Grand Prix, just days after the official introduction of the 289 V-8 in the Bronco and won first place finishes in both the 6-cylinder and V-8 classes. Harvick, driving the 6-cylinder Bronco, won the Top Eliminator Award and took home the top prize: a brand-new Jeep CJ-5. Ironically, in the 1967 event, Carl Jackson, who later drove for Stroppe, won the event in his Jeep and took home a new Bronco as his top prize.

Stroppe's Broncos competed in the Grand Prix event for several more years, with Ray Harvick and Larry Minor winning many top honors.

National Off-Road Racing Association

In 1962, motorcyclists Dave Ekins and Bill Robertson completed a publicity run down the length of the Baja Peninsula from Tijuana to La Paz, Mexico, finishing the journey in less than 40 hours and gaining publicity for Honda's new dirt bikes in the process. Ekins's and Robertson's run also caught the eye of other adventurers who wanted to set records traversing the peninsula. After completing the trip in 1966, Ed Pearlman decided to hold a race from Tijuana to La Paz and

The second Stroppe Bronco entered in the 1967 Mexican 1000 was driven by Cliff Brien and ace fabricator Dick Russell (Russell is sitting in the passenger seat). Note that the drivers are riding on stock 1966 Bronco seats. A small shield has been installed above the front bumper to protect the radiator. A radiator screen was also installed. The rocker exhaust was a feature carried over from Stroppe's stock car racing days and was incorporated on other Stroppe racers. (Photo Courtesy Motor Trend Group LLC)

Stroppe Bronco race driver Larry Minor leans into the driver compartment of the 1966 Bronco that Ray Harvick and Bill Stroppe drove in the inaugural NORRA Mexican 1000 in 1967. Harvick sits in the driver's seat wearing an STP jacket. These early race trucks were surprisingly stock in their setup. Note the lack of fiberglass flares on the rear of the truck; the flares are molded into the metal. (Photo Courtesy Motor Trend Group LLC)

This was the Stroppe Racing Team at the 1967 NORRA Mexican 1000. Left to right: Cliff Brien, Dick Russell, Bill Stroppe, and Ray Harvick. Russell went on to build Big Oly for Parnelli Jones a few years later. Harvick was Stroppe's first Bronco race driver and also drove Ford stock cars on the West Coast. (Photo Courtesy Motor Trend Group LLC)

This is what that pristine, shiny Bronco looked like at some point during the race. During my 2006 interview with Harvick, he recalled how he and Stroppe rolled the truck, got lost, and generally had all kinds of crazy adventures on their run in the inaugural Mexican 1000. Lessons were learned, and the team did much better the following year. (Photo Courtesy Motor Trend Group LLC)

soon founded NORRA, the National Off-Road Racing Association, with Don Francisco and Pete Condos.

In 1967, the first Mexican 1000 was held by NORRA with 68 vehicles starting the race. Bill Stroppe entered two Broncos, one driven by Ray Harvick and Stroppe and the other handled by Dick Russell and Cliff Brien. Neither vehicle finished the race, but Stroppe was hooked.

Bill Stroppe's Broncos were always known for their immaculate preparation prior to a race. Here, before the start of the 1968 Stardust 7-11, Larry Minor and Jack Bayer's Bronco looks as if it had just pulled out of a car wash. The Nevada silt ensured that the truck and its occupants soon looked as if they had driven through a huge bowl of flour. (Photo Courtesy Motor Trend Group LLC)

For 1968, *ABC's Wide World of Sports*, hosted by Jim McKay, brought some recognition to the event, and TV viewers saw Broncos driven by Larry Minor, actor James Garner, Parnelli Jones, and Stroppe. Minor won his class as the Bronco's legendary status in Baja was just beginning.

In 1968, NORRA also hosted a race in Las Vegas called the Stardust 7-11. Brutally hot and dusty, few competitors finished, but Minor and Jack Bayer managed to win that race. They also raced in the Mint 400 near Las Vegas, which also began in 1968.

In 1969, Stroppe added Rodney Hall to his team of drivers, and for the 1969 Mexican 1000, Larry Minor and Hall were teamed in a Bronco together. Minor's proven record and Hall's skills as a driver (he had raced previous years in a Jeep) proved to be an unbeatable combination as the two accomplished a feat that has never been duplicated in Baja racing history. They managed to beat every other vehicle, including the motorcycles, with a 4WD vehicle and win the race overall. 2WD trucks have managed the feat numerous times in the intervening years, but never another 4WD vehicle. Hall and Minor crossed the finish line in their #56 Bronco with a time of 20 hours and 48 minutes.

The off-road racing scene was becoming more organized and more professional, and Stroppe's efforts had become the epitome of the large, well-organized, well-funded team. In an era when most race vehicles arrived at a race under their own power, on a tow bar, or perhaps on a trailer, Stroppe's team arrived on one or more transporters, a virtual armada of immaculately prepped and painted vehicles ready to do battle on the course. He had also hired an army of capable drivers and codrivers, including Jones, Minor, Hall, Jim Loomis, Carl Jackson, Bud Wright, Jim Fricker, Bill Rush, and Walker Evans.

The lessons learned in competition were also invaluable. Stroppe's first racing Broncos started with very simple roll cages and modifications to basic Broncos. With more races under his belt, he quickly discovered the Bronco's weak points and compensated accordingly. To allow the fitment of larger tires, Stroppe employee Whitey Clayton developed the first pair of rear fender cutouts and flares for the Bronco. Dual shocks were added at each corner to help control the pony's bouncing tendencies and better bushings for the front end were developed to replace the stock rubber pieces.

In a 2006 interview, Ray Harvick recalled Dana 30 front-axle failures at an early race in Denver that resulted in an airlifted pallet of axles to keep the Broncos competing in the event. Stroppe's team helped in the early development of the Dana 44 front axle, using early versions of the axles before they became available from the factory. Stroppe also developed an automatic transmission conversion and power steering

One of the most iconic racing images in Bronco racing history features Rod Hall and Jim Fricker in their 1969 1000-winning rig, busting through the silt at the 1972 Baja 500. Hall and Fricker went on to have a nasty rollover at this race, collapsing the passenger-side cage precariously close to Fricker's head. (Photo Courtesy Trackside Photo)

Carl Jackson's fatigue is evident in this picture taken about halfway through the 1971 Baja 500. It was hard enough to race a basically stock Stroppe Baja Bronco and almost unthinkable to attempt it towing a travel trailer, but that's exactly what Jackson and codriver Jim Fricker did.

conversion for his race trucks several years before they became available to the public in his Baja Bronco models.

Stroppe's success with Broncos also inspired a generation of other drivers to race the little bobtails as well. In the 1970s, Kurt Strecker of El Cajon, California, developed the Viva Broncos race team in addition to building modified street Broncos and aftermarket parts. Bob "Uncle Bob" Lewis had a popular Bronco as part of his racing team for many years in the 1970s and 1980s as well. Another early racer was James Duff, who, like Stroppe, developed and tested parts on his race truck that found their way into his Duffy's Bronco Service parts catalog.

Many other Bronco racers in those early years tested their machine's mettle and their stamina in the rough courses of the Southwest and Baja.

For the 1971 Baja 500, Stroppe found himself with an out-of-the-ordinary challenge. Wayne Lindsey, a Southern California travel trailer dealer, contacted him about towing a travel trailer behind one of his Broncos in the race as a publicity stunt to prove the trailer's durability. Stroppe found this request unusual, but never one to turn down an opportunity, he agreed to do it and asked one of his more gentle drivers, Carl Jackson, to drive it.

Rod Hall and Jim Fricker race down course in the 1972 Mexican 1000. Note the lettering on the windscreen denoting that this truck was the overall winner of the 1969 Mexican 1000. When a truck won a significant race like the Baja 500 or Mexican 1000, Stroppe lettered the victory on the truck, where it often remained for years. Hall/Fricker took second in class at this event. (Photo Courtesy Trackside Photo)

sprite

FIRST TO ATTEMPT AND
COMPLETE THE JUNE
1971 BAJA MEXICO
500 OFF-ROAD
RACE

Carl Jackson and Jim Fricker are shown at the finish line of the 1971 Baja 500, just over 26 hours after they started. The Sprite travel trailer then went on a publicity tour around the country, highlighting the fact that the Bronco and trailer combo had beaten Parnelli Jones in the race.

By 1987, the second generation of the Pike family was racing their Bronco, and the formerly open rig had gained a windshield and a half cab. Family patriarch Gale Pike had been hit in the mouth with a rock while racing and the windshield followed shortly thereafter. The Bronco is seen in action here at the season-opening Parker 400 race. (Photo Courtesy Trackside Photo)

Lindsey provided a Baja Bronco, and Stroppe added the required safety equipment to tow the trailer. NORRA officials didn't quite know what do with the entry, so they started them last, with 225 entries leaving the starting line before they did.

Early in the race, Jackson and his codriver, Jim Fricker, discovered that the Bronco's transfer case wouldn't shift into low range, so they ended up running the entire race with a hot-running engine and transmission. The trailer got five flat tires during the race, and Jackson sometimes had to tow it for quite a distance until they could pull over and change the tires. High winds meant that Fricker had to hold the trailer on the jack while Carl changed the tires.

Other challenges included welding the bolt-on hitch to the frame and pit crews that didn't want to give them gas because they didn't think the pair were a real race entry.

Jackson and Fricker ended up finishing the race in 26 hours and 2 minutes, well under the limit of 30 hours. Other than the flat tires, the only damage to the trailer was a curtain rod that had come loose! Jackson still likes to say he "beat *Big Oly* with a camp trailer," as Jones did not finish the race that year.

Plans to race the trailer again in the Mexican 1000 did not come to pass, as NORRA felt that towing a travel trailer in a race was not good publicity for the roughness of their courses. The trailer has been lost to history, but the Bronco was re-discovered in 2002 and is now owned by a private collector.

By the mid-1970s, the Bronco's day in the sun as far as off-road racing was concerned was fading. The short wheelbase, narrow track, and limited suspension travel meant that

Steve Mizel's race Broncos often stretched the limit (and not just their wheelbase) of what folks considered a "Bronco." Shown here in action at the 1987 Parker 400, Mizel's beast has 1980–1986 door panels but little else to suggest that it's a Bronco. Again, the wing on top seems to be a design element incorporated into many Bronco racers. (Photo Courtesy Trackside Photo)

it was being overtaken by faster trucks and buggies. Privateers Gale Pike and Ken Rice/Hal Sealund soldiered on throughout the 1970s and 1980s, running their little bobtails in Class 3 in the SCORE series with some success. Occasionally, other Broncos came out to race as well.

Gale Pike launches his Bronco over a rise at the 1979 Mint 400 outside Las Vegas, Nevada. The truck began life as a Stroppe Baja Bronco, which Pike purchased and took to Stroppe to build into a racer. It is said to be the last racing Bronco built by Stroppe. (Photo Courtesy Trackside Photo)

Ken Leavitt has Anger Issues! Well, maybe not, but that's what he calls his longtime off-road racing team. Driving into the sun and battling dust, Ken is shown here doing battle at the SCORE Laughlin Desert Challenge race in the early 2000s. Ken is one of the most passionate drivers in the sport, racing on a much more limited budget than most. (Photo Courtesy Trackside Photo)

Long before Don and Ken Moss began their racing streak with their second-generation Bronco, Franco Martinez was busing through the silt at the 1979 Mint 400. Many people regard the 1978–1979 trucks as the toughest Broncos ever built. (Photo Courtesy Trackside Photo)

Kirk Kovel raced this early Bronco in the SCORE desert racing series in the 1990s and early 2000s. Shown here at a Laughlin Desert Challenge race, Kovel's Colorado Springs–based Bronco raced at a time when its class had very few entries. Kovel usually drove solo and tragically lost his life in a car accident in Florida in 2015. (Photo Courtesy Trackside Photo)

Early Bronco parts vendor Chuck Atkinson and his son Jason raced this Bronco in patriotic livery at several Baja 1000 races in the early 2000s. Shown here at the 2003 race, Atkinson used his experiences to launch a series of "Baja Proven" parts sold through his business, BC Broncos. (Photo Courtesy Trackside Photo)

In the late 1960s, Hal Sealund purchased a 1966 Bronco that had originally been built for the Hearst family by Bill Stroppe. Sealund built the truck into a racer, and for about 20 years, it had many iterations and became the longest-racing early Bronco in history. Here, Hal poses after a race in Mexico in the late 1960s. (Photo Courtesy Ed Gudenkauf)

By the late 1970s, the Sealund truck had a lot more fiberglass on it, and the Rice Brothers were racing it for Sealund. Lessons learned over the years had made it a very different truck from when the decade began. (Photo Courtesy Ed Gudenkauf)

Bronco enthusiast Ed Gudenkauf rescued the the Sealund truck from Texas and treated it to a full restoration. Happy days are here again for the truck now known as Thunder. (Photo Courtesy Ed Gudenkauf)

In the mid-1980s, the Sealund truck was sponsored by K Bar S Bronco Specialties, and future Trophy Truck racer Steve Olliges got behind the wheel for the first time in this Bronco, now with a longer wheelbase. It last raced in the late 1980s and then went to Texas where it languished with neglect. (Photo Courtesy Ed Gudenkauf)

Big Oly II

In the late 1980s, *Off Road* editor Rick Sieman decided to build an off-road racing Bronco called *Big Oly II*. Based on the 1987–1991 bodystyle, Sieman had Garman Fabrication build the Bronco, which featured a modified Twin-Traction Beam front suspension with coil-over suspension and a unique rear suspension modeled after a motorcycle swing arm. The build was documented in a series of articles in the magazine in 1987 and 1988.

With a strong 351W engine and a lot of suspension travel, the truck held a great deal of promise as a Class 3 contender. Like many racing rigs, the truck suffered a great deal of development teething issues and took quite a while to sort out before it arrived in strong fashion. After only a few short years of racing, *Big Oly II* was retired.

Rough Riders

Dick Landfield had an idea. One of off-road racing's pioneers, the Southern California Ford dealer had helped start the First Association of Independent Racers (FAIR) pit-support organization in the early years and then went on to race for many years in a variety of Fords. In the late 1990s, he came up with the idea to put all the top-tier Ford racing teams together on one super team to conquer off-road racing in a big way. Ford went for Landfield's proposal and the Rough Riders were born. Not since the heyday of Bill Stroppe's domination had such an ensemble with such talent ruled the desert.

The Rough Riders' Class 3 entry was a Bronco fielded by Enduro Racing, the racing team associated with Landfield's dealerships. The Bronco had first been raced by two women in the 1989 Baja 1000. After that race, Landfield acquired the Bronco and his team went to work. Piloted by Dave Ashley, a former motorcycle racer, the Enduro Bronco went on to dominate the Class 3 ranks for the next four or five years.

A few years later, Ashley moved to a pickup, and the Bronco was piloted by motorcycle racer Dan Smith. The Bronco featured a highly modified Twin-Traction Beam front suspension with coil-over shocks. Out back, the rear axle was located by a four-link

In the mid-1980s, Off Road *editor Rick "Superhunky" Sieman teamed with Garman Fabrication to build* Big Oly II *to race in Class 3. With Jeeps winning most of the class races, Sieman figured that a Bronco with a longer wheelbase and a better suspension could clean up. Teething problems and development issues kept the truck from dominating the class, but it was still a fan favorite, and the buildup was featured in* Off Road. *(Photo Courtesy Trackside Photo)*

One of the most successful racing Broncos of all time, the Enduro Racing Bronco is shown here in its first livery early in its career. Originally entered in the 1988 Baja 1000 with two female drivers, Enduro Racing owner Dick Landfield purchased the truck shortly thereafter, removed the fiberglass top, and launched a powerful race team. (Photo Courtesy Trackside Photo)

In the early 1990s, Southern California Ford dealer Dick Land-field organized the Ford Rough Riders, a factory-based team of trucks meant to dominate off-road racing. And dominate they did with an armada of trucks including this Class 3 Bronco driven by Dave Ashley and Dan Smith. Note that the Twin-Traction Beam front suspension is backward from the production version: The passenger-side beam is in front of the driver-side beam. (Photo Courtesy Trackside Photo)

and suspended by quarter-elliptic leaf springs and large racing shocks.

With the engine pumping out close to 700 hp, the Bronco was a competitor to be reckoned with. Its reign lasted until the Rough Riders disbanded in the mid-1990s. It was then sold to a Mexican race team and eventually burned to the ground in a racing accident.

NORRA Returns

In 2009, Mike Pearlman, Ed Pearlman's son, set out to revive NORRA. His vision was a rally-type race with special emphasis on making the event friendly to vintage vehicles. In April 2010, the first running of the revived NORRA Mexican 1000 was held, starting in Mexicali, Baja California. Several early Broncos entered and captured the eye of many enthusiasts hungry for a race where a vintage race car could be entered and raced on a course that wasn't impractical for something less than a Trophy Truck.

Soon, early Broncos were being rescued, revived, and raced. Vintage race Broncos and late-model full-size prerunners alike have found a home where owners can enjoy their vehicles in a competitive environment that still proves to be extremely challenging for the drivers and crews. Younger enthusiasts have found it exhilarating to race their vehicles alongside such legends as Parnelli Jones (2010 Grand Marshal), Walker Evans, and Rod Hall (who raced a Stroppe Bronco himself for two years).

Once again, Broncos are bombing down the Baja Peninsula, helping make memories for a new generation of racers. As in the early days, parts tested on the racers are found again in vendors' catalogs, following that axiom of "Race on Sunday, Sell on Monday" that rang so true so many years ago and still does today.

After racing the 1969 Baja 1000-winning Stroppe Bronco in the 2010 NORRA Mexican 1000, Chris Wilson and Glen Straightiff decided to build a race Bronco for themselves. They combined the classic looks of an early Bronco with the higher-speed capability of a full-size Bronco frame and suspension. The earlier body was lengthened and widened to fit the frame. With a nod to Big Oly, a wing was added. (Photo Courtesy Trackside Photo)

Another Bronco racer in the modern era who combined an early Bronco body (or body panels) with a more modern drivetrain is Don Hatch. Shown here in action at the 2015 NORRA Mexican 1000, Hatch's Bronco features a tubular frame and Twin-Traction Beam front suspension with coil-over shocks at each wheel. (Photo Courtesy Trackside Photo)

Starting life as an original Stroppe-prepped Bronco, the Kaysinger Racing/Baja Broncos Unlimited Bronco has been a regular NORRA contender since 2012 and has never failed to finish a race. With the bright blue waters of the Sea of Cortez in the background, the hard-charging Bronco nears the finish line in San José del Cabo, Baja California Sur. (Photo Courtesy Trackside Photo)

Randy "Rapido" Ludwig of Rancho Cucamonga, California, is the owner and driver of this true multi-purpose Bronco, which has raced numerous times in the NORRA Mexican 1000. In addition to racing in Baja each year, Ludwig also uses the street-legal truck for activities as varied as trail riding and trips to the local ice-cream shop. (Photo Courtesy Trackside Photo)

Boyd Jaynes and Brian Godfrey have participated in every NORRA 1000 since 2010. After a few years of teething problems, they've been unstoppable, winning their class for a record six times in their 1968 Bronco known as El Caballo del Diablo. No other NORRA competitor has won as many times. (Photo Courtesy Boyd Jaynes)

The indefatigable Rod Hall was the only driver to complete all 50 Baja 1000 races through 2017; winner of more races and championships than he can probably count! This former Stroppe racing Bronco was sinking further into the sand in a Barstow, California, salvage yard for 20 years before it was rescued. Hall resurrected it and raced it in the NORRA Mexican 1000 in 2015 and 2016.

Parnelli Jones

There is no figure more central to the popularity of the Bronco in off-road racing lore than Parnelli Jones. One of America's most versatile and well-known race car drivers, Jones was at the height of his popularity when the Bronco was introduced. Having won the Indianapolis 500 a few years earlier and finishing near the top in recent years, Jones had become a household name among racing enthusiasts and the general public alike.

Although moving from the Brickyard to Baja seems like a huge stretch, Broncos were not Jones' first adventure in the dirt. In fact, he cut his racing teeth on the dirt tracks of the West Coast, racing jalopies and sprint cars long before his time on paved tracks. Jones had his first association with Bill Stroppe in the dirt, driving one of Stroppe's Mercury stock cars at Pikes Peak in 1963 and 1964. In 1962, he captured the championship on a road that was dirt at the time.

At *Hot Rod* publisher Ray Brock's Christmas party in 1967, Stroppe, perhaps with a bit of craftiness, suggested that Parnelli race one of his Broncos. Parnelli replied that he had

done his time in the dirt and didn't need to spend any more of his career sucking dust. Stroppe retorted that perhaps Jones wasn't man enough for off-road racing anyway. As Jones has stated, this was the equivalent of "waving a red cape in front of a bull" and the challenge was on. Parnelli told Stroppe to get a Bronco ready and he'd drive it!

This publicity photo was likely taken soon after Parnelli Jones decided to drive one of Bill Stroppe's Broncos in an off-road race. Resplendent in a bright orange windbreaker and fancy green jeans, Jones poses with one of Stroppe's short-course Broncos, which he never drove. (Photo Courtesy Stroppe Performance)

In recent times, Parnelli poses for a photo with Big Oly *in his museum in Torrance, California. Now the elder statesman of off-road racing, Jones looks back on his racing career with an immense amount of pride and satisfaction. (Photo Courtesy Boyd Jaynes)*

1968 Mint 400

Jones's first race was the 1968 Mint 400. His impact by entering the race was phenomenal. In a 2018 article in the *Las Vegas Sun*, Mint 400 cofounder Norm Johnson recalled that until Jones signed up for the race, there were 56 entries. After he entered, Johnson noted, "the entries just poured in" and they ended up with 109 entries.

Stroppe honored his word and had a Bronco ready for Jones. In the codriver's seat was Ray Harvick, charged with coaching Jones on the course. Before the race started, Jones told Harvick to hit him on his right thigh with his fist if he wanted him to slow down.

To hear Jones and Harvick tell the story in recent times, Harvick nearly beat Jones's leg to a pulp before they had traveled far in the race, and Harvick was a hard-charging driver in his own right. Along the course, an unseen drop into a wash caused the Bronco to slam to a stop with both front tires flattened and the rims cauliflowered around the brake drums. The wheels were so badly bent that Stroppe had to use a torch to cut them off.

Thus ended Parnelli's debut in the desert, but he had tasted enough to know that he liked it. In the dirt, he found that he could relax a bit and do the racing for himself, not to satisfy anxious sponsors, which took the pressure off and allowed him to have fun. The desert scratched Jones's itch of always wanting to see what was over the next hill.

1968 NORRA Mexican 1000

In November 1968, Stroppe and Jones teamed up in one of Stroppe's Broncos for the second running of the NORRA Mexican 1000 race. This race caught the attention of the general public when it was filmed for an episode of *ABC's Wide World of Sports*. Setting a speed record of 90 mph in the first pavement section, Jones charged hard. Before long, the Bronco was bouncing across the barren Baja peninsula's arid desert.

Stroppe's longtime engine builder, Verne Houle, used to say that "Parnelli could break an anvil with a rubber mallet," and that saying held true again for this race when the Bronco's front end broke about 15 miles from Laguna Chapala. Hailing a ride in the back of actor James Garner's Bronco to the Chapala pit, Jones admitted in a recent interview, "My hands probably made dents in the roll cage—I was hanging on so tightly!"

1969 Season

The year 1969 brought little consolation in terms of Parnelli's racing success. At the Mint, he and Stroppe were disqualified for using the Unser brothers' Bronco on the second day of racing after wadding their truck on the first day (competitors were not allowed to switch vehicles in the multi-day event). Jones switched to a fiberglass-bodied 4WD Bronco called *Colt* for the next two races, but the results were predictable. Both were DNFs due to engine issues and a broken front end.

1970 Baja 500

After seasons of frustration, everything clicked for Jones and Stroppe at the 1970 Baja 500, as they finally roared to victory in the 2WD truck, named *Pony*. They finished in a time of 11 hours and 55 minutes and won the race overall. When Jones had finally reached the winner's circle, he knew what he needed to win.

There was only one problem: he needed a vehicle.

Big Oly

Bill Stroppe liked Broncos that were close to stock or resembled stock Broncos, and felt that since Ford was financially backing his efforts, he should be racing trucks that closely resembled their showroom counterparts. Jones's idea for a new race truck ran counter to that idea. Over several lunches, he and Stroppe fabricator Dick Russell sketched some

Arguably the most iconic off-road racer of all time was a Bronco. Big Oly is still owned by Parnelli Jones, more than four decades after it last roared through the desert in pursuit of victory. The truck epitomizes Broncos and off-road racing to many people. (Photo Courtesy Boyd Jaynes)

This is a rare photo of Big Oly under construction at Stroppe's shop in Long Beach, California. Dick Russell and Joe Fukushima work on the truck under Jones's watchful eye. The body panels bore Johnny Lightning colors and livery because the truck was then known as Crazy Colt. (Photo Courtesy Jeff Bennett)

ideas on napkins on what the new race truck should look like. 2WD, a tube frame, a 351 Windsor engine set back in the frame, more suspension travel, and a fiberglass body to keep weight to a minimum were integral to the design they came up with. Knowing that Stroppe would not bless such a project coming out of his shop, Russell started on the new truck in his home garage.

In 1970, Jones was at the Indianapolis 500 where he, in his words, "blabbed" about the new project to Mickey Thompson. Thompson soon called Stroppe and told him what was going on. Stroppe was furious! Today, Jones says that the ensuing fight about the Bronco almost ended their friendship. With a little time, however, emotions cooled and Stroppe told Russell to bring the project to his Signal Hill facility to finish it.

The resulting masterpiece has become one of the most iconic vehicles in off-road racing history. Drawing on his experiences in a wide variety of race cars, Jones incorporated a number of new and innovative ideas into the Bronco. The rear axle was a full-floating 9-inch axle similar to stock car and Trans Am car assemblies. If the axle shaft broke, the wheel stayed on the car. That axle carried disc brakes, also a carry-over from the Trans Am beasts.

Jones knew that the truck needed a roof, so he decided to make it a movable wing. It made a difference in how the truck flew off jumps in Baja and helped keep the Bronco planted at high speeds. Russell and Jones also incorporated powerful driving lights into the leading edge of the wing.

At the base of the windshield area, Russell built a two-piece

DUNE BUGGY PROJECT

"I was just too damn hard on the equipment," Jones ruefully admits today, but in 1970, a new vehicle arrived that he knew might be a better match for his driving style. Ford skunkworks builder Kar-Kraft in Brighton, Michigan, had built a "Bronco dune buggy" concept that, according to Tom Madigan's Stroppe biography Boss, was intended to be a special-edition Bronco in kit form.

The Bronco kit had a Twin I-Beam front end, plastic body, and engine set back in the chassis. According to Madigan, the project died when Bunkie Knudsen was fired from Ford in 1969, and the remains of the concept were offered to Stroppe. Stroppe brought the remains to Long Beach, and Jones immediately recognized the potential of the rig to be built into a race Bronco.

This is Ford designer Kenneth Dowd's dune buggy sketch from the late 1960s. Several dune buggy sketches from Ford's design team served as an impetus for a Bronco-based dune buggy project at Kar-Kraft in 1969. When Bunkie Knudsen was fired from Ford, the project was scrapped, and the remains went to Bill Stroppe, who built it into a Bronco racer known as Pony. *(Photo Courtesy Kenneth Dowd)*

Hard-charging Larry Minor, with longtime Stroppe wrench Jaime Martinez onboard, noses into the Nevada desert during the 1973 Mint 400. Minor piloted Pony *in more races than any other driver, often finishing not far behind Parnelli Jones in* Big Oly. *(Photo Courtesy Trackside Photo)*

channel that ducted air into the windshield space, creating a virtual air curtain that kept dust out of the cab. This was an idea borrowed from Colin Chapman's Lotus race cars that Jones had raced years earlier. The front end used the modified Twin I-Beam front suspension used on *Pony* but with a twist. The beams were located by trailing arms rather than leading radius arms, which allowed the front wheels to more naturally travel over bumps in the road. When the Bronco was finished, Stroppe not only gave it his blessing but agreed to continue to be Jones's codriver.

In its earliest iteration, the new Bronco was known as *Crazy Colt* and sported Johnny Lightning livery, which was Jones's Indy car sponsor at the time. In some of its earliest races, it also ran on propane power.

When Stroppe first received Pony *from Kar-Kraft, it looked like the basis for a fairly simple 2WD Bronco. After Stroppe worked his magic, it was ready for a thrashing at the hands of Parnelli Jones.*

Parnelli Jones and Bill Stroppe look clean and crisp in the Pony *Bronco following their 1970 Baja 500 win.* Pony *finally allowed Jones to finish and win an off-road race. (Photo Courtesy Stroppe Performance)*

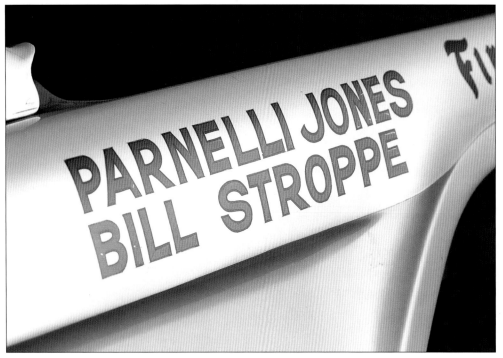

1970 Mexican 1000

Big Oly's first Baja race was the 1970 Mexican 1000, and Jones thought he was doing well. At a pit stop at Santa Ynez, Jones saw a dune buggy go roaring by and exclaimed, "That's Drino Miller!" the top buggy driver in the race that year. Jones roared out of the pit in hot pursuit, not realizing that it was Drino's prerunner scouting the course, and not the race car. In an effort to catch up with the buggy, Jones drove over his head and ended up breaking the rear end housing on some rocks. Frustrated, Parnelli eventually finished the race after extensive repairs. Drino did eventually win the race, setting a new course record.

Jones's luck was about to change, and in 1971, the stars aligned for the Mexican 1000.

One of the classic pairings in all of off-road racing history: Parnelli Jones was the hard-charging racing superstar who was the man's man of desert racing behind the wheel of his mighty Bronco. Bill Stroppe was the ace mechanic and the tempering influence on Jones's flames, although Jones often said that Stroppe turned into a different man when they were racing in the desert. (Photo Courtesy Boyd Jaynes)

This was state of the art in off-road racing in the early 1970s. Big Oly used a 9-inch rear end with full-floating axles borrowed from the stock car world. Suspended on coil springs and damped by two shock absorbers, body roll was limited by an anti-sway bar, and things were brought to a stop by disc brakes. The tube frame is also visible in front of the shock absorbers. (Photo Courtesy Boyd Jaynes)

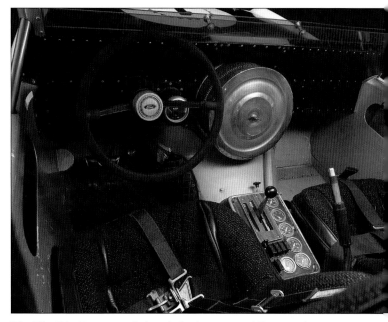

The Big Oly Bronco cockpit only had two actual Bronco pieces in it: the padded Baja Bronco steering wheel and the glove box door. The interior air filter, a Stroppe signature item, was easily changed by the codriver. Critical functions were monitored by gauges in the center console, and the handle to the left of the codriver's seat controlled the angle of attack of the wing. (Photo Courtesy Boyd Jaynes)

1971 Mexican 1000

With $5,000 in sponsorship funds from the Olympia Brewing Company, *Crazy Colt* was rechristened *Big Oly*, and a legend was born. As the Mexican 1000 matured and vehicle

Parnelli Jones and Bill Stroppe are shown at speed in the 1971 Mexican 1000. This was the vehicle's second Mexican 1000 and the first as Big Oly. Jones knew that the previous record was more than 16 hours and thought he might be able to make it in about 15 hours. He finished in 14:59 and won the race overall. (Photo Courtesy Trackside Photo)

Placing 1st overall in the 1971 "Baja 1000" were Parnelli Jones and Bill Stroppe in a highly modified Whittaker Baja Team Bronco. Their elapsed time was 14 hours 59 minutes, bettering last year's record time by an hour and 8 minutes.

Jones's and Stroppe's overall win in the 1971 Mexican 1000 generated an incredible amount of publicity for Ford and Broncos. This iconic photo of Big Oly at speed was used in promotional materials, a magazine cover (right), and a postcard (below), among others.

Sponsor: OLYMPIA BREWING CO.   BIG OLY BRONCO   Drivers: PARNELLI JONES

technology and speeds increased, Jones knew that his ultimate goal was to beat the motorcycles with a four-wheeled vehicle.

Before the 1971 race, Nico Saad, an Ensenada hotel owner, asked Jones how long he thought it would take for him to finish the race that year. Jones replied, "I think I can do it in 15 hours." On a flight with race officials, bets were placed on the first-place finishing time, and Saad, recalling his conversation with Jones, placed his money on 15 hours. The others thought he was crazy for such a quick pace.

Despite some problems with a front-brake caliper and a few broken pieces on the front end, Jones made a winner of Saad, finishing in an astonishing 14 hours and 59 minutes, well over an hour better than the previous record. Parnelli Jones was the new king of Baja. The resulting media coverage in print ads, newspaper coverage, and magazine articles was unparalleled in the Mexican 1000's history and assured Jones's legendary status on the peninsula.

1972 Mexican 1000

The 1972 race started in Mexicali that year and once again Jones and Stroppe were racing down the peninsula, looking as if they would repeat the previous year's victory. All went well until the last pit stop outside Ciudad Constitución, where a rookie pit helper accidentally poured gasoline in the thermos jugs designed to hold drinking water. In the ensuing confusion, water and gas got mixed up and Jones and Stroppe weren't quite sure how much gas they had but decided to go for it anyway.

That night, in total darkness on a mesa high above La Paz, *Big Oly* sputtered and coasted to a stop. Jones and Stroppe could see the lights of La Paz, only 15 or 20 miles away, but when you're leading the race, it looks a lot farther!

Jones recalls that while they were standing there wondering what to do, they saw a faint single light coming toward them in the distance. He at first thought it was a bicycle because it was moving so slowly. It turned out to be two locals in an aging Volkswagen. Jones yelled at them to see if they had gasoline and pulled a $20 bill out of his racing suit to help them give the right answer. Yes, they did! But no one had a container or siphon. Stroppe noticed the two Mexicans had a bottle of tequila and money was quickly exchanged for it. The tequila was poured out in front of its former owners' sad faces and Jones yanked the windshield washer hose off the VW for a siphoning hose.

After about a dozen bottles of gasoline were siphoned out of the car, Stroppe decided that they had enough gas to make it the rest of the way to La Paz, and they roared off. Despite the tequila adventure, *Big Oly* won the race overall that year, albeit almost 2 hours slower than in 1971.

Any record of the story of Jones, Stroppe, and *Big Oly*

Although leading the 1972 Baja 1000, Big Oly sputtered to a stop, out of gas, with the lights of La Paz in the distance. Jones managed to purchase a bottle of tequila from some passing locals and siphon enough fuel out of their VW with this tequila bottle to fire Big Oly to life and go on to win the race. Bill Stroppe kept the bottle and Willie Stroppe passed it on to Jones following Bill's passing.

Covered in silt at the 1972 Mint 400, Parnelli Jones appears to be giving the photographer some advice, perhaps something along the lines of, "Why don't you put down that camera and help push me out of here!" Note that there is no passenger seat as Jones and Walker Evans took turns behind the wheel of Big Oly for this race. (Photo Courtesy Trackside Photo)

would not be complete without mention of the human dynamics involved among a vehicle, its driver, and its codriver. As anyone who knew Stroppe will tell you, he was one of the kindest, most gentle human beings you could ever hope to meet. That all changed when he was in *Big Oly* with Jones.

According to Jones, Stroppe's personality changed once Jones stomped on the gas pedal, vainly trying to serve as a governor to Jones's right foot and trying to get him to slow down to save the truck. The normally docile Stroppe would cuss and

At the 1972 Baja 500, Bill Stroppe was nursing a broken leg, so Big Oly *fabricator Dick Russell co-drove with Jones in* Big Oly. *Pounding through the silt,* Oly *displays its new-for-1972 front end as Jones keeps throttling through the soft terrain. (Photo Courtesy Trackside Photo)*

Even the best get stuck in the Nevada silt! With Big Oly's *body-work wrinkled, dust hanging in the air, and spectators lending a hand, Parnelli Jones takes a moment to consider his predicament during the 1972 Mint 400. They eventually extracted the winged wonder and Jones roared to the finish line. (Photo Courtesy Trackside Photo)*

yell at Jones, threatening to get out of the truck if he didn't slow down, to which Jones would retort, "Well, how do you think we got out in front . . . it wasn't because I was going slow!"

Jones states that he threatened to leave Stroppe in the des-

The 1973 running of the Mint 400 was a cold affair, as evidenced by the low-hanging clouds in the sky and the moist dirt in the foreground. Jones and Stroppe encountered rain, mud, and snow that day en route to their victory. (Photo Courtesy Trackside Photo)

ert more than once when he had to work on the truck, and Stroppe often told Jones to slow down because they didn't want to spend the night in the desert with the snakes and coyotes.

Jones and Stroppe remained close friends long after their Baja adventures were over.

1973 Mint 400 and Baja 500

The year 1973 was also good for *Big Oly* and Parnelli Jones. In direct contrast to his first effort in Las Vegas five years earlier, Stroppe and Jones won the Mint 400 that year, battling a snowstorm. A few months later, despite multiple rollovers and the truck looking as if it had been in a demolition derby, they managed to win the Baja 500 in what was *Big Oly*'s last visit to the winner's circle.

A year later at the 1974 500, Jones and Stroppe were involved in a head-on collision with a motorcycle heading the wrong way on the course in the middle of a huge dust cloud. Although not at fault, it marked the end of *Big Oly*'s run in Baja. It raced one last race later in US Indy Mags livery and then officially retired.

Although *Big Oly*'s time in Baja lasted only about five years, its legendary status was cemented forever in the hearts and minds of racing enthusiasts, Bronco fans, and residents of the Baja peninsula. Pay a visit to modern-day La Paz or other Baja towns during races and you'll still hear locals talk of Jones and *Big Oly*.

Big Oly was restored by Dick Russell shortly after its retirement from racing and is today owned by Parnelli Jones.

After a long racing career, the overall winner of the 1969 Mexican 1000 enjoys a tranquil life these days. It raced to a class victory again at the 2010 NORRA Mexican 1000, raced (and rolled) in the 2012 running of the race, and appeared as an understudy in the Need for Speed movie. It now wears the livery it had in the 1972 Mexican 1000 race and is shown at various car shows and events in the West. (Photo Courtesy Dave Loewen)

A high-performance small-block provides the motivation for the Stroppe racer now fondly referred to as Red Racer. The stock air filter was modified to pull air from inside the cab in front of the codriver. Note the coil spring holding the dipstick in place. The inner fender panels were built by Stroppe fabricators and gave more fenderwell clearance for shocks at the expense of working room in the engine compartment. (Photo Courtesy Jay Kopycinski)

Veteran racer Rod Hall with codriver Jim Fricker stop at a checkpoint at Mike's Sky Ranch in the mountains of Baja California during the 1974 Baja 500. Hall's race-seasoned Bronco bore a new moniker, Halls Ass, on its windshield panel for this year. Based on his race record, it was well deserved! (Photo Courtesy David Kier)

At the rear is a big bearing 9-inch rear end with a heavy-duty plate strap truss spanning its width. The rear frame horns have been sectioned and reduced in section height as they sweep toward the rear. This feature was a key item in identifying this truck's previous life: Spring shackles were once mounted to the frame horns and were mounted on the spring perches still visible inboard from the existing ones. When the springs were moved back outboard in the mid-1970s, a reinforcement crossmember provided additional strength. (Photo Courtesy Jay Kopycinski)

Additional books that may interest you...

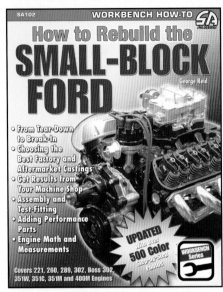

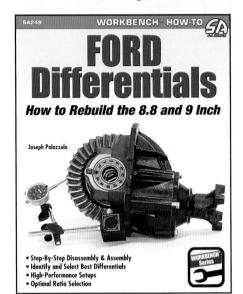